TC 3-04.7 (FM 3-04.500)
2 February 2010

Army Aviation Maintenance

DISTRIBUTION RESTRICTION: Approved for public release; distribution is unlimited.

DESTRUCTION NOTICE: Follow procedures in Army regulation (AR) 380-5, chapter 6, section V.

Headquarters, Department of the Army

Published by Books Express Publishing
Books Express Publishing, 2011
ISBN 978-1-78039-948-5

Books Express publications are available from all good retail and online booksellers. For
publishing proposals and direct ordering please contact us at: info@books-express.com

*Training Circular
No. TC 3-04.7 (FM 3-04.500)

Headquarters
United States Army Aviation Center of Excellence
Washington, DC, 2 February 2010

Army Aviation Maintenance

Contents

Page

*This publication supersedes FM 3-04.500, dated 23 August 2006.

Figures

Tables

Preface

Training circular (TC) 3-04.7 outlines requirements concerning aviation maintenance structure, organizations, and functions. The intended audiences are aviation maintenance commanders, leaders, officers, technicians, noncommissioned officers (NCOs), and aircraft repair and maintenance personnel.

TC 3-04.7 applies to all active, Army Army National Guard (ARNG)/Army National Guard of the United States (ARNGUS), United States Army Reserve (USAR), civilian, and contract maintenance personnel unless otherwise stated. Commanders must consider the contents of this document and the particular circumstances in which they find themselves (national military objectives, available forces, threat capabilities, and rules of engagements) when planning maintenance operations.

The term 'aircraft' refers to all Army aircraft types (rotary-wing, fixed-wing, and unmanned aircraft systems [UAS]), unless a specific aircraft has been identified in this publication.

The proponent for this publication is Headquarters, United States Army Training and Doctrine Command. Send comments and recommendations on Department of the Army (DA) Form 2028 (Recommended Changes to Publications and Blank Forms) directly to Commander, United States Army Aviation Center of Excellence, ATTN: ATZQ-TDD-D, Fort Rucker, AL 36362-5263. Email comments to DOTD at av.doctrine@us.army.mil.

This publication has been reviewed for operations security considerations.

This page intentionally left blank.

Chapter 1

Maintenance Fundamentals

This chapter addresses doctrinal guidance and maintenance fundamentals for aviation units. It discusses efficient and effective sustainment functions needed by aviation units to conduct operations while maintaining optimum combat capability. Army aviation is a critical combat multiplier. To ensure vital assets remain ready and available to the unit, a thorough Aviation Maintenance Management Program must be in place with quantifiable measures to report and track.

SECTION I – GENERAL

1-1. The Army maintenance program has two levels of maintenance: field and sustainment.

1-2. The goal of Army aviation field maintenance is to support the operations and objectives of the maneuver commander. The primary purpose of the maintenance plan is to enable maintainers to provide the maximum number of operational aircraft available to support the tactical battle.

Contents

1-3. Commanders tailor and position maintenance assets and capabilities within the area of operations (AOs) to best support the unit. The maintenance-supply interface is the commander fusion point between field and sustainment maintenance management echelons. Sustainment maintenance managers ensure the maintenance system supports and sustains theater forces down to the individual Soldier.

SUSTAINMENT IMPERATIVES

1-4. Sustaining the operational unit requires aviation commanders and staffs to adhere to the sustainment imperatives—responsiveness, simplicity, flexibility, attainability, sustainability, survivability, economy, and integration. These imperatives apply, across the spectrum of conflict, to units conducting offense, defense, and stability and civil support operations (FM 1, FM 3-0, FM 3-07, and FM 4-0).

RESPONSIVENESS

1-5. Responsiveness is the key characteristic. It means providing the right support, in the right place, at the right time and meeting changing requirements on short notice. Responsiveness includes the ability to anticipate operational requirements. Aviation logisticians must anticipate future events and requirements by reviewing and understanding the Aviation Maneuver Commander Operation Plan. While supporting current operations, aviation logisticians plan for future operations and consider variations based on changes in the current, unfolding operations.

SIMPLICITY

1-6. Simplicity means avoiding complexity in planning and executing sustainment operations. Standardized mission orders, drills, rehearsals, and standing operating procedures (SOPs) contribute to simplicity.

FLEXIBILITY

1-7. Flexibility is the adaptation of sustainment operations to changing situations, missions, and concepts of operations. Logistics plans and operations must retain responsiveness and economy, while remaining flexible. An attribute of flexibility is improvisation. Improvisation is to make, invent, or substitute something that is available in lieu of what is needed. Improvisation can maintain sustainment continuity when the preferred item is not available or attainable.

ATTAINABILITY

1-8. Attainability is ensuring the minimum essential supplies and services necessary to begin operations are available and on-hand. Commanders determine the minimum acceptable level of supplies and support necessary to initiate operations.

SUSTAINABILITY

1-9. Sustainability is the ability to maintain continuous support during all phases of conflicts and major operations. Aviation logistics planners anticipate sustainment requirements over time and synchronize the delivery of sufficient sustainment stocks and levels to sustain ongoing operations or missions.

SURVIVABILITY

1-10. Commanders determine how much of their logistical support assets are focused on sustainment operations versus security. The larger the number of aviation support Soldiers committed to operations other than sustainment the less effective sustainment maintenance operations are. The commander must weigh the threat against the desired level of support and determine the acceptable level of risk. In some cases, ground forces may be available or required to augment security. Being able to protect support functions from destruction or degradation equates to survivability. Robust and redundant security contributes to survivability but may deter economy of operations.

ECONOMY

1-11. Resources are always limited. Economy is the most efficient use of available resources in accomplishing the mission. Commanders must consider economy in prioritizing and allocating resources. Emerging information and communication technologies continue to enhance the economy of critical aviation resources.

INTEGRATION

1-12. Integration consists of synchronizing sustainment operations within Army maneuver and aviation operations in a unified action environment. Effective sustainment operations are achieved through an understanding of and synchronization with the maneuver and aviation commander's intent and concept of operations. Aviation maintenance units must be organized and trained to conduct split-based operations.

FUNCTIONAL RESPONSIBILITIES

1-13. The functional responsibilities of Army aviation maintenance are—
- Providing the user with safe, reliable, and fully mission capable (FMC) aircraft.
- Sustaining materiel in an operational status and/or restoring equipment to a FMC condition.
- Enhancing or upgrading aircraft functional usefulness through modification work orders (MWOs), materiel changes, and product improvement.

SECTION II – OBJECTIVES

1-14. The objective of aviation maintenance is to safe maintain readiness at an optimal level with the fewest resources. Leaders must decide which resources most effectively support specific mission requirements and advise the commander on the sustainment effect of various courses of action.

1-15. Maintenance management uses the following factors to channel maintenance efforts:
- Command emphasis.
- Measures of effectiveness (MOE).
- Management skills.
- Supervision.
- Motivation.
- Technical skills.

COMMAND EMPHASIS

1-16. The commander sets the tone for what is important within the command. Soldiers in the unit translate this tone into action. To place command emphasis on maintenance operations, the commander takes an active interest in these operations and in the materiel readiness of unit equipment. Maintenance leaders use command emphasis and the MOE to influence the maintenance mission. To achieve quantifiable standards, commanders and leaders must aggressively pursue resources and equipment required to perform each mission. By actively tracking the unit MOE, commanders, officers, and NCOs identify strengths and rapidly address weaknesses, improving unit performance and enhancing its capabilities.

MEASURES OF EFFECTIVENESS

1-17. MOE provide the yardsticks to assess a field maintenance operation ability to generate combat power in support of the commander's tactical goals and missions. The maintenance team, and specifically the maintenance leaders, can direct organizational efforts toward these commonly understood goals by clearly defining these measures and capturing them in quantifiable reports and records. The common maintenance operating picture and measures ensure maintenance personnel can pursue mission goals with minimum guidance and retain high confidence in the direction of their efforts.

1-18. The aviation field maintenance MOE fall into four categories: combat power measures, maintenance measures, technical supply measures, and core unit measures.

COMBAT POWER MEASURES

1-19. Combat power measures quantify a unit's ability to perform its core-mission essential task list (METL) and directed-METL tasks. There are three combat power measures:
- Operational readiness (OR) rates or ready-to-launch (RTL) rates.
- Fleet bank time.
- Aircraft recovery operation responsiveness, capabilities, and training.

1-20. OR/RTL rates provide quantifiable status for immediate planning and trend analysis. Commanders establish RTL standards in combat by considering type of aircraft, unit TTP, and mission equipment packages required to support operations. Fleet bank time, linked with operational requirements, provides maintenance leaders and commanders the ability to forecast scheduled service requirements. These measures work in synchronization to provide the commander a representation of his maximum sustainable combat power generated by available maintenance resources.

1-21. Units reporting high OR/RTL rates, but not supporting high operational requirements, mask inadequate combat power generation. Additionally, high bank time percentages without corresponding combat or training flight hour execution demonstrates under utilization and reduced combat presence in sustained operations. Units executing high flight hours against strong OR/RTL rates while sustaining or improving bank time ensure flexibility, predictability, and combat power generation.

1-22. Using existing regulatory standards and applying known mission considerations, the appropriate level commander will specify his goals for readiness rates and bank time by a percentage. Commanders will report aircraft recovery operations status by unit standards established for deploying a fully-loaded, organic, deliberate recovery operation by air and ground in accordance with (IAW) FM 3-04.513, as well as the date of the full dress rehearsal. These measures will be reported (figure 1-1) at least monthly and historically tracked for analysis of improvement, degradation, and goals achieved.

Combat Power Measures Report

	Oct	Nov	Dec	Jan	Feb	Mar
Operational readiness or Ready to launch rate	83%	85%	79%	82%	88%	
Bank time % = $\frac{X}{12000}$	50%	52%	51%	53%	55%	
DART equipment readiness	95%	97%	98%	96%	98%	
DART training status (% of unit personnel trained)	15%	18%	18%	20%	17%	
Date of last full dress DART rehearsal	Air	12 Aug XX		Ground	8 Nov XX	

Figure 1-1. Combat power measures reporting example

MAINTENANCE MEASURES

1-23. Maintenance measures directly affect the unit's ability to regenerate combat power through repair and scheduled services. The seven maintenance measures are—

- Production index.
- Scheduled maintenance/phase completion standards.
- Annual internal or Army command aviation resource management survey (ARMS) results and corrective progress.
- Special tools acquisition, serviceability status, and replenishment.

- Test, measurement, and diagnostic equipment (TMDE) delinquency and instrument master record file (IMRF) data matching percentages.

- Specially qualified Soldier and personnel status such as nondestructive inspection (NDI), welder, hazardous material (HAZMAT), confined space, or protective clothing and equipment (PCE) (Army term)/personal protective equipment (PPE) (Occupational Safety and Health Administration term).

- Work-order rejection rate percentage (monthly and annually).

1-24. The production index quantifies a unit's ability to complete work orders in a timely fashion and reflects its ability to reduce or eliminate backlogs. Completion of back logged work orders is a maintenance command goal. The production index is the ratio of work orders accepted by a maintenance unit compared to the number of work orders completed over a given period, generally the calendar month. The goal is 100 percent of accepted work orders completed in the period; this precludes generation of a backlog. If a unit falls below 100 percent in any given period, a backlog is created that must be mitigated as soon as possible. Once a backlog is generated, the maintenance unit must exceed 100 percent for one or several reporting periods to recover from the backlog, or the backlog remains or expands. Successive periods below 100 percent indicate a systemic issue and demands command analysis and attention. Successive periods over 100 percent show positive results against a backlog of work orders and indicate a healthy maintenance operation.

1-25. Unit commanders must set reasonable standards for the completion time allowed to complete scheduled or "phase" maintenance operations. Days allowed or windows of acceptability for progressive phase maintenance (PPM) completion programs specify standards for unit personnel to work toward. These operations generate bank time for aircraft fleets and can rapidly enhance or cripple combat power. Competition between units is healthy and should be encouraged in achieving or exceeding the goal. Safety is always the primary consideration. Adjustments to shorten the timelines may be considered if timelines are frequently and easily met. If timelines are habitually missed, the maintenance team must analyze the causes and mitigate the challenges to bring the program back in compliance to support required flying hours.

1-26. Units will conduct internal ARMS surveys annually or substitute the Army command ARMS for the annual requirement. The results establish benchmarks for sustainment and improvement. Commanders will ensure all passing areas retain their satisfactory status and work toward commendable levels of performance. For failing areas, commanders will establish a recurring reporting process to indicate progress on bringing substandard areas into compliance as rapidly as possible. This recurring requirement allows commanders to assess the overall performance of the unit and bring focus to areas needing attention. All major areas below standard should be in compliance by the subsequent evaluation and sustained indefinitely thereafter. Inspectable area progress will be reported to the support operations aviation cell every four months for analysis and assistance. The support operations officer or designated representative will re-inspect unsatisfactory and marginal areas prior to the first post-inspection tri-annual progress report.

1-27. Commanders will monitor the status of their special tools compliment and work diligently toward filling the shortages to achieve 100 percent of the commander-approved levels, with matching serviceability ratings. Additionally, the commander will continually update the logistics staff officer (S-4) on funding necessary to acquire all required special tools. Special tools will be incorporated into property book unit supply enhanced (PBUSE) tracking and included in the command supply discipline program (CSDP) for monitoring and accountability.

1-28. Unit leaders will monitor and facilitate the calibration of TMDE within the organization IAW this manual, unit SOPs, and supporting regulations. Commanders receive delinquency rate reports and match rate reports between the unit internal TMDE inventory quantity and identity and the supporting calibration center IMRF. Missing or additional items will be identified and addressed immediately to ensure the IMRF report coincides with the unit inventory. The IMRF serves as a quality check against the unit-generated list, not as a unit inventory. Unit TMDE lists and the IMRF reconciliation match rate goal is 98 to 102 percent of the IMRF. The unit TMDE delinquency standard is two percent delinquent or less relative to the IMRF.

1-29. Maintenance units demand specially qualified Soldiers and personnel to perform unique functions. These include but are not limited to maintenance test pilots (MPs), 151AEs, NDI technicians, certified welders, confined spaced trained technicians, PCE/PPE certified users and maintainers, HAZMAT inspectors, and technicians. The commander will track required positions by grade and qualification to assess the impact on mission performance and assist human resources personnel in prioritizing fills or operations staff officer (S-3) personnel with securing necessary training for currently assigned Soldiers. The percentage filled of these specially trained Soldiers directly impacts unit capabilities. The leadership must monitor and work toward increasing this percentage until capacity and requirements are reached.

1-30. Work orders failing to meet standards and not performing to the customer requirements will be rejected, cataloged, assessed, and mitigated by the unit leadership responding appropriately to prevent recurrence. The number of rejections against the number of completed work orders will be tracked and reported monthly and annually for possible trend analysis.

1-31. Maintenance measures will be reported (figure 1-2) in brief format to higher commands up to brigade level at least monthly and historically tracked for analysis of improvement, degradation, and goals achieved.

Maintenance Measures Report						
	Oct	Nov	Dec	Jan	Feb	Mar
Production index/ workorders over 60 days	98% /20	101% /12	103% /1	100% /0	97% /8	
500 hour service completion average (standard = 15 days)	17 (+2)	15	15	14 (-1)	14 (-1)	
Workorder rejection rate	0%	0%	0%	.0014%	0%	
Special tools serviceable on hand %	75%	75%	77%	78%	80%	
TMDE delinquency % / IMRF match %	.5% / 100%	1% / 101%	1% / 101%	3% / 97%	.7% / 100%	
Specially qualified personnel on hand %	65 %	65 %	77 %	77 %	83 %	

Last annual ARMS date/ rating %	Jul XX/89%	Current tri-annual ARMS progress rating	96%

Figure 1-2. Maintenance measures reporting example

TECHNICAL SUPPLY MEASURES

1-32. Technical supply measures provide immediate support to the maintenance measures and further enable combat power generation through conservation of time and funding. Technical supply measures exploit success and expose inefficiencies by right sizing parts stockage, minimizing excess, and ensuring funding is applied both for and against unit budget accounts. Technical supply measures include—

- Average customer wait-time.
- Rates for zero balance items with due out requests against them.
- Inventory accuracy and excess management.
- Aviation Class IX (air) budget reconciliation.

1-33. Technical supply sections will track and report monthly the average wait time in days required to satisfy standard and high-priority parts requests. This provides an indication to the commander of how well the unit parts and supplies requirements are addressed with items on-hand. This reporting assists in determining when unsatisfied demand rates are low and items are appropriate in the unit and authorized stockage list (ASL).

1-34. Zero balance items with due-out requests against them affect average customer wait times. These items are normally stocked by technical supply for the customer shop, platoon, or unit, but existing quantities are exhausted and require replenishment. Low zero balance with due-out rates indicates a healthy and properly tailored technical supply operation, where high rates may justify increasing quantities on-hand or expediting certain items experiencing unusual delivery delays.

1-35. Frequent inventories of technical supply operations ensure quantities match automation information reports and the request and fill process will continue to function properly. The inventory match rate for all stockage is 95 percent, which demonstrates good stewardship of parts and supplies. Commanders will set a schedule IAW Army regulation (AR) 710-2 to ensure inventories occur frequently to generate useful data for operations analysis. Commanders will resource technical supply operations appropriately to improve and ensure inventory accuracy and consistency. The more accurate the inventory the less idle and excess items remain in possession of the unit. The retention of serviceable and unserviceable excess items ties up funds and assets needed by other units and must be avoided. Leaders will ensure excess items receive immediate turn-in actions according to the unit SOP to improve unit mobility and technical supply budget fidelity.

1-36. Technical supply officers will constantly manage and balance the unit Class IX (air) budget. The Class IX (air) budget includes Class IX and limited items of other classes of supply in direct support of aviation maintenance missions. This is an on-going process and should be updated immediately as expenditures and credits occur. Commanders will review the budget monthly to ensure projections and statuses remain in line with available funding. However, since the budget is managed as events occur, the budget report must be available upon demand. Additionally, face-to-face comptroller reconciliations may be required to correct errors detected during budget management or command review. These reconciliations can return unapplied credits to a unit and improve its budget posture.

1-37. These measures will be reported (figure 1-3, page 1-8) in brief format to higher commands up to brigade level at least monthly and historically tracked for analysis of improvement, degradation, and goals achieved.

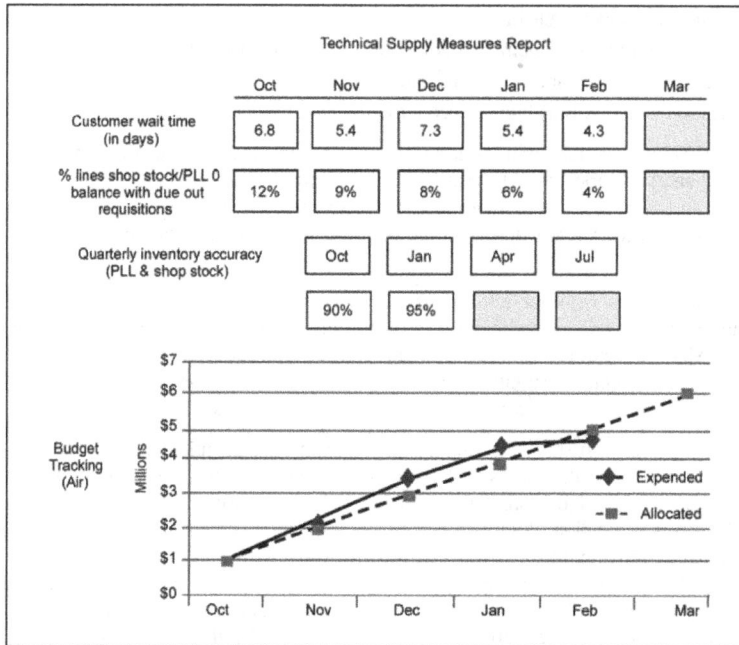

Figure 1-3. Technical supply measures reporting example

CORE UNIT MEASURES

1-38. While not unique to aviation field maintenance units, core unit measures enable leaders to assess the underlying operations of a maintenance unit supporting both maintenance and tactical operations. Individual Soldier training is significant and reportable but is not included in maintenance unit core measures due to the amount of regulations and guidance available in other publications. Those statistics and requirements are best tracked and reported (figure 1-4 and figure 1-5, page 1-9) to higher commands as training specific goals and measures. With that understanding, core unit measures establish rhythm, pulse, and Soldier identification with unit goals of a maintenance unit. Core unit measures are—

- Vehicle and non-flying system readiness rates.
- Semi-annual safety survey results and hazard log management.
- Monthly individual flying and safety awards presentations.
- CSDP results:
  - Shortage annex reduction status.
  - Property accountability (cash collection voucher, statement of charges, financial liability investigation of property loss).
  - Unit budget status (Classes II, IV, and VII).
- Unit reenlistment mission accomplishment.
- Uniform Code of Military Justice (UCMJ) action rate.

Core Measures Report — Part A

	Oct	Nov	Dec	Jan	Feb	Mar
Non-aviaton systems and vehicle operational rate	98%	94%	88%	95%	91%	
Individual/safety/flight awards	2/4/1	4/5/0	6/10/1	3/4/3	1/2/1	
Unfilled shortages/ funds needed for 100% fill	400/ $89K	332/ $74K	310/ $69K	303/ $68K	301/ $67K	
Open hazard log entries	12	12	8	7	7	

Last semi-annual safety survey	Dec XX		Next semi-annual safety survey	Jun XX+1

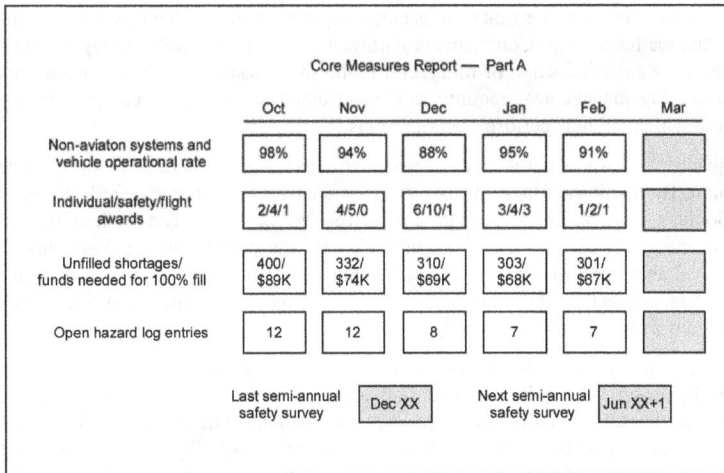

Figure 1-4. Core unit measures reporting-part A example

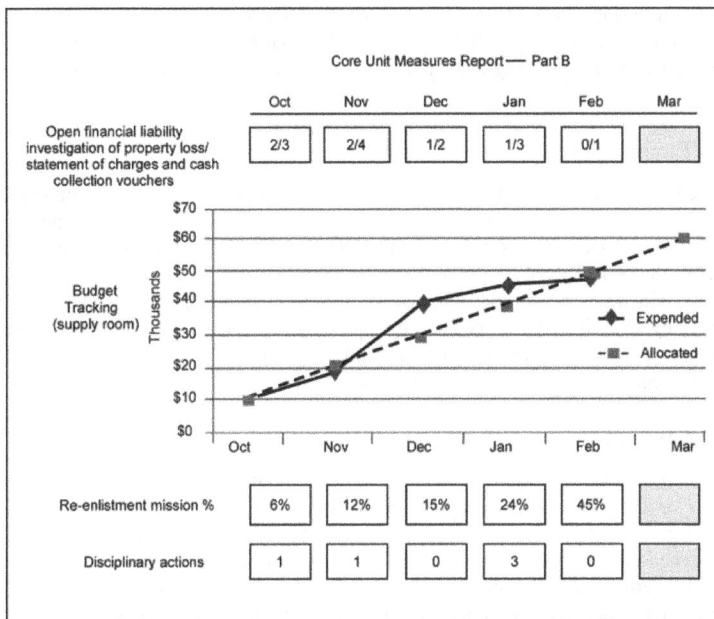

Core Unit Measures Report — Part B

	Oct	Nov	Dec	Jan	Feb	Mar
Open financial liability investigation of property loss/ statement of charges and cash collection vouchers	2/3	2/4	1/2	1/3	0/1	

Budget Tracking (supply room)

Thousands

$70
$60
$50
$40
$30
$20
$10
$0

Oct   Nov   Dec   Jan   Feb   Mar

— ◆ — Expended
— ■ — Allocated

	Oct	Nov	Dec	Jan	Feb	Mar
Re-enlistment mission %	6%	12%	15%	24%	45%	
Disciplinary actions	1	1	0	3	0	

Figure 1-5. Core unit measures reporting-part B example

1-39. Commanders traditionally monitor their motor pools, but in aviation maintenance units, additional emphasis must be placed on enablers to ensure availability. Downed aircraft recovery team (DART) systems, material handling equipment (MHE), power generation and ground support equipment (GSE) and peculiar ground support equipment (PGSE) readiness should receive separate enumeration up the chain of command since their missions directly generate combat power, and unique repair requirements often demand maintenance team supporting member assistance to accomplish.

1-40. Semi-annual safety survey results and accident reports establish reference points for the unit and can rapidly populate the hazard log. Commanders will track semi-annual safety survey results and hazard log entries progress toward elimination or mitigation in the same fashion as the production index work order backlog. Hazard log management requires command emphasis to ensure compliance and improve the environment in which Soldiers perform their missions.

1-41. The quantity of awards across the spectrum of individual, safety, and flying indicates the positive health of a unit. By monitoring these quantities, leaders ensure appropriate awards are not neglected, and deserving Soldiers receive timely recognition. Excessive quantities can undermine their value, and insufficient quantities display a lack of consideration for the performance of individuals. By positively tracking these numbers and establishing a history, units can maintain the proper balance and increase unit health. By looking across the MOE, units can identify Soldiers who uniquely contribute to improving those measures and may award them appropriately.

1-42. The CSDP for aviation maintenance units is a critical program and demands direct leader involvement. By ensuring acquisition, retention and maintenance of resources, tools and equipment, leaders reduce the burdens on individuals, sections, and platoons to accomplish their missions. Having the right compliment of serviceable items to perform a maintenance task directly improves the ability, morale, and effectiveness of maintenance units. They ensure equipment needed is on hand and functional. This mentality applies to our maintenance units and the technicians who repair our systems. They deserve and require all equipment on hand and serviceable to perform their combat missions. The Soldiers retain the requirement for securing those items, but the commander owns the acquisition and replenishment responsibility and must meet it through their CSDP. The three pillars of achieving a productive CSDP are shortage annex elimination, reducing loss of accountability actions, and balancing and monitoring the unit budget.

Shortage Annex Elimination

1-43. Once the change of command inventory is complete, the maintenance unit commander possesses a starting point for the shortage annex elimination process. The PBUSE unit shortage annex will include all components, items, and special tools needed for tracking and elimination through acquisition. This includes new additions to the shortage annex generated by unserviceable turn-ins to unit supply. Each month, the supply sergeant will delineate for the commander progress, additions, and setbacks to eliminating the shortage annex, by quantity, class, accounting requirements code (ARC), acquisition advice code, and funding required. This enables commanders to apply appropriate resources and surge if necessary to eliminate the shortages. This is an easily quantifiable measure.

Reducing Loss of Accountability Actions

1-44. Loss of accountability of items demands action IAW AR 710-2. Whether an accepted loss, simple cash collection voucher, statement of charges, or a complete financial liability investigation of property loss, maintenance commanders must implement a vehicle to confirm and conclude the reason for loss. The initiation of the chosen vehicle allows integration onto the shortage annex of the item(s) for replenishment and serves as a deterrent to negligence by users and hand receipt holders. A solid commitment to proper accounting prevents carelessness and preserves systems, tools, and special tools for future use. It precludes the frequent repurchasing of lost or damaged items allowing the commander to focus budget resources on additional unit priorities including automation and quality of life requirements.

Balancing and Monitoring the Unit Budget

1-45. The executive officer or supply sergeant will constantly monitor the unit Class II, IV, and VII budget. This is an ongoing process and should be updated immediately as expenditures and credits occur. Commanders will review the budget monthly to ensure projections and statuses remain in line with available funding. However, since the budget is managed as events occur, the budget report must be available upon demand. Additionally, face-to-face comptroller reconciliations may be required to correct errors detected during unit supply budget management or command review. These reconciliations can return unapplied credits to a unit and improve its budget posture.

Unit Reenlistment Mission Accomplishment

1-46. The reenlistment mission accomplishment of a unit exemplifies its quality. With the assistance of first sergeants, reenlistment NCOs and career counselors, maintenance unit commanders possess the tools to establish, validate, and improve retention operations. Positive trends in reenlistment should be recognized and highlighted, while negative trends that jeopardize mission accomplishment must be assessed, addressed, and mitigated. Healthy aviation maintenance units generally experience little to no difficulty meeting retention goals. Healthy units are easily identified by the reports of their MOE. Those units with high MOE assessments show little difficulty retaining quality Soldiers.

Uniform Code of Military Justice Action Rate

1-47. Consequently, if maintenance units experience low incidents of UCMJ infractions, it is likely they are a high functioning unit with very solid MOE assessments. The converse is also true. Leader engagement in ensuring maintenance Soldiers are mentored, challenged, and properly resourced moves UCMJ infraction rates down as Soldiers align themselves with the goals and Soldiers of the unit, and witness their contributions to mission accomplishment. This is one of the significant factors in quantifying MOE and exposing aviation maintenance personnel to the goals of the organization. If units experience high UCMJ infractions, commanders and leaders should make a full assessment including what MOE fall short of objectives.

1-48. These core unit measures will be reported in brief format to higher commands up to brigade level at least monthly, and historically tracked for analysis of improvement, degradation, and goals achieved.

> *Note.* Units generating monthly MOE reports, the support operations aviation section, and the brigade aviation materiel officer (BAMO)/SAMO will maintain MOE report archives for the period covering the previous commander of the unit generating the report or one year (whichever is greater). Additionally, they will maintain the entire period of the current commander to capture trends, and assess and integrate any lessons learned IAW AR 11-33. Component II and III units will report the cumulative data for the preceding semi-annual period until mobilized. Once mobilized, monthly reporting and active duty archiving requirements take effect.

MANAGEMENT SKILLS

1-49. Maintenance managers continually look for ways to improve planning, organizing, coordinating, directing, and controlling. Managers must also be proactive (influencing events before they happen) rather than reactive (reacting to events as they happen). Feedback and after-action reviews (AARs) are proactive tools used by maintenance managers.

1-50. Small improvements in the overall sustainment system produce greater, lasting results than a concentrated effort directed toward one or two specific areas. The maintenance manager must be careful that changes to maintenance operations do not undermine other unit initiatives.

SUPERVISION

1-51. First-line supervisors are the commanders' first-line of defense in the prevention of accidents. Reducing or eliminating accidents will retain available manpower and equipment to execute the unit maintenance mission. The commander depends on first-line supervisors to accomplish the day-to-day mission and ensure the welfare of the troops.

1-52. First-line supervisors are the individual Soldier's primary source of assistance and further professional development. The first-line supervisor's major challenge lies in ensuring that the people they supervise accomplish the mission correctly the first time. These supervisors need to know the standards and MOE objectives set by the chain of command to direct their Soldiers' efforts.

1-53. First-line supervisors must be aware of mission requirements and the capabilities and limitations of the Soldiers under their control. They must continuously train their subordinates to support the needs of the Soldier. Next to the mission, the welfare and professional development of Soldiers is paramount in the supervisor's mind.

MOTIVATION

1-54. The leadership demonstrated by commanders and supervisors directly influences the motivation of Soldiers. Effective leaders define objectives, communicate them, evaluate how well they are achieved, and provide feedback to Soldiers doing the work. Most Soldiers want to perform well. They need to know the objectives and standards, and receive performance feedback. Superior achievement must receive recognition, and substandard performance rapidly corrected. Leaders will also focus on resourcing their Soldiers appropriately to improve effectiveness. Maintenance managers may underestimate the importance of this process and the dramatic benefits and improved enthusiasm proper resourcing can generate.

TECHNICAL SKILLS

1-55. Technical skills involve the ability to perform tasks associated with duty positions. On-the-job training (OJT) enhances these technical skills. A technically and tactically trained Soldier is one of the commander most important assets. The commander must continuously strive for high levels of training to provide adequate maintenance support to operational units.

1-56. The Army training system depends on the unit commander continuing the training process begun during advanced individual training (AIT). Training resources must be identified and made available to ensure quality training for assigned Soldiers. To the commander and maintenance manager, training on technical tasks is as important as training on tactical skills. Unit task lists (UTLs) and Soldier training publications (STPs) establish the requirements for technical maintenance training.

1-57. Contract maintenance can potentially diminish Soldier technical skills if improperly managed. Over-reliance on contractor maintenance may continue to erode Soldiers' experience level. The loss of maintenance experience will negatively affect all aviation Soldiers as they progress to higher levels of responsibility. Every experience gained by Soldiers enhances their future leadership qualities and capabilities. Maintenance tasks conducted by contractors can provide training opportunities for assigned Soldiers and their supervisors. Contractors with specialized skills or high levels of experience can effectively serve as trainers, improving Soldier skills. When practical, commanders/leaders should coordinate and create training opportunities involving Soldiers, as well as contractors, performing maintenance procedures.

SECTION III – PRINCIPLES

POSITIONING MAINTENANCE SUPPORT

1-58. Maintenance managers will ensure the proper mix (type and location) of maintenance support meets the commanders' requirements. Early arrival of maintenance support in theater ensures deployed aircraft are made operational in a timely manner upon arrival into theater.

1-59. Each aviation maintenance company (AMC)/aviation maintenance troop (AMT) and aviation support company (ASC)/aviation support troop (AST) can conduct split-based operations by deploying mission specific field maintenance teams (FMTs) within a single theater of operations. Each AMC/AMT is responsible for performing field maintenance on its assigned/attached aircraft. ASCs assigned to aviation support battalions (ASBs) and ASTs assigned to air cavalry squadrons (ACSs) provide field maintenance support by conducting intermediate aviation maintenance according to the maintenance allocation chart (MAC).

1-60. Aircraft must be prepared and repaired quickly and as far forward as possible. This requirement implies a forward thrust of maintenance within the combat aviation brigade (CAB)/ACS AO Maintenance assets will move as far forward as the tactical situation permits to repair unserviceable and damaged aircraft to return them to the fight as quickly as possible.

AVIATION MAINTENANCE PLANNING AND EXECUTION

1-61. Field maintenance operations must be conducted according to ARs, policies, and procedures. An aviation maintenance unit relies on an efficient and effective maintenance program. A sound maintenance plan, at its core, has a dedicated group of maintainers and technicians who apply the sustainment imperatives to the planning and execution of scheduled and unscheduled maintenance.

1-62. This maintenance approach takes into consideration the following elements: problem, plan, people, parts, time, tools, and training (P4T3). P4T3 is a management tool for leaders at all levels. This management tool serves as a common-sense platform for effective leadership, oversight, and management of maintenance.

SECTION IV – PROBLEM, PLAN, PEOPLE, PARTS, TIME, TOOLS, AND TRAINING

PROBLEM

1-63. The maintenance event or problem must first be identified. This process can be as simple as identifying a particular scheduled maintenance event, such as a 300-hour service that an assigned/attached aircraft is approaching or replacing rivets in a driveshaft cover.

1-64. The failure of an operating aircraft system or subsystem, resulting from improper maintenance procedures, can have catastrophic and deadly consequences to personnel and equipment. Aviation maintainers must adhere to the most current applicable aircraft technical manuals (TMs) and references when conducting maintenance on aircraft.

1-65. While conducting scheduled and unscheduled maintenance, maintenance managers or maintainers may encounter problems. Unanticipated/unscheduled maintenance may surface; affecting a mission after the mission has been accepted and planned for execution. Similarly, maintenance teams, when conducting scheduled maintenance (phase maintenance), may encounter problems that hinder timely completion of a scheduled maintenance phase.

1-66. When unforeseen problems are encountered during scheduled or unscheduled maintenance, OR, and mission accomplishment is hindered. Likewise, unforeseen problems encountered during scheduled maintenance will affect units' OR rates. Maintenance managers must devise a maintenance plan that returns unserviceable aircraft to an FMC status.

1-67. Prescribed troubleshooting procedures are the first maintenance task the crew and maintenance personnel must complete to standard, particularly during unscheduled maintenance:
- Are maintainers diagnosing the faults using established troubleshooting procedures?
- Are the components causing the aircraft fault properly identified and repaired?

1-68. Disciplined use of TMs and adherence to troubleshooting procedures and MACs are critical to aircraft readiness rates. Incorrect diagnosis at the start of maintenance troubleshooting procedures will waste time, repair parts, and ultimately, affect Class IX (air) budgets. If the maintainers cannot diagnose the problem, experts (maintenance officers/technicians, technical representatives, and aircraft maintenance contractors) should be involved early.

1-69. The ASC or AST maintenance support personnel or logistics assistance representatives (LARs) will assist when requested. They will also provide maintenance support throughout the troubleshooting process.

PLANNING

1-70. Planning involves implementing measures and devices to correct the problem without discontinuing the mission. The unit maintenance SOP and maintenance plan are the first steps toward ensuring a solid basis for quality control (QC). In planning maintenance, the production control (PC) officer-in-charge (OIC) will ask—

- How will we accomplish the task?
- What is the maintenance plan for performing the task to completion?
- Who is responsible for performance of the task?
- Can the maintenance be performed by the owning unit, or will it have to be performed by the AMC/AMT or ASC/AST?
- Can the maintenance be performed on site, or must the aircraft be relocated?

1-71. The leadership must enforce and execute the maintenance plan. The maintenance plan is continuously reviewed and updated. The planning process continues until the task or event is resolved.

1-72. The maintenance plan for scheduled services must contain adequate details to ensure uniformity. Such details could include the maintainer—

- Reviewing the maintenance task.
- Anticipating mandatory replacement parts.
- Gathering all of the parts in one location.
- Ensuring required consumable material is on hand.
- Ensuring tools are available in sufficient quantity and type.
- Ensuring TMDE calibration is current.

1-73. Planning for unscheduled maintenance is a team effort calling for platoon leaders and company/troop maintenance personnel to identify necessary resources needed to do the job. Junior leaders can initiate the planning process simply by asking and obtaining answers to P4T3 questions outlined in this chapter.

1-74. Technical supply coordinates with the supply support activity (SSA) to see if parts/components are available locally. If the part is not available at the SSA, check with other aviation units or activities. PC coordinates with similar units with the same mission-design-series (MDS) aircraft to see if parts are available. PC also coordinates with QC, airframe repair platoon (ARP), component repair platoon (CRP), and maneuver companies to work after normal duty hours if extended maintenance is required.

1-75. PC should coordinate with the ASC/AST for maintenance support or with contractor field service representatives (CFSRs), maintenance contractors, and LARs for assistance and guidance on accomplishing repair and ordering parts/components if necessary.

PEOPLE

1-76. Maintenance managers will assess available resources to ensure adequately trained personnel and the required level of expertise is available to conduct maintenance (scheduled/unscheduled). The maintenance manager and commander should minimize conflicts between maintenance events and scheduled training (such as weapons qualification and driver training) when they are preparing for major maintenance events. Trained personnel will have the military occupational specialty (MOS) classification or additional skill identifier authorizing them to perform the repairs.

1-77. The MAC will show the level of maintenance required to perform repairs. The maintenance manager uses the MAC to determine if repairs can be done internally (AMC, AMT, or externally [ASC/AST/contractors]).

1-78. Supervision is an on-going process and must be accomplished throughout the entire phase of the repair. Section sergeants are responsible for the direct supervision of maintenance personnel who are performing specific jobs or repairs.

1-79. AMC/AMT and ASC/AST commanders and first sergeants must continually manage the use of low-density MOS Soldiers. Leaders should ensure the priority is for Soldiers to perform jobs that hone their technical skills instead of working on non-job-related details or duties.

1-80. At every opportunity, new Soldiers should be placed with more experienced Soldiers to conduct specific tasks. This training practice will ensure the new Soldiers get the training and experience needed to perform the task on their own in the future.

PARTS

1-81. Before performing maintenance, PC personnel should verify they have the correct type and quantity of parts. Parts assessments are necessary to determine what is required and available to correct deficiencies. If parts/components are not available, a request for the necessary parts/components must be processed immediately.

1-82. Before beginning scheduled maintenance events, to reduce not mission capable supply (NMCS) time, PC will ensure owning unit personnel order time-change components with ample lead-time. Additionally, crew chiefs and maintenance personnel must accurately identify the correct types and quantities of parts/components required to facilitate the maintenance action.

1-83. If the primary stock number is not available, check federal logistics (FEDLOG) data for substitute or interchangeable stock numbers. In some cases, parts, components, and common hardware may have multiple stock numbers because more than one manufacturer produces the same part.

Note. QC personnel will notify maintenance officers and NCOs when 100 hours remain until replacement of hourly components and/or when two months remain until replacement of calendar components. Obtain this information from the Unit Level Logistics System-Aviation (Enhanced) (ULLS-A [E]) system.

1-84. Aircraft maintainers and crew chiefs must ensure removed components are properly cleaned and inspected to determine serviceability. They must properly tag and store serviceable parts removed from an aircraft and inspected by a technical inspector (TI) to ensure parts are on-hand and serviceable when it is time to reinstall them. Aircraft maintainers and crew chiefs must properly tag unserviceable components, have QC technically inspect and sign the tag, and promptly turn in components to the technical supply section.

1-85. If repairs are beyond their capability, then a DA Form 2407 (Maintenance Request) is generated by ULLS-A (E) and submitted to the ASC/AST PC for support. Prompt submission of an ULLS-A (E) generated DA Form 2407 to a higher-level maintenance support is essential to facilitate ASC/AST personnel in acquiring the necessary parts. This form can be used by ASC/AST maintainers to record accomplishment of maintenance requested on the work order.

1-86. Maintenance managers will encounter maintenance or sustainment challenges that may ultimately affect the unit assigned mission. Maintenance managers must consider time and tools to minimize or eliminate these challenges.

TIME

1-87. For the maintenance manager, time is critical to mission accomplishment. Maintenance managers must accurately evaluate time constraints when determining if the available time to accomplish a maintenance repair is adequate.

1-88. Maintenance managers should consider the following questions when conducting maintenance procedures:

* How much time is required to complete the maintenance action?
* Is there sufficient time free from detractors to affect the repair?

1-89. The estimated completion date of maintenance that brings an aircraft to mission capable status is crucial in forecasting combat power availability. Leaders must allow adequate time for aircraft maintainers to perform maintenance on the equipment.

1-90. If additional problems or shortages of resources occur resulting in an extension of the estimated completion date, platoon leaders must inform the PC OIC immediately.

TOOLS

1-91. The maintenance manager, when assessing maintenance procedures, should consider if the unit has the correct type and quantity of tools to perform the maintenance tasks. This is especially true during split-based operations.

1-92. Supervisors must identify tools required to do a job and make sure they are on-hand, serviceable, and, if required, calibrated. Leaders must educate themselves on the different tools and enforce TM/technical bulletin (TB) standards when aircraft maintenance is performed.

TRAINING

LEADER TRAINING AND DEVELOPMENT

1-93. Commanders must afford junior maintenance leaders the opportunity to develop an understanding of maintenance operations and management. This leadership training is an essential building block critical to leadership development. Maintenance leadership skills taught and reinforced every day in garrison translate well to a field environment, to include a tactical and combative environment. Leaders must know the maintenance standard to enforce it and the MOE to improve them.

1-94. Fundamentals of maintenance management can be observed and learned by involvement in regularly scheduled PC meetings. Attendance and involvement in the battalion or ASC/AST PC meeting is only one level of maintenance management and is an enabler in the development of junior leaders. Another enabler is time management. Time management is critical to maintenance planning, preparation and execution of maintenance support missions.

1-95. Competent maintenance leaders should mentor junior leaders in the many facets of developing a sound maintenance plan and timeline. Once trained, junior maintenance leaders should, at a minimum—

* Know the aviation maintenance MOE and quantify them into a usable report(s) IAW the units SOP.
* Assess the maintenance mission and maintenance requirements in support of the operational maneuver battalion.

- Compare the time needed to accomplish the maintenance objectives with allocated time, personnel, and equipment and ensured they are aligned before a maintenance action begins.
- Compare the time needed for maintenance actions with the allocated time and determine if additional courses of actions are available to safely expedite maintenance procedures.
- Maximize the skill and experience of assigned maintenance personnel to minimize supported units aircraft downtime.
- Be assertive in providing guidance to maintenance personnel.

1-96. Maintenance development at all levels is an important aspect of leadership. Maintenance management affects mission training/execution of essential warfighting missions. Development of junior leaders is critical for their professional development; it also prepares them for the next level of responsibility. Junior maintenance leaders are functional members of the maintenance team. Preparing them to operate in a fluid maintenance environment enables them to be in synchronization with the unit maintenance support plan and achieve aviation maintenance MOE goals.

TECHNICAL TRAINING

1-97. Technical training is conducted at three training bases: the United States Army Aviation Logistics School, Fort Eustis, Virginia; the United States Army Aviation Center of Excellence, Fort Rucker, Alabama; and the Military Intelligence Center, Fort Huachuca, Arizona.

1-98. AIT should not be considered the end of individual training. At the conclusion of AIT, the training the Soldier has received is equivalent to that of an apprentice. The gaining aviation unit commander is then responsible for enhancing and expanding the training Soldiers received in AIT. This enhanced unit training will increase the maintainers' ability, skill, and knowledge. This training includes the integration of airframe and supportive maintenance specialties. An apprentice possesses entry-level knowledge and a skill set that must be carefully groomed and honed to develop into a master or seasoned maintainer.

1-99. The commander/leader, maintenance officers/technicians, and NCOICs must identify training resources and make training meaningful for their Soldiers. To a maintenance company/troop commander, training on technical tasks is as important as training on tactical skills. UTLs and STPs establish the requirements for technical maintenance training.

1-100. Commanders must initiate and maintain a viable MOS sustainment and continuation training program. Maintenance supervisors must coordinate efforts to establish effective training. IAW the commander's guidance, subordinate leaders, and supervisors will identify critical or high frequency tasks, and establishes their recurring training requirements. MOS training must encompass the use of TMs to reinforce proper maintenance procedures. Supervisors will ensure critical tasks in support of the METL and unit mission receive formal training at a frequency outlined in the appropriate STP for each skill level. If no current STP exists, supervisors will establish a critical task-training plan.

Note. Interface with the technical training bases to assists in unit program development when STPs are not available.

1-101. While deployed, commanders must continue this process to sustain or retrain certain tasks as needed. The commander's program will include individual training for Soldiers in the unit to routinely evaluate and document their MOS proficiency. The MOS training program must integrate individual training with phase and progressive maintenance operations, and other collective training. The MOS training plan will maximize utilization of sister unit integration (for low density MOS), cross training, train-up, and sustainment programs.

1-102. Conducting daily maintenance operations provides opportunities for NCOs (primary trainers) to conduct formal MOS sustainment training, based on established procedures, with applicable standards from approved publications. Increased risk of damage to equipment and injury to personnel could result when approved procedures are not followed. To develop an effective unit training program, commanders will employ a seven-step cycle:

- Step 1. Establish maintenance-training objectives.
- Step 2. Plan resources (personnel, time, facilities, and training aids).
- Step 3. Train the trainers.
- Step 4. Provide resources.
- Step 5. Assess risk and safety considerations.
- Step 6. Conduct training.
- Step 7. Evaluate results based on the objectives.

1-103.   Training individual tasks to standard and relating individual training to collective mission essential tasks remain the responsibility of trainers. Trainers of all grades must use the following steps to plan and evaluate training:

- Identify individual training needed. The trainer determines required subordinate tasks. The unit's METL, Army training and evaluation program, and MOS training plan assist the trainer in defining the individual training needed.
- Plan the training. Trainers can usually integrate or conduct training concurrently with other training or during opportune periods of low activity. The unit's Army training and evaluation program assists trainers in identifying individual tasks for training and evaluation concurrently with collective tasks.
- Gather training references and materials. The MOS training plan lists the required references for each task.
- Apply composite risk management (CRM) principles to identify and mitigate safety concerns. Analyze the risk involved in training a specific task. Use the risk assessment matrix in FM 5-19. If the planned training anticipates a high risk, allow the commander to exercise risk reduction options, if available.
- Train each Soldier. Show each Soldier the task to standard and explain, step-by-step, how to perform the task. Give each Soldier at least one chance to perform the task.
- Emphasize training in mission-oriented protective posture-level 4 (MOPP-4). Soldier performance in a chemical, biological, radiological, and nuclear (CBRN) environment is difficult and demands familiarization. The combat effectiveness of the Soldier and the unit can degrade quickly when performing a task in mission-oriented protective posture-level 4 (MOPP-4).
- Check each Soldier. Evaluate how well each Soldier performs the tasks in the manual. These evaluations may be conducted during individual training sessions or while evaluating individual proficiency during the conduct of unit collective tasks. The MOS training plan determines how often to evaluate Soldiers on each task to ensure they sustain proficiency.
- Retrain and evaluate. Work with each Soldier until each task performance meets specified standards.

1-104. Leaders at all levels must ensure Soldiers are rotated through as many positions in their respective and associated field of training as possible to develop well-rounded skill sets. Upon reception and in processing, Soldiers and NCOs should be screened for their past duty positions and given different jobs to ensure they are as well rounded as possible.

1-105. Maintenance training is an integral component to combat readiness training in an aviation unit. It must be incorporated into scheduled training periods. Maintenance management training may be scheduled as a part of leader development training. Hands-on instruction by maintenance supervisors must be incorporated into scheduled and unscheduled maintenance periods.

1-106. Maintenance training is often best achieved when "learning by doing." OJT, with carefully provided supervision, provides huge dividends to aviation units in the long term. When conducting OJT, maintenance supervisors are required to keep good records to ensure critical tasks are not overlooked in the training plan.

1-107. Soldiers proficient in certain tasks may oversee apprentice Soldiers in execution of maintenance tasks. For example, an aviation maintainer may gain proficiency under the supervision of an experienced phase maintenance team chief before becoming a crew chief. Cross-training maintenance tasks are also important, especially in low-density MOSs.

1-108. Leaders at all levels must understand basic maintenance management principles. This understanding includes how to plan for and manage flow charts, bank time, scheduled and unscheduled maintenance, aircraft performance deficiency write-up procedures, when to defer (annotated as delay in ULLS-A[E]) maintenance, and the Army supply system. Training must also include cross training of enlisted maintenance personnel to maximize their benefit to the unit and their own professional development.

P4T3 vignette

During the PC meeting, sergeant first class (SFC) Vasquez, the aircraft maintenance platoon sergeant, was informed her platoon would receive aircraft 15862 from the 1-224th Aviation Brigade the following day for a 300-hour inspection. SFC Vasquez notified the platoon leader, first lieutenant (1LT) Rodgers, and then asked staff sergeant (SSG) Polmanteer to accompany her and the platoon leader to the PC meeting, having identified him as the most qualified leader in her platoon for a supervisory position. SFC Vasquez and SSG Polmanteer made note of the tail number and after the PC meeting went to prepare the platoon brief.

SFC Vasquez supervised numerous 300-hour inspections; prior to every job, she thoroughly planned and reviewed how to conduct the work. SFC Vasquez emphasized to SSG Polmanteer the importance of treating each work order with the highest degree of regard and preparation. With two new Soldiers on her team, she and SSG Polmanteer reviewed the plan and decided which portions of the inspection the new Soldiers would work and with whom the Soldiers would be placed to receive the most effective mentoring.

SFC Vasquez and SSG Polmanteer confirmed with the technical supply sergeant that a 300-hour service pack was available for the following day. The technical supply sergeant, who was present at the PC meeting, anticipated their visit and confirmed a 300-hour service pack was complete and available. After the visit, the technical supply sergeant assembled another 300-hour service pack to replace the one set out for the maintenance platoon.

SFC Vasquez also ensured aviation support equipment section (ASES) had all required support systems available during the scheduled service to preclude delays.

SFC Vasquez reviewed the training schedule with 1LT Rodgers and SSG Polmanteer to determine if any other requirements had the potential to impact the planned period of time to complete the inspection.

SFC Vasquez and SSG Polmanteer used a locally produced 300-hour inspection check sheet to ensure the tools needed were available and calibration was up-to-date.

After a complete review of the maintenance plan and satisfied that preparation had been completed, SFC Vasquez informed SSG Polmanteer that he would lead this inspection. SSG Polmanteer then received guidance to prepare a brief for the platoon leader to approve the planning and resource any shortfalls. Following receipt of the platoon leader approval of the plan, SSG Polmanteer called in the team and briefed them for the next job.

This page intentionally left blank.

Chapter 2
Maintenance Levels, Structures, and Roles

A comprehensive unit maintenance program is critical for the sustainment of weapon platforms, aircraft systems and subsystems, and GSE. A well-established and managed maintenance program exponentially increases the availability of operational assets for aviation maneuver commanders conducting training and tactical missions.

SECTION I – TWO-LEVEL MAINTENANCE

2-1. AR 750-1 and Department of the Army pamphlet (DA PAM) 750-1 outline the concepts, roles, responsibilities, and authority requirements of the Army maintenance program. Field- and sustainment-level maintenance comes under the Army national maintenance program (NMP). The CAB/ACS commander has command and control (C2) authority for field-level maintenance.

2-2. The aviation logistics maintenance plan provides maintainers with the ability to replace forward and repair in the rear. In contiguous and noncontiguous areas, the rear is generally defined as an area with higher security and capability. Aviation maintainers will continue to repair limited items forward within the ASB, returning repaired components to the customer or the unit prescribed load list (PLL).

Contents

FIELD MAINTENANCE

2-3. Field maintenance is performed by CAB/ACS personnel assigned to maneuver companies/troops, AMCs/AMTs, and ASCs/ASTs. Flight companies perform authorized maintenance procedures within their capability. AMCs/AMTs assigned to aviation maneuver battalions and squadrons provide maintenance support to maneuver companies. Aviation maneuver battalion AMCs and squadron AMTs are more agile, flexible, and mobile than ASCs and ASTs because of reduced sets, kits, outfits, and tools (SKOT).

2-4. The AMC/AMT and ASC/AST are authorized to perform field-level maintenance. The AMC/AMT performs unit maintenance only, according to the MAC. The ASC/AST performs unit and intermediate maintenance.

SUSTAINMENT MAINTENANCE

2-5. According to FM 4-0, sustainment maintenance is the Army strategic support. The strategic support base is the backbone of the NMP and the sustainment maintenance system. At this level, maintenance supports the supply system by economically repairing or overhauling components. Maintenance management concentrates on identifying the needs of the Army supply system and managing programs to meet the supply system demands.

2-6. Sustainment maintenance support is divided and primarily performed by three separate entities: the original equipment manufacturers (OEMs) and their CFSRs; Army sustainment facilities, located at fixed-bases in the continental United States (CONUS); and by the national maintenance (NM) source of repair (SOR).

2-7. On a case-by-case basis, the CAB/ACS may request a letter of authorization (LOA) asking for specialized repair authorization (SRA), one time repair (OTR), or aircraft repair authorization (ARA) from Aviation and Missile Command (AMCOM) LARs to perform limited sustainment-level repairs on specific equipment classified as sustainment-level according to the MAC. Figure 2-1 depicts two-level maintenance illustrating the supported and supporting relationships of field and sustainment maintenance.

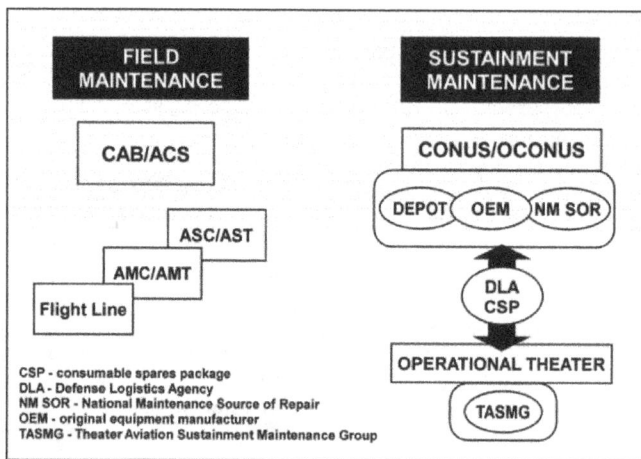

Figure 2-1. Two-level maintenance

SECTION II – AVIATION FIELD MAINTENANCE STRUCTURE

FIELD MAINTENANCE CHARACTERISTICS

2-8. CAB/ACS assets primarily perform field maintenance. Field maintenance includes unit and intermediate maintenance. Aviation field maintenance is characterized by "on-system maintenance," generally replacing components or performing component repair and return to the user. Aviation field maintenance capabilities vary based on SKOT, personnel assigned, and the authority directed by AR 750-1.

FIELD MAINTENANCE TEAMS

2-9. CAB/ACS maintenance unit flexibility is enhanced through the formation of FMTs. FMTs vary in composition depending on the support requirements, duration, and availability of personnel. Maintenance managers must know the estimated duration of a mission and the supported aircraft type to plan, forecast, and compose FMTs. Since most heavy tools, sophisticated TMDE, and shop sets are single or low density and generally cannot be divided; these FMTs provide the specialized split-based operations capability resident in the aviation maintenance units.

2-10. Commanders and maintenance managers send FMTs, parts, TMDE, and tools forward to conduct maintenance. FMTs also conduct battle damage assessment and repair (BDAR) and/or DART operations. See FM 3-04.513 for specific aircraft recovery operations.

2-11. When employing contractor FMTs, positioning them within the maintenance operational facilities can produce many teams consolidated in one location, multiple teams distributed across a geographic area, or a combination of heavy consolidation with some distributed teams. The aviation maintenance team will address the contractor employment considerations in the logistics estimate and planning for the organization, and continually evaluate effectiveness to determine any required adjustments.

FLIGHT LINE AND COMPANY/TROOP OPERATIONS

2-12. Maneuver company/troop maintenance activities primarily focus on operational inspections (preflight, post flight, and daily) and unscheduled maintenance. When deficiencies are identified and entered in the aircraft logbook, company/troop personnel must initiate corrective action, submit the entry for work order assignment, or confirm a document number against the entry as quickly as possible (no longer than 96 hours). Crew chiefs and aviation maintenance personnel also perform aircraft launch and recovery operations, maintenance operational checks (MOCs), vibration analysis, and maintain aircraft logbooks. Battalion maneuver companies and squadron maneuver troops receive support from the AMC/AMT when performing scheduled and unscheduled maintenance.

AVIATION MAINTENANCE COMPANY/TROOP

2-13. The AMC/AMT (formerly aviation unit maintenance) manages the battalion/squadron maintenance program, operates a centralized tool room, and performs field-level maintenance and scheduled services. In coordination with elements of the forward support company/forward support troop, the AMC/AMT conducts battalion-/squadron-level forward arming and refueling point (FARP) operations according to FM 3-04.104. The AMC/AMT troubleshoots airframe and component malfunctions, performs maintenance and repair actions, removes and replaces aircraft components, and performs maintenance test flights (MTFs) and MOCs.

2-14. The AMC/AMT provides sustainment support by processing, requesting, and storing Class IX (air) aircraft repair parts. Technical supply personnel operate unit-level Standard Army Management Information System (STAMIS), requisition Class IX (air) serviceable spares, and manage the battalion/squadron Class IX (air) PLL. The AMC/AMT performs unit-level repairs on aviation life support systems (ALSS). Aviation maintainers operate and maintain GSE.

2-15. The transportability requirement of the AMC/AMT is 100-percent and the unit transports 100 percent of their table of organization and equipment (TOE) in one movement using organic vehicles.

2-16. The AMC/AMT commander and PC OIC coordinate and schedule maintenance at forward locations of the battalion/squadron using FMTs. The members of these forward elements must be able to diagnose aircraft damage or serviceability rapidly and accurately. FMT operations follow these principles:

- FMTs may be used for aircraft, structural, component, avionics, or armament repair.
- When the time and situation allows, FMTs repair on site, rather than evacuate aircraft; these repairs includes BDAR.
- FMTs must be 100 percent mobile and transported by the fastest means available (usually by helicopter) or temporarily attached to customer units for extended repairs.
- FMTs may be oriented and equipped for special tasks to include recovery operations; type of aircraft recovery will depend on the assets available.

2-17. The AMC/AMT conducts BDAR and aircraft recovery operations and can be assisted by the ASC/AST. Soldiers from the AMC/AMT can repair aircraft onsite or prepare them for evacuation if necessary. In these situations, maintenance procedures may be expedited to meet operational objectives. In such cases, the unit commander may authorize the use of BDAR.

2-18. BDAR uses specialized assessment criteria, repair kits, applicable TMs, and trained personnel to return damaged aircraft to the battle as soon as possible. These repairs are often a short-term solution; temporary repair methods are used to meet operational needs only. Temporary repair methods will not be used if the tactical situation allows application of standard repair methods. When the tactical situation allows, permanent repairs are conducted on aircraft that received temporary repairs.

2-19. The AMC/AMT is organic to aviation battalions/squadrons. Figure 2-2 (page 2-4) depicts an AMC organic to a general support aviation battalion (GSAB). AMCs and AMTs (figure 2-3, page 2-4) are comprised of a headquarters (HQ) platoon, ARP, and CRP. The AMC of the attack reconnaissance battalions (ARBs) and AMTs retain a nearly identical structure as a GSAB or assault AMC. However, the ARB AMC and AMT add an armament repair capability to the avionics and electrical repair section under the CRP resulting in a systems repair section.

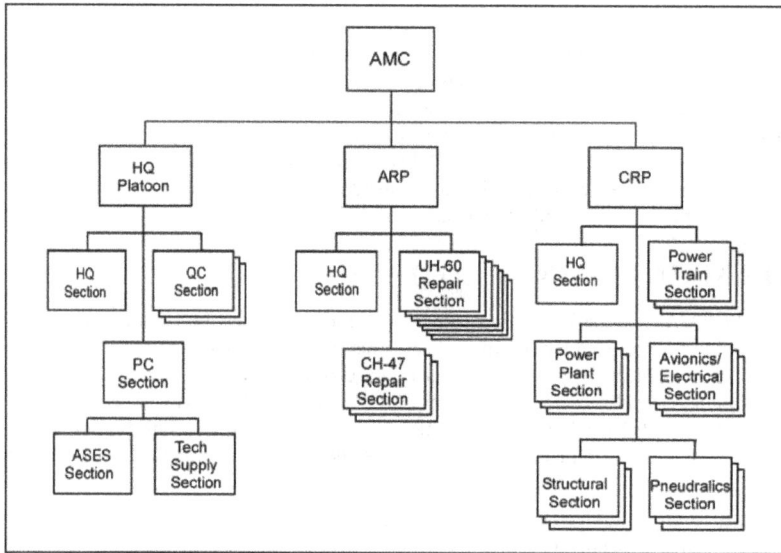

Figure 2-2. Aviation maintenance company

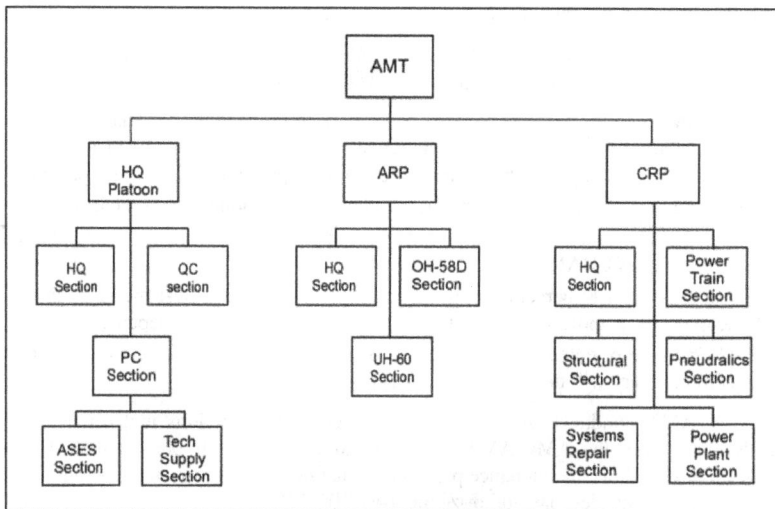

Figure 2-3. Aviation maintenance troop

HEADQUARTERS PLATOON

2-20. The HQ platoon consists of a PC, QC, ASES, and technical supply section (figures 2-2 and 2-3).

Headquarters

2-21. The HQ of the maintenance company/troop contains the command team and performs administrative and unit functions including personnel actions, training management, information management, reenlistment, safety, unit supply and arms room, CBRN, and communications support.

Quality Control Section

2-22. The QC section is accountable directly to the commander, thereby eliminating potential conflicts of interest among the PC section, the maintenance shops, and the supported units. This accountability structure allows the inspectors to maintain objectivity in the performance of their inspection duties. QC should be composed of the most qualified and technically proficient maintainers.

2-23. QC enforces standards in repair, overhaul, modification, safety-of-flight (SOF), and other required maintenance functions. QC follows the priorities that PC provides and maintains constant communication pertaining to the status and progress of maintenance. QC is also responsible for oversight of compliance with safety regulations in maintenance areas.

Production Control Section

2-24. The PC manages maintenance production within the AMC/AMT. The PC performs the following:

- Receives and processes work requests.
- Coordinates, schedules, and prioritizes maintenance and shop workloads.
- Maintains the status of aircraft parts and shop reports.
- Coordinates inspections, MOCs, and MTFs.
- Returns repaired aircraft and equipment to supported units.
- Directs ASES operations.
- Directs technical supply operations.

Aviation Support Equipment Section

2-25. ASES consolidates several support functions under one organization increasing performance and readiness. Placing the tool room, HAZMAT, TMDE, GSE, MHE, and DART under the leadership of a single formation, the commander ensures a higher level of training, readiness, performance, and regulatory compliance. ASES preserves combat power by allowing the HQ, ARP, and CRP to focus exclusively on aviation maintenance. ASES provides routine aviation maintenance support to the AMC/AMT under the direction of the PC section to ensure accomplishment of the AMC/AMT customer support goals. To function effectively, ASES at the AMC/AMT level usually consists of six to twelve Soldiers including an NCOIC appointed on orders by the commander. Due to its rotational nature, this is a non-modified table of organization and equipment (MTOE) section built from Soldiers within the unit. Soldiers are rotated into the ASES from the platoons within the company/troop and returned after serving approximately one year. This time line can be shorter in the focused mission saturation environment of unaccompanied short tours or combat. Commanders and first sergeants should time rotations to ensure a majority of experienced ASES Soldiers remain in the section to train newly assigned Soldiers. ASES Soldiers in the AMC/AMT perform six functions:

- Tool room operations.
- GSE maintenance and support.
- TMDE coordination management.
- MHE operations.
- Package petroleum, oils, and lubricants (POL) and HAZMAT operations and planning.
- Deliberate recovery DART support (unit maintenance aircraft recovery kit operations) and training.

2-26. ASES maintains the AMC/AMT compliment of aviation ground power units (AGPUs), generic aviation nitrogen generators, pressure washers, cranes, hoists, tractors, tugs, forklifts, aviation electrical power generators, jacks and recovery assets (unit maintenance aircraft recovery kit, DART trucks), as well as the tool room. ASES coordinates calibrations tracking, as well as equipment turn-in and receipt for the entire company/troop. ASES also maintains the AMC/AMT spill contingency plan and manages the company/troop HAZMAT storage and disposal operations.

Technical Supply Section

2-27. Technical supply section obtains, stores, and issues Class IX (air) repair parts, special tools, PLL, bench stock, and shop stock. The technical supply OIC manages the Class IX (air) budget for the commander. See chapter 7 for more information on technical supply operations.

AIRFRAME REPAIR PLATOON

2-28. The ARP provides supported aviation units (maneuver company/troop) field-level scheduled and unscheduled maintenance support when requested (figures 2-2 and 2-3, page 2-4). Daily and operator-level scheduled maintenance is the primary responsibility of the maneuver company/troop. Prolonged scheduled maintenance such as aircraft phases or compliance with aviation safety action messages (ASAMs) is best performed by the ARP and can be requested by the maneuver company/troop through the PC office. Unscheduled maintenance is also the primary responsibility of the maneuver company/troop. If the maneuver company/troop cannot complete the unscheduled maintenance in one day or less, it should contact the PC office and request maintenance support.

2-29. Maneuver company/troop maintenance managers, PC OICs, and QC should communicate daily in scheduling and prioritizing scheduled and unscheduled maintenance support. Coordination must also include the technical supply officer to ensure required aircraft repair parts and components are available before commencing maintenance procedures. If required aircraft repair parts and components are not available in the technical supply section, the maintenance manager, with the technical supply officer assisting, must obtain the required parts before the aircraft is work ordered to the AMC/AMT and, ultimately, the ARP.

General Support Aviation Battalion

2-30. A GSAB AMC ARP has a headquarters and two repair sections (figure 2-2, page 2-4). The repair sections are CH-47 and UH-60.

Assault Battalion

2-31. The assault battalion AMC ARP has a headquarters and a UH-60 repair section (figure 2-4, page 2-6). The assault battalion AMC HQ platoon and CRP are structured as depicted in figure 2-2, page 2-4.

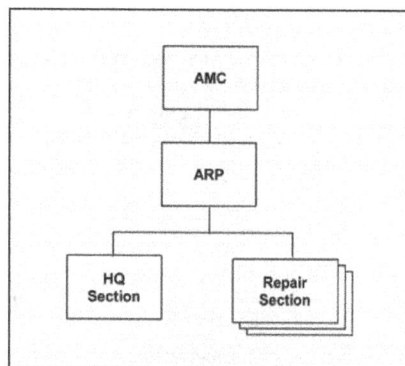

Figure 2-4. Assault battalion AMC ARP

Attack Reconnaissance Battalion/Squadron

2-32. The ARB (AH-64) AMC ARP and attack reconnaissance squadron (ARS) (OH-58D) AMT ARP are structured as depicted in figure 2-4.

Air Cavalry Squadron

2-33. The ARP of the AMT in the ACS contains one OH-58D or AH-64 maintenance section and one UH-60 maintenance section to support the ACS organic assault troop.

COMPONENT REPAIR PLATOON

2-34. The CRP assigned to an AMC/AMT provides component repair support functions to their supported unit assigned aircraft (figures 2-2 and 2-3, page 2-4). Component repairs to aircraft systems entail field-level maintenance repairs according to applicable TMs and the MAC.

2-35. The CRP contains specialized sections to repair subsystems associated with their supported aircraft including power plant, power-train, structural, pneudraulics, avionics/electrical, and systems repair sections. The systems repair sections, organic to the ARB AMC and AMT CRPs, perform armament, avionics, and electrical repairs.

General Support Aviation Battalion and Assault Helicopter Battalion

2-36. A GSAB and assault helicopter battalion (AHB) AMC CRP contains a headquarters and five shop sections (figure 2-2, page 2-4). The five shop sections are power plant (engine), power train, structural (airframe), pneudralics (hydraulics), and avionics/electrical. Each shop section is comprised of three teams.

2-37. Each shop section performs maintenance of aircraft components and structures requiring specialized technical skills. Assigned maintainers perform scheduled and unscheduled maintenance, troubleshoot components, remove and replace aircraft components and line replaceable units (LRUs), perform BDAR procedures, and manage deployment support kits (Class IX aviation spares and shop stock) at the platoon level.

Attack Reconnaissance Battalion/Squadron and Air Cavalry Squadron

2-38. The CRP (figure 2-5, page 2-8) contains a headquarters, four shop sections, and a system repair section. The four shop sections are power plant (engine), power train, structural (airframe), and pneudraulics (hydraulics). Each shop section is comprised of three teams. The system repair section, led by a 151AE armament trained maintenance technician, is subordinate to the CRP and separate from the shops section. The system repair section consists of three teams of armament/electrical/avionics systems repairers.

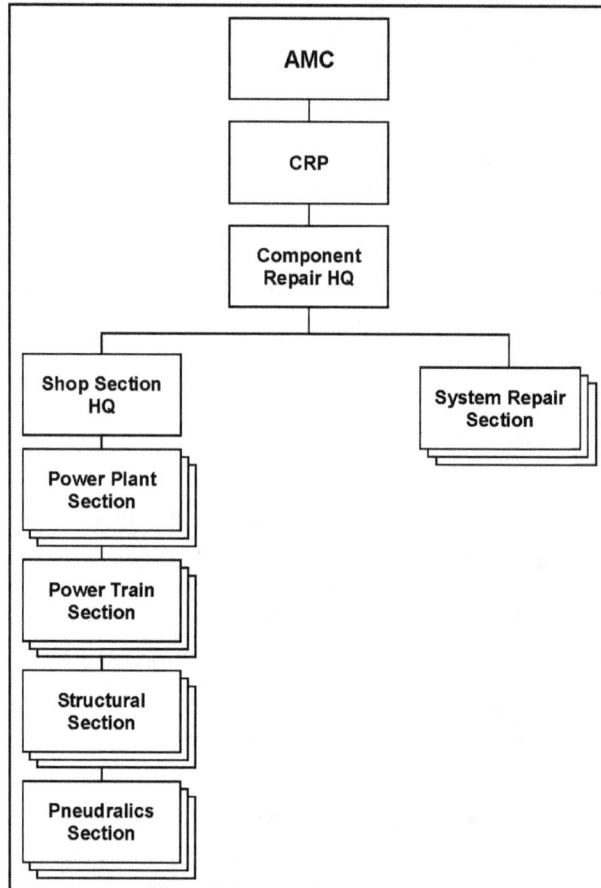

Figure 2-5. ARB, ARS, or ACS AMC/AMT CRP

AVIATION SUPPORT COMPANY/TROOP

2-39. The ASC/AST (formerly aviation intermediate maintenance) provides field-level maintenance, up to intermediate-level maintenance, support to AMCs/AMTs. The ASC/AST primarily performs intermediate maintenance support IAW the applicable TM MAC and reinforces unit maintenance support upon request.

2-40. The ASC/AST performs PC maintenance management and quality assurance of CAB/ACS aircraft to ensure airworthiness, and conducts work ordered system/subsystem component repairs. The ASC/AST is capable of supporting CAB/ACS split-based and aviation logistics support operations. The transportability requirement of the ASC/AST is 100-percent and the unit transports 50-percent of their TOE in one movement using organic vehicles.

2-41. The ASC consists of a HQ platoon, ARP, and CRP (figure 2-6, page 2-9) (figure 2-7, page 2-12, for AST). The three platoons of the ASC perform similar functions as the corresponding AMC/AMT platoons.

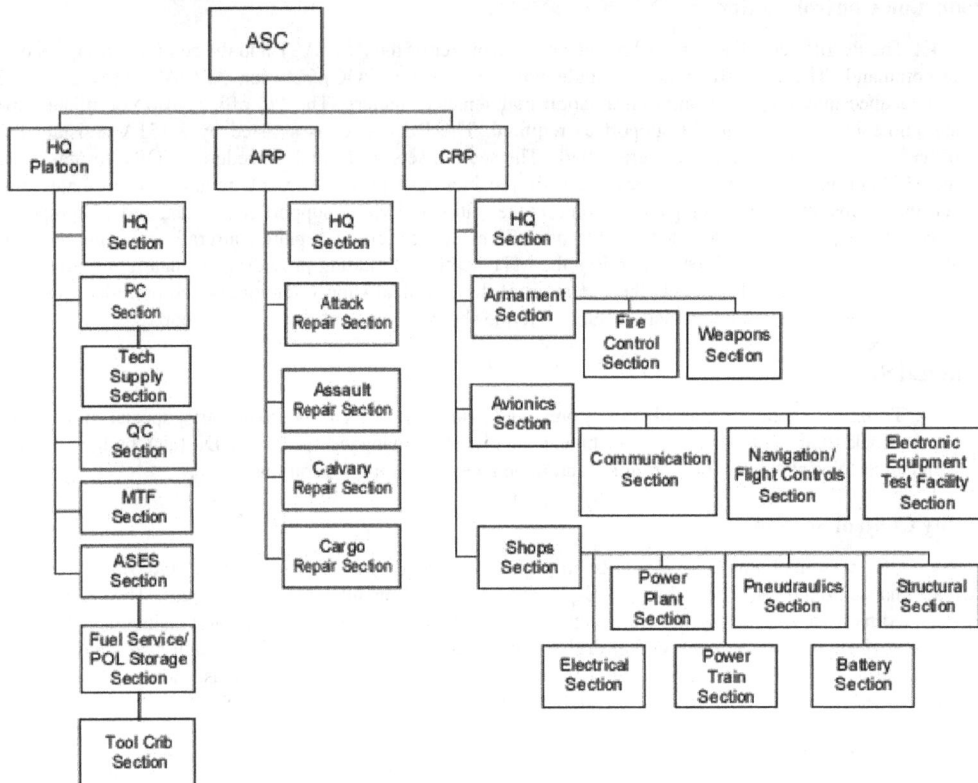

Figure 2-6. Aviation support company

COMPANY/TROOP HEADQUARTERS

2-42. The ASC/AST headquarters provides C2, administration, and logistics support required to conduct aviation maintenance operations. The commander has direct control over the company/troop administrative functions. The commander coordinates training and operational matters and conducts consolidated training for low-density maintenance MOSs authorized in the ASC/AST and in forward support company/forward support troop of aviation battalions and squadrons assigned to the CAB/ACS. The commander is also responsible for the care, maintenance, and accountability of ASC/AST equipment. Key functions of the company/troop headquarters include, but are not limited to:

- Perform route reconnaissance.
- Organize the unit for movement and issue movement orders to ASC/AST personnel.
- Request additional transportation through the ASB S-4.
- Maintain situational awareness and understanding of CAB/ACS aviation operations in coordination with the ASB intelligence/operations staff officer (S-2/3).
- Provide C2 of ASC/AST in response to an air or ground attack.
- Coordinate base defense.
- Establish communications.
- Determine placement of CBRN assets in the headquarters area.
- Information systems management.
- QC functions.

Production Control Section

2-43. The PC officer is the principal maintenance manager of the ASC/AST and the company/troop second in command. The PC officer is the single point of contact (POC) between ASC/AST-provided field maintenance and supported units on aviation maintenance matters. The PC officer also coordinates for sustainment level maintenance support as required. The PC officer is assisted by a 151A assistant PC officer, a 15K NCOIC, and a 15-series clerk. The section sets up formal procedures (SOPs) to maximize the efficient use of maintenance resources. It receives and processes work requests, coordinates and schedules jobs into various shops, and monitors the status of TMDE, support equipment, and shop reports. It coordinates inspection and test flights as well as the return of repaired aircraft and equipment to supported units. The PC officer supervises the MTF section, including providing evaluators for supported units. The PC section also directs the operation of the technical supply section, which provides Class IX repair parts and special tool requisition support to the shops and the entire company/troop.

Technical Supply Section

2-44. Technical supply section obtains, stores, and issues Class IX (air) repair parts, special tools, PLL, bench stock, and shop stock. The technical supply OIC manages the Class IX (air) budget for the commander. See chapter 7 for more information on technical supply operations.

Quality Control Section

2-45. QC personnel enforce standards in repair, overhaul, modification, SOF, and other required maintenance functions. They are also responsible for safety in all maintenance areas. The QC section reports directly to the company/troop commander; this avoids conflicts of interest and maintains objectivity in the performance of their inspection duties. Among other functions, the QC section also maintains the master technical library, performs safety inspections of the work and shops areas, monitors compliance with ASAMs, and ensures compliance with the Army oil analysis program (AOAP).

Maintenance Test Flight Section

2-46. The MTF section performs test flights on aircraft to troubleshoot problems, confirm repairs, and conduct initial break-in of major components. The section can perform scheduled MTFs or limited test flight support after aircraft repairs are accomplished. The section also provides maintenance test pilot evaluator (ME) support for the MPs in the AMCs/AMTs and maneuver companies/troops of the CAB/ACS aviation battalions/squadrons.

Aviation Support Equipment Section

2-47. At the ASC/AST level, large quantities of aviation support equipment and DART responsibilities mandates an ASES with 15 to 35 Soldiers including an OIC and NCOIC (both appointed on orders by the commander) to function efficiently and effectively. As in the AMC/AMT, Soldiers are rotated into the ASES from the platoons within the company/troop and returned after serving approximately one year. This time line can be shorter in the focused mission saturation environment of unaccompanied short tours or combat. Commanders and first sergeants should time rotations to ensure a majority of experienced ASES Soldiers remain in the section to train new Soldiers before their subsequent replacement.

2-48. The ASC/AST ASES is a combination of the tool crib section and the fuel service and POL section, augmented with aviation Soldiers from within the company/troop to perform six functions:

- Tool room operations.
- GSE maintenance and support.
- TMDE coordination management.
- MHE operations.
- Deliberate air and ground DART operations.
- Aircraft fueling/defueling operations, package POL support, and HAZMAT operations and planning.

2-49. ASES provides routine aviation maintenance support to the ASC/AST under the guidance of the PC section to ensure accomplishment of the ASC/AST customer support goals. However, because of its combat DART responsibilities to the entire CAB/ACS and diverse capabilities, the ASC/AST ASES reports directly to the commander. ASES maintains the ASC/AST compliment of AGPUs, generic aviation nitrogen generators, pressure washers, cranes, hoists, tractors, tugs, forklifts, aviation electrical power generators, jacks and recovery assets (prime movers and trailers), as well as the tool crib shelter. ASES leads and executes ASC/AST aircraft recovery operations, and coordinates calibrations tracking, turn-in, and receipt of equipment for the entire company/troop. ASES also maintains the ASC/AST spill contingency plan and manages the company/troop HAZMAT storage and disposal. Using its cranes, forklift, trailers, and prime movers, ASES can perform MHE missions in support of the ASC/AST, ASB, or the CAB/ACS.

AIRFRAME REPAIR PLATOON

2-50. ASC/AST ARP (figure 2-6, page 2-9) provides field-level maintenance, to include intermediate-level maintenance, and limited sustainment-level maintenance support to AMC/AMT assigned aircraft. The ASC/AST ARP can also provide technical assistance and maintenance support when requested by the AMC/AMT PC section and coordinated through the ASC/AST PC office. The ASC/AST ARP can perform field-level and limited sustainment-level maintenance repairs according to applicable TMs and the MAC. When requested by the ASC/AST PC section, AMCOM LARs will issue a LOA enabling ASC/AST ARP maintainers to perform a one-time sustainment-level maintenance repair.

2-51. The ARP is capable of supporting aviation units through contact maintenance teams using shop equipment contact maintenance vehicles. ARP contact maintenance teams provide in-depth troubleshooting and diagnostics of aircraft systems, subsystems, and components. The ARP also provides repair personnel for technical assistance, contact teams, and recovery teams.

2-52. The ASC/AST ARP has a headquarters and four repair sections (figure 2-6, page 2-9). The headquarters has a 15A platoon leader and a 15-series platoon sergeant. The four repair sections are—
- Attack reconnaissance (AH-64 and/or OH-58D) with six repair teams.
- Assault (UH-60) with three repair teams.
- GSAB (UH-60 and HH-60) with two repair teams.
- Heavy lift (CH-47) with three repair teams.

COMPONENT REPAIR PLATOON

2-53. ASC/AST CRP (figure 2-6, page 2-9) provides field-level maintenance component repair support functions, to include intermediate-level maintenance, to the AMC/AMT supported aircraft. The ASC/AST CRP can also provide unit-level component repair support when requested by the AMC/AMT PC section and coordinated through the ASC/AST PC office. The ASC/AST CRP can perform limited sustainment-level maintenance repairs according to applicable TMs and the MAC. When requested by the ASC/AST PC section, AMCOM LARs will issue an LOA enabling ASC/AST CRP maintainers to perform a one-time sustainment-level maintenance repair.

2-54. The ASC/AST CRP has a headquarters, six shop sections, two armament repair sections, and three avionic repair sections. The headquarters contains a platoon leader and a platoon sergeant. The six shops sections are power plant (engine) repair, structural (airframe) repair, power train repair, pneudraulics (hydraulics) repair, electric repair, and battery repair. The two armament sections are fire control repair and weapons systems repair. The three avionics repair sections are communications/equipment repair, navigation/flight control repair, and the electronic equipment test facility (EETF).

Note. EETF systems will remain in ASC/ASTs until completion of their retrograde and assignment to sustainment level organizations by AMC.

2-55. The CRP sections are capable of supporting aviation units through contact maintenance teams using shop equipment contact maintenance vehicles. CRP contact maintenance teams provide support to all subordinate AMCs/AMTs and can extend support outside to other aviation units with approval from the ASC/AST PC office.

AVIATION SUPPORT TROOP

2-56. The AST is assigned to the ACS and provides field-level maintenance, to include intermediate-level maintenance, support to the AMT (figure 2-7). The AST primarily performs intermediate maintenance support according to the applicable TM MAC. When requested by the AMT, the AST also provides unit maintenance support.

2-57. The AST performs PC maintenance management and quality assurance of ACS aircraft ensuring airworthiness and conducts work ordered system/subsystem component repairs. The AST is capable of supporting ACS split-based maintenance and aviation logistics support operations. The AST consists of a headquarters platoon, ARP, CRP, and supply platoon (figure 2-7). The headquarters platoon, ARP, and CRP of the AST perform similar functions as the corresponding ASC platoons (figure 2-5, page 2-8).

2-58. The supply platoon manages the requisition, receipt, storage, issue, and stock control for all classes of supply; not just aviation repair parts for the ACS (figure 2-7). The platoon consists of a headquarters section, technical supply operations (squadron) section, shipping and receiving section, storage and issue section, and reparable exchange (RX)/quick supply store (QSS) section.

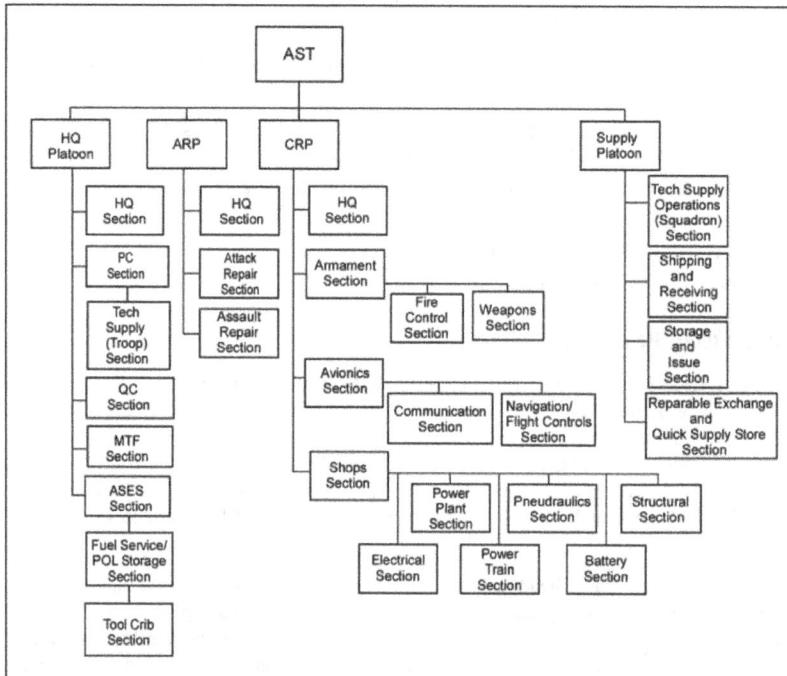

Figure 2-7. Aviation support troop

SUPPLY PLATOON HEADQUARTERS

2-59. The headquarters has a platoon leader and a platoon sergeant. The platoon headquarters supervises and controls platoon functions in support of the AST and ACS.

Technical Supply Operations Section

2-60. This section has a technical supply operations officer and a section NCOIC. The technical supply operations officer and NCOIC monitor and direct the daily supply activity in support of all units assigned or attached to the ACS, not solely the AST. The technical supply section in the AST headquarters platoon performs technical supply functions for the AST headquarters and repair platoons (see chapter 7).

Shipping and Receiving Section

2-61. The shipping and receiving section receives and accounts for all Class IX (air) repair parts coming from supply sources, field returns, and shipment redirects. It also packages and crates supplies when required.

Storage and Issue Section

2-62. The storage and issue section stores supplies and performs warehouse storage operations such as shelf-life monitoring, protection from weather, and security against pilferage. It assigns storage locations, maintains stock location systems, and administers document control procedures. It is also responsible for selecting materiel for issue or shipment and for preparing materiel release orders.

Reparable Exchange and Quick Supply Store

2-63. The RX/QSS section provides exchange of selected reparable items to supported units and receives, stores, and issues QSS items. The section may maintain a QSS for customers to get low-cost, high-demand, consumable parts (light bulbs, wiper blades, and common bolts) without formal requests. QSS service improves availability of low-cost, consumable items. RX of selected reparable is handled as a simple exchange of an unserviceable for a serviceable item. Unserviceable reparables must accompany any requests for reparables.

SECTION III – AVIATION MAINTENANCE TEAM COMPOSITION, RESPONSIBILITIES, AND ROLES

TEAM COMPOSITION

MAINTENANCE LEADERSHIP MEMBERS

2-64. Maintenance leaders are those officers and NCOs assigned to positions in the aviation maintenance structure possessing direct authority and responsibility over maintenance personnel, equipment, and operations. This includes commanders, platoon leaders, aviation maintenance technicians, command sergeants major, first sergeants, platoon sergeants, and repair section sergeants. These are the members with decision authority and implementation responsibility.

MAINTENANCE TEAM SUPPORTING MEMBERS

2-65. These members provide subject matter expertise and logistics integration information to the maintenance team to ensure the team leadership decisions support their responsibilities. These members include, but are not limited to the support operations officer and staff, BAMO/squadron aviation materiel officer (SAMO), PC personnel, QC personnel, S-4, LARs, CFSRs, contractors, sustainment level representatives or attachments.

MAINTENANCE TEAM RESPONSIBILITIES

2-66. The maintenance team leadership and supporting members will work together to achieve maintenance goals and standards. This informal unification of skilled Soldiers and personnel provides a capability to meet mission demands and reduce or eliminate friction points in maintenance operations. Responsibilities include but are not limited to:

- Recommend monthly, quarterly, and semiannual planning objectives and conduct reviews.
- Recommend fiscal year (FY), calendar year, and multi-year planned objectives and conduct reviews.
- Review and facilitate the aviation MOE reports.
- Monitor maintenance automated systems.
- Ensure aviation maintenance follows brigade, theater, and DA technical guidance.
- Participate in BDAR and DART planning and risk assessment (FM 3-04.513).
- Monitor supply execution and vigorously pursue CSDP objectives. Ensure compliance with SOF messages and ASAMs affecting assigned brigade/battalion airframes.
- Assess manning shortfalls and mitigate their effects on mission execution.
- Monitor daily execution of the following aircraft contracts (brigade level and, on a limited basis, at the battalion level):
    - Project officer.
    - Contracting officer representative (COR).
    - Administrative contracting officer representative (ACOR).
- Assess the following aviation systems' maintainability and performance:
    - Aircraft systems and subsystems; for example, weapons, communications, survivability equipment, and special mission equipment.
    - GSE.
    - Maintenance facilities.
    - STAMIS.
- Monitor unit Class II, IV, VII, Class IX (air) budgets.
- Monitor and analyze monthly and FY aircraft readiness trends.
- Monitor maintenance training operations in support of unit METL and MOE.
- Ensure reporting of quality deficiency report (QDR)-affected items.
- Track RX performance and the use of ASC/AST repair and return.
- Monitor aircraft resource management and budget reports affecting aircraft assets and flight hours to include—
    - Track flying-hour dollars for support needs.
    - Track short-term, nonstandard equipment purchases and sustainment.
    - Oversee maintenance services contracting if appointed as COR or ACOR.
- Identify resources and co-develop aircraft and equipment maintenance operations requirements and supporting plans for the unit. To accomplish these objectives the team will—
    - Participate in Army command policy development.
    - Participate in Training and Doctrine Command (TRADOC) doctrine development and review.
    - Verify compliance with maintenance and sustainment automation updates (software and hardware).
- The leadership co-develops long-term maintenance training plans and identifies supporting resources.
- The unit S-3, S-4, BAMO, SAMO, and ASB staff will participate in—
    - Initial Army command coordination issues.
    - Leader reconnaissance to help determine facilities and infrastructure to conduct maintenance.
    - Program manager, AMCOM, life-cycle management command planning conferences.

- Determining requirements and coordinating training and frequency for new equipment.
- Emergency change proposal (ECP) development.
- MWO planning.

COMMANDERS

2-67. Officers in command of aviation maintenance units must serve as advocates for the officers, NCOs, and Soldiers in their organization, as well as set quantifiable standards of performance.

BRIGADE AND AIR CAVALRY SQUADRON

2-68. The brigade and ACS commanders establish and enforce maintenance standards according to applicable regulatory policies and procedural guidance. They prioritize and allocate resources, provide training guidance, and retain responsibility for safely executing the maintenance mission, QC, and materiel readiness.

2-69. As the overall maintenance team leader, the brigade or ACS commander sets the maintenance priorities for their subordinate units in support of mission requirements, balances operational pace/tempo against maintenance and sustainment capabilities and resources their subordinate maintenance structure to assure high ratings across the MOE. They receive the MOE roll up reports from the BAMO or SAMO for review and consideration and usually lead aviation resource council meetings to ensure a common picture and vision for the entire maintenance team. Additionally, when MOE require reinforcing, the ACS commander directly applies assets and resources appropriately to achieve the desired results in concert with his aviation maintenance team vision.

BATTALION AND ATTACK RECONNAISSANCE SQUADRON

2-70. Battalion and ARS commanders execute the brigade commander maintenance priorities in support of mission requirements, balance operational pace/tempo against maintenance and sustainment capabilities and resource their subordinate maintenance structure to assure high ratings across the MOE. They receive the MOE roll up reports from the ASC or AMC/AMT commanders for review, consideration, and submission to the BAMO. When MOE require reinforcing, these commanders directly apply assets and resources appropriately to achieve the desired results in concert with the aviation maintenance team vision.

MAINTENANCE AND SUPPORT COMPANY/TROOP

2-71. The company/troop commander plans, directs, and supervises the operations and employment of the company/troop through skilled application and synthesis of all unit Soldiers and assets to achieve the MOE goals established by their higher commanders. These leaders provide the battalion and squadron commanders with status and recommendations regarding all maintenance operations of their unit, and serve as the single point of entry for all issues related to maintenance in support of their parent organizations. They are the primary advisor to their battalion or squadron commanders regarding all maintenance issues. Maintenance and support company and troop commanders present the MOE reports to the battalion or squadron commander identifying progress, negative trends, and required resources to maintain or improve the MOE. Maintenance and support company and troop commanders make direct coordination with battalion and squadron staff sections in pursuit of MOE goals.

MAINTENANCE OFFICERS

BRIGADE AVIATION MATERIEL OFFICER

2-72. The BAMO is the primary adviser to the brigade commander on the brigade aviation maintenance program. In concert with the ASB, ASC, and AMC/AMT commanders and PCs, the BAMO recommends actions and forecasts future capabilities based on the existing maintenance posture.

2-73. The BAMO coordinates maintenance actions based on operational necessities and consultation with the brigade/squadron aviation maintenance leadership, and reviews the daily status of all aircraft in the CAB. The BAMO is normally a ME, responsible for the following:

- Provides advice to the brigade/ACS commander on aviation maintenance and sustainment issues.
- Assists in resolving aircraft maintenance standardization issues.
- Attends the brigade/ACS safety and standardization meeting.
- Supports internal safety and ARMS evaluations.
- Consolidates the MOE reports.

BATTALION/SQUADRON AVIATION MATERIEL OFFICER

2-74. The ASB's chief warrant officer five (CW5) aviation materiel officer (AMO) serves in the support operations section of the HSC to facilitate any brigade-level sustainment expediting or special staff actions in support of aviation maintenance. He also participates in the concept of support planning as a key advisor and subject matter expert. The ACS's chief warrant officer four (CW4) SAMO also performs these support operations duties for the squadron and works in concert with the AST, AMT, commanders, and unit maintenance officers. The SAMO also provides the same support to the ACS commander as the BAMO does to the CAB commander. The battalion/squadron chief warrant officer three (CW3) AMO of the maneuver battalions/squadrons leads the technical supply section of the AMC/AMT. Specific duties and mission goals are covered in chapter 7.

SUPPORT OPERATIONS OFFICER

2-75. The support operations officer (logistics corps major) operates under the supervision of the ASB commander. The support operations officer provides technical supervision of daily sustainment functions and supervises his aviation section led by the aircraft maintenance officer, an aviation captain who should be a graduate of the aviation maintenance course. If not attached to the ASC/AST as an augmentation leader performing duties such as executive officer or platoon leader, the aircraft maintenance officer in the support operations office coordinates and provides technical advice relating to intermediate maintenance conducted within the ASC/AST. The support operations officer, aircraft maintenance officer, and ASB AMO interface with the brigade and battalion/squadron supply officers (S-4s) and BAMO to assist in accomplishing maintenance priorities and resolve maintenance support issues. The supply and services cell in the ASB support operations section assists the aviation maintenance officer and aviation material officer by tracking distribution and availability of Class IX (air) repair parts and any special tools or equipment.

2-76. The support operations section provides centralized, integrated, and automated C2 and planning for all distribution management operations within the ASB. The support operations section coordinates with sustainment operators in the fields of supply, maintenance, and movement management for the support of all units assigned or attached in the brigade area. The primary concern of the support operations section is customer support and increasing the responsiveness of support provided by subordinate units.

MAINTENANCE TEST PILOTS

2-77. MPs are responsible for conducting MTFs to determine the airworthiness of the unit's aircraft IAW TM 1-1500-328-23. Maneuver unit MPs manage and execute the unit commander's maintenance program. They also provide advanced troubleshooting skills within their specific mission, type design, and series aircraft to facilitate efficient repairs and maintenance. The unit commander appoints qualified aviators to duties as MPs. The unit commander can further appoint MPs the duties of PC, QC, technical supply, ASES leader, or repair platoon leader. MPs who possess the ME designation train, develop, and evaluate MPs to enhance skills and increase overall technical proficiency.

MAINTENANCE PLATOON AND SECTION LEADERS

2-78. Maintenance platoon and section leaders ensure the operation of their respective platoon or section supports unit mission goals, priorities, and MOE. They ensure standardization IAW regulations and publications and monitor maintenance procedures for strict compliance with the TMs. They constantly receive reports, monitor progress, and provide specific missions and tasks to their warrant officers and NCOs. They track and report the movement of the MOE assessment in support of their commander guidance and actively pursue necessary resources to ensure and improve platoon performance. They are the senior advisor to the PC officer and retain control over the employment of their formations in support of mission accomplishment. The platoon leader provides administrative direction for the platoon as well as serves as the primary resource manager for their organizations ensuring accountability, maintenance, and serviceability of assigned assets.

AVIATION MAINTENANCE TECHNICIAN

2-79. These highly skilled warrant officers assist the platoon leader and direct the daily operations of their assigned sections according to the platoon leaders guidance and goals. They prepare reports supporting the MOE for the platoon leader to review for presentation to the commander, and manage the work-order load. They also provide advanced troubleshooting in their area of expertise to facilitate efficient repairs and maintenance. Aviation maintenance technicians are uniquely qualified and positioned as advanced trainers for their sections. The unit commander can further appoint aviation maintenance technicians the duties of PC, QC, technical supply, ASES leader, or repair platoon leader.

NONCOMMISSIONED OFFICERS

COMMAND SERGEANT MAJOR

2-80. As the senior enlisted leader in any formation, the command sergeant major ensures the right NCO leaders and Soldiers receive assignment to appropriate positions. With their extensive background, they serve as the primary advisor to the battalion, squadron, or brigade commander on all issues related to Soldiers assigned to maintenance positions and units. Commanders will always consider their input when formulating decisions against the maintenance MOE.

FIRST SERGEANTS

2-81. The company or troop first sergeant serves as the senior enlisted leader in any ASC/AST or AMC/AMT formation. The first sergeant ensures the right NCO leaders and Soldiers receive assignment to appropriate positions. With their extensive background, they serve as the primary advisor to the company or troop commander on all issues related to Soldiers assigned to maintenance positions and units. Commanders will always consider their input when formulating decisions against the maintenance MOE. The first sergeant also directs the headquarters operations supporting administrative functions of the company or troop.

PLATOON SERGEANTS

2-82. Platoon sergeants direct the performance of assigned Soldiers through their section sergeants. Platoon sergeants serve as first-line supervisors, responsible for ensuring all assigned aircraft receive maintenance according to regulatory policies, standards, and procedures. Platoon sergeants ensure accountability of all platoon resources and that maintenance operations meet or exceed the established MOE. They prepare reports supporting the MOE for the platoon leader to review for presentation to the commander, and manage the work-order load. Additionally, they perform administrative support functions for the platoon in concert with the platoon leader.

SECTION SERGEANTS

2-83. The section sergeant monitors individual Soldier activities and assists with new or unfamiliar tasks. Section sergeants mentor Soldiers on procedures and their connection with the maintenance MOE. They assess, develop, and counsel individual Soldiers to ensure appropriate progression, growth and skill improvement. Section sergeants ensure Soldiers under their charge complete required individual tasks related to aviation maintenance operations and the MOE.

TEAM LEADERS

2-84. Team leaders have overall responsibility for assigned scheduled/phase maintenance operations. They coordinate special tools, repair parts, and personnel to facilitate and expedite maintenance actions.

ADDITIONAL STAFF

PRODUCTION CONTROL OFFICER AND NONCOMMISSIONED OFFICER-IN-CHARGE

2-85. The PC OIC is the principal maintenance manager and coordinator in the ASC/AST or AMC/AMT and coordinates maintenance at the company/troop and battalion/squadron level. The PC OIC is the AMC/AMT or ASC/AST commanders' primary maintenance advisor for all internal production and maintenance activities. The PC OIC (captain) in the ASC/AST also serves as the second in command for those organizations and must possess sufficient maintenance experience and background to direct these large operations, as well as command the ASC/AST in the commander absence.

2-86. The PC NCOIC coordinates all maintenance actions in the absence of the PC OIC. The PC NCOIC assists the PC OIC; and in the PC OIC absence, coordinates and establishes priorities of work with QC, ARP, CRP, technical supply, and maneuver companies as required.

Note. See chapter 6 for a detailed explanation of PC activities.

QUALITY CONTROL OFFICER AND NONCOMMISSIONED OFFICER-IN-CHARGE

2-87. The QC OIC is responsible for the internal management of the QC section to include quality assurance of all work performed by the TIs. The QC OIC will coordinate priority of work with the unit PC OIC/NCOIC. To avoid conflict of interest, the QC OIC is accountable to the commander.

2-88. The QC NCOIC is directly responsible for the operational management of the QC section. He assists the QC OIC, in his absence, coordinates, and establishes priority of work with the PC OIC. The NCOIC distributes the work and supervises the TIs for quality assurance of work assigned.

Note. See chapter 9 for a detailed explanation of QC activities.

TECHNICAL SUPPLY OFFICER AND NONCOMMISSIONED OFFICER-IN-CHARGE

2-89. The technical supply officer is responsible for and performs oversight of the internal management and daily operations of the technical supply section to include requesting, processing, issuing, stockage, and turn-in of Class IX (air) repair parts, special tools, and components. He or she coordinates high-priority urgency of need (UND) A and B parts requests, such as aircraft on ground (AOG), with the unit PC OIC. If authorized by the commander, he or she certifies and authorizes all high-priority Class IX (air) requests. The technical supply OIC balances the unit Class IX (air) budget in detail for review by the commander.

2-90. The technical supply NCOIC coordinates high-priority (UND A and B) requisitions with the technical supply officer. He or she directs and supervises all technical supply actions assigned to the logistics clerks. The technical supply NCOIC is directly responsible to the technical supply officer.

Note. See chapter 7 for a detailed explanation of technical supply activities.

SECTION IV – AVIATION SUSTAINMENT MAINTENANCE STRUCTURE

2-91. Generally, sustainment maintenance refers to all maintenance performed on equipment above and outside of the CAB/ACS. The OEM CFSRs may be placed within the CAB/ACS to provide a limited forward sustainment maintenance capability.

2-92. In special circumstances (normally caused by the lack of repair parts or components in the supply pipeline), the CAB/ACS may obtain a SRA, OTR, or ARA. This authorization, requested through the AMCOM LAR, will enable the CAB/ACS to perform limited sustainment-level repair(s) on specific equipment classified as sustainment maintenance, if approved by AMCOM engineering.

UNITED STATES ARMY MATERIEL COMMAND

2-93. The United States Army Materiel Command (USAMC) mission is to provide technology, acquisition support, and sustainment. The USAMC operates research, development, and engineering centers; Army Research Laboratory; sustainment facilities; arsenals; ammunition plants; and other facilities. Subordinate commands provide specific aviation support within the USAMC structure. These commands include AMCOM and the Army Communications-Electronics Command (CECOM).

2-94. The USAMC—

- Overhauls and upgrades Army equipment.
- Produces and provides ordnance for the military services.
- Provides on-the-ground logistics support assistance to every unit in the Army.
- Provides new equipment training.
- Maintains the Army pre-positioned stocks on land and at sea.
- Researches, develops, and acquires conventional ammunition for the Department of Defense (DOD).
- Supports acquisition of end items and parts for military weapon systems.

UNITED STATES ARMY AVIATION AND MISSILE COMMAND

2-95. AMCOM is a major subordinate command of the USAMC. It is responsible for commodity management of aeronautical equipment, including—

- Design, research, and development.
- Maintenance engineering.
- Supply and stock control.
- Logistics assistance for all Army aviation and aerial delivery equipment.

2-96. AMCOM has direct operational control of the NM sources of repair, Corpus Christi Army Depot, Letterkenny Army Depot, Aviation Field Maintenance Directorate (AFMD), and new equipment training teams.

NATIONAL MAINTENANCE SOURCES OF REPAIR

2-97. The NM manager is responsible for managing all sustainment-level reparable and selected field-level reparable items according to AR 750-1. The NM manager uses various sources of repair. The national maintenance program (NMP) distributes sustainment maintenance workload across sustainment-level and non-sustainment-level activities based on national needs. The NMP manager may establish the use of a theater aviation sustainment manager within a specific theater. The theater aviation sustainment manager provides a unified aviation maintenance life-cycle management command focused on the use of theater assets providing airframe maintenance, overhaul of aviation subassemblies, and crash/battle damage repair.

CORPUS CHRISTI ARMY DEPOT

2-98. Corpus Christi Army Depot is the Army's organic facility for the repair and overhaul of rotary-wing aircraft. Corpus Christi Army Depot provides worldwide readiness, sustainment, and training support for all Army rotary-wing aircraft. Corpus Christi Army Depot is partnered with industry to overhaul, repair, modify, retrofit, and modernize Army aircraft and related engines and components. Corpus Christi Army Depot also provides hands-on training for Reserve, National Guard, and active-duty personnel. On a case-by-case basis, Corpus Christi Army Depot provides additional on-site sustainment maintenance support for crash damage analysis and repair. Sustainment maintenance is employed primarily in CONUS. However, it projects itself worldwide through maintenance support teams using organic assets and through contract programs.

2-99. Corpus Christi Army Depot provides the following maintenance support:
- Overhauls, repairs, modify, retrofits, and modernize aircraft systems.
- Maintains a mobilization and training base to provide capability for missions.
- Provides maintenance support services for aeronautical equipment worldwide.
- Provides project development and design services for special projects, as assigned.
- Provides worldwide telephone hot line and on-site technical assistance for the inspection, maintenance, and repair of customer aircraft and engines.

LETTERKENNY ARMY DEPOT

2-100. Letterkenny Army Depot provides a variety of support to the Army. Two aviation-specific systems that are overhauled and returned to the NMP are the AH-64 target acquisition designation sight/pilot night vision sensor and resetting and overhaul of AGPUs. AGPU reset and overhaul are functions of the service life extension program. Letterkenny Army Depot also provides sustainment-level maintenance for Hellfire launchers and air-to-air Stinger pressure bottle refurbishment.

AVIATION FIELD MAINTENANCE DIRECTORATE

2-101. The AFMD executes United States Army rotary-wing aircraft maintenance missions above unit level and below sustainment (depot) level. The field maintenance missions include but are not limited to:
- Leave behind equipment maintenance.
- Mobilization support.
- Aviation brigade pass-back maintenance support.

2-102. Sustainment maintenance missions include but are not limited to:
- Preset mission equipment package installation.
- MWO installation.
- Aviation reset program.
- NMP.
- Foreign military sales maintenance support.

2-103. The AFMD consists of several aviation field maintenance activity (AFMA) facilities located in CONUS and outside the continental United States (OCONUS). AFMA facilities are staffed by maintenance support contractors who perform the AFMD maintenance mission. CONUS AFMA facilities are operationally controlled via regional aviation sustainment managers (RASM):
- RASM-East, Fort Stewart, Georgia.
- RASM-West, Fort Hood, Texas.
- RASM-Pacific, Fort Lewis, Washington.

2-104. OCONUS sites are operationally controlled via a theater aviation sustainment manager (TASM) or an AFMA:

- TASM-Europe, Coleman Barracks, Germany.
- AFMA-Korea.

Note. The AFMD web site is located on Army Knowledge Online (AKO) at https://www.us.army.mil/suite/page/416874.

NEW EQUIPMENT TRAINING TEAMS

2-105. The logistics assistance and new equipment training division is a subordinate division of the directorate for readiness. Its mission is staff supervision and operational control of worldwide logistics assistance programs (LAPs) for Army aircraft and related support equipment. The division also provides representatives to make command staff visits and to manage all aspects of the new equipment training and support services.

2-106. Army aircraft mobile training teams are made up of either specialists or contract technical services personnel trained in the support of a particular aircraft. These teams are controlled by AMCOM and assist the commander in improving the proficiency of maintenance personnel at the AMC/AMT and ASC/AST. When the team completes a job, it prepares and forwards a report to AMCOM with consolidated findings.

DEFENSE LOGISTICS AGENCY

2-107. The Defense Logistics Agency (DLA) provides supply support and technical and logistics assistance to the BAMO and battalion/squadron AMO. DLA manages, stores, and distributes hardware and electronics used in the maintenance and repair of equipment and weapons systems. Refer to DLA customer assistance handbook for assistance in contacting the various sources of supply managers. To obtain an online version of this handbook, go to http://www.dla mil/j-4/login.aspx.

2-108. DLA maintains three supply centers in the following locations:

- Defense Supply Center, Richmond (DSCR), Virginia.
- Defense Supply Center, Columbus (DSCC), Ohio.
- Defense Supply Center, Philadelphia (DSCP), Pennsylvania.

2-109. DSCR is the designated aviation supply chain manager. Contact DSCR at http://www.dscr.dla mil.

2-110. With internet access to DSCR the following functions are possible:

- View current flight safety critical parts list.
- Input requisitions through direct online ordering option; using this option does not preclude inputting/submitting the requisition into the user appropriate command requisitioning system.
- Query the system for back-ordered items.
- Access the asset visibility (AV) system (formerly defense supply expert [DESX] system).

2-111. DSCC is the designated land and maritime supply chain manager and manages electronic items. Contact DSCC at http://www.dscc.dla mil.

2-112. DSCP is the Soldier support and construction supply manager providing food, clothing, textiles, medicines, medical equipment, and construction supplies and equipment. The general and industrial commodities (nuts and washers, bolts and studs, screws, packing and gaskets, pins, rivets, and springs), are managed by DSCC and DSCR detachments located at DSCP. Contact DSCP at http://www.dscp.dla mil.

2-113. The following agencies support the BAMO tracking and managing sustainment, maintenance, and supply transactions:

- DLA at http://www.dla mil or DOD E-Mall at https://dod-emall.dla mil.

- DLA national item identification number (NIIN) and national stock number (NSN) search at https://www.webflis.dlis.dla.mil/WEBFLIS/pub/pub_search.aspx?niin.
- DLA part requisition tracking system at http://wegal.ogden.disa.mil/mrostatus.
- CECOM NSN and part number search at http://lrc3.monmouth.army.mil/nsn/index.cfm.
- Logistics and Readiness Center at http://www.monmouth.army.mil/cecom/lrc/lrc.html.
- Global transportation network (track any part, equipment, and household goods traveling in the DOD transportation network) at https://www.gtn.transcom.mil.
- General Services Administration (GSA) approved products and services from GSA contracts at https://www.gsaadvantage.gov/advgsa/advantage/main/start_page.do.

ARMY COMMUNICATIONS-ELECTRONICS COMMAND

2-114. The CECOM mission is to develop, acquire, and sustain information technologies and integrated systems. CECOM controls and operates Tobyhanna Army Depot. Tobyhanna Army Depot is the largest, full-service electronics maintenance facility in DOD This depot's mission is total sustainment, including design, manufacture, repair, and overhaul of hundreds of electronic systems. These include satellite terminals, radio and radar systems, telephones, electro-optics, night vision and anti-intrusion devices, airborne surveillance equipment, navigational instruments, electronic warfare, guidance, and control systems for tactical missiles, and Blue Force Tracking installation kits.

AVIATION DEPOT MAINTENANCE ROUNDOUT UNIT PROGRAM

2-115. The aviation depot maintenance roundout unit (ADMRU) program consists of the ADMRU HQ and four aviation classification repair activity depots (AVCRADs). Location of the—

- ADMRU HQ is Edgewood, Maryland.
- 1106th AVCRAD is Fresno, California.
- 1107th AVCRAD is Springfield, Missouri.
- 1108th AVCRAD is Gulfport, Mississippi.
- 1109th AVCRAD is Groton, Connecticut.

2-116. The primary mission of the ADMRU is to provide backup regional aviation maintenance support for ARNG aircraft for a 13 to 15 state regional area. The Army aviation support facility provides field and limited sustainment-level maintenance in support of ARNG aviation units. The ADMRU program provides backup support to the Army aviation support facilities. The ADMRU program provides NMP repairs, limited sustainment (depot) airframe repair, aircraft painting, major airframe repair, repair of components classified as sustainment (depot) level reparables, and the identification and classification of aviation receipts and stocks in storage.

2-117. The ADMRU program was designed to mobilize multiple AVCRADs with the ADMRU HQ acting as the C2 of multiple AVCRADs during deployments from an Army HQ such as AMCOM. The ADMRU HQ is also responsible for establishing liaison officer (LNO) positions as required.

2-118. The ADMRU provides—

- NMP repairs as directed by USAMC.
- Backup field-level maintenance.
- BDAR.
- Estimated cost of repair assessments.
- Tailored maintenance contact teams for deployment.
- Engine repairs.
- Airframe repairs.
- Welding.
- Main rotor blade repair and balance.
- Composite material repairs.

- Electrical systems repairs.
- Avionics and armament repairs.
- Hydraulic component repairs and fabrication of lines.

2-119. The AVCRADs are fixed-base, limited sustainment (depot) facilities and initially mobilize in place but can deploy to a theater of operations. The AVCRADs are able to deploy limited, task-organized support using maintenance contact teams and classification support teams. In theater, an AVCRAD provides fixed-base support and must receive transportation support assets external from the unit. The AMCOM theater aviation maintenance program (TAMP) equipment package is movable but not mobile. The AVCRAD, with additional attachments to perform its wartime mission, forms the Theater Aviation Sustainment Maintenance Group (TASMG) supporting the TAMP.

2-120. The four AVCRADs are in the process of transforming from table of distribution and allowances (TDA) into a TOE for executing the TAMP and performing sustainment-level (depot-level) repairs as directed by USAMC, in an operational environment or theater of operation. The TOE organizations will become TASMGs. Upon conversion of the AVCRADs to TASMGs, the primary and backup support mission remains the same. AVCRAD conversion to TASMG occurs for the—

- 1107th AVCRAD on 1 January 2010.
- 1106th AVCRAD on 1 September 2010.
- 1108th AVCRAD on 1 September 2011.
- 1109th AVCRAD on 1 September 2012.

2-121. The ADMRU HQ is converting from a TDA to a TOE unit, named the theater aviation sustainment maintenance HQ, and will retain the same missions. They will also develop the capability, through contractor and ARNG support, to become a fifth TASMG for unit rotational purposes. The theater aviation sustainment maintenance HQ and the four TASMGs will make up the theater aviation sustainment maintenance program.

THEATER AVIATION SUSTAINMENT MAINTENANCE GROUP

2-122. The TASMG can support manned and unmanned aviation assets. The TASMG focuses on the repair of specified components in support of the NMP as directed by USAMC. The repaired components are returned to the supply system. The TASMG may assist in port-opening operations but is not solely responsible for this function. The TASMG can perform repair and return of components and end items when required.

2-123. The TASMG consists of—

- Headquarters and headquarters detachment.
- ASC.
- Group support company (GSC).

2-124. The TASMG provides theater-level support for all aviation sustainment and maintenance requirements, including—

- Sustainment maintenance of airframes and components in theater as directed by USAMC.
- Field-level maintenance to support theater surge requirements.
- Repair and return of depot-level reparable components to the theater ASL.
- Selected depot-level airframe repair.
- Oil analysis.
- Calibration of TMDE.
- Limited rapid parts fabrication capability and selective circuit card repair.

2-125. The TAMP tasks executed by the TASMG are—

- Provide technical assistance.

- Provide SSA for Class IX (air) in the theater of operations and a storefront for aviation sustainment at echelon above corps.
- Provide limited sustainment and backup field maintenance.
- Support the sustainment classification mission.
- Assist units in reception, staging, onward movement, and integration (RSOI) at aerial port of debarkation and/or sea port of debarkation.
- Provide contact teams.
- Validate estimated cost of repair.
- Provide application of MWOs.
- Forecast and support theater aviation maintenance surge requirements in support of operations plan.
- Provide special test and troubleshooting capability.
- Establish/manage staging areas, wash points, and inspections.
- Repair crashed or battle-damaged aircraft.
- Receive, manage, and distribute ASL (aviation) within theater.
- Obtain special repair authority from AMCOM liaison.
- Facilitate and coordinate engineer requirement and authorization before repair.

Chapter 3

Programs and Equipment

This chapter provides Army aviation maintenance commanders/leaders, maintenance officers, maintenance technicians, and maintainers with a "how-to" on practices, procedures, and guidelines related to Army aviation programs and equipment.

SECTION I – PROGRAMS

AVIATION RESOURCE MANAGEMENT SURVEY PROGRAM

3-1. The ARMS program provides aviation personnel with expert technical assistance and on-site evaluations, as mandated by AR 95-1, to all units assigned to Forces Command (FORSCOM), TRADOC, Eighth United States Army, Intelligence and Security Command, and United States Army European Command aviation units. Inspectable areas of the ARMS include, but are not limited to:

Contents
Section I – Programs.................................3-1
Section II – Equipment.........................3-13

- Safety.
- Command support programs.
- Maintenance and aviation support equipment operations.
- POL.
- Warehouse, tech, and unit supply.
- Training and command programs.
- Aviation night vision devices.
- Flight operations.
- ALSS management (TC 3-04.72 [FM 3-04.508]).
- Aviation medicine.
- Air traffic services.
- Standardization.
- Tactical operations.

Note. Annual internal ARMS for UAS units are performed by the brigade aviation element.

3-2. The ARMS program is a comprehensive survey of aviation units conducted every 24 to 36 months IAW AR 95-1. These surveys assist aviation unit commanders in evaluating their unit ability to conduct its mission safely and effectively.

3-3. FORSCOM units or units evaluated and inspected by FORSCOM ARMS teams can obtain ARMS information, assistance, or download the FORSCOM ARMS guide at https://www.us.army.mil/suite/page/592726. An AKO login and password is required to access this web site. For all other Army command units in need of their corresponding ARMS checklists, see the Army command ARMS inspection team designated POC.

3-4. Commanders of maintenance companies and troops will ensure compliance with their Army command ARMS standards and include satisfactory evaluations as a unit MOE goal. Commanders, in cooperation with the support operations section, will conduct annual internal ARMS reviews of their units to validate SOPs and operational compliance. Tri-annual (every four months) progress updates will be provided to the support operations section and the command team for analysis and archiving. Assistance from sister units provide a skilled outside look when the formal ARMS team evaluation is off cycle for a particular unit.

LOGISTICS ASSISTANCE PROGRAM

3-5. The USAMC LAP provides aviation users and maintainers of USAMC-managed equipment with logistical and technical assistance. This assistance can be requested by supported units when materiel problems might adversely affect aircraft OR rates.

Note. For more information and guidance concerning the USAMC LAP, refer to AR 700-4. In addition, refer to AR 700-138 and AR 750-1 for more information on the LAP. For logistics assistance, contact logistics support activity (LOGSA) at https://liw.logsa.army.mil/index.cfm?fuseaction=login.main.

3-6. Aviation maintenance commanders/leaders and maintenance officers/technicians may, while conducting aircraft maintenance, encounter the NMCS conditions. NMCS conditions may be the direct result of logistical problems beyond their resource capability to resolve or clearly not within their responsibility. In cases beyond their resource capabilities, assistance is provided to commanders/leaders and maintenance officers/technicians in analyzing readiness, identifying problems, determining responsibility for resolutions, and, when appropriate, resolving problems.

RESPONSIBILITIES

3-7. LAP responsibilities include providing commanders and unit maintainers with the technical guidance necessary to resolve logistic problems. These responsibilities include identifying and reporting, through channels, all logistic conditions that have an adverse effect on aircraft readiness. The LAP provides a means for logistic support activity managers to observe and to identify materiel and logistic system problems in the field.

3-8. The LAP is not intended to be a permanent augmentation to the aviation maintenance commander. LARs, when available, provides assistance in resolving specific logistical problems. They can also provide limited training to assigned unit personnel when requested. When appropriate, LARs provides logistics support resolution (normally on new equipment) to aviation maintenance units.

FUNCTIONALITIES

3-9. Logistics assistance is the advice, assistance, and training provided by qualified logisticians. They may be military or civilian employees of the Army or employees of industrial or commercial companies serving the Army under contract.

3-10. The LAP provides solutions to problems of supply and equipment, installation, operations, and maintenance. The program provides a pool of knowledgeable and experienced personnel from which all aviation units may request and draw assistance.

3-11. Logistics assistance personnel will coordinate actions with the commander and keep him fully informed of their findings and recommendations. Some functions of logistics assistance personnel are to—

- Give a hands-on demonstration to show how to perform a given procedure.
- Advise technical and nontechnical personnel.
- Help users replace unserviceable equipment that cannot be repaired.

- Visit AMC/AMT and ASC/AST activities to help improve supply, repair parts distribution, and maintenance support for using organizations.
- Collect, evaluate, and exchange technical information.
- Instruct units in records management and preparing unit supply records, PLL, and ASL.
- Instruct units in preparing equipment for field exercises and overseas deployment.
- Provide assistance on the care and preservation of stored material.
- Work with the AMCOM liaison engineers to facilitate and authorize maintenance to be performed at the unit or intermediate level that would otherwise be performed at a sustainment facility.
- Coordinate with the major support command (MSC) item managers to expedite repair parts delivery wherever possible.
- Monitor the performance of assigned contractor personnel to ensure the work being performed is according to the statement of work.

PERSONNEL AND SERVICES

3-12. LAP personnel are highly trained, experienced, physically qualified, and well versed in the missions, equipment, and procedures of the unit. According to AR 700-4, they are assigned or attached to the appropriate geographical logistics assistance office (LAO) when deployed to field command areas. Logistics assistance personnel are employed by, or under contract to, one of the major subordinate commands under the USAMC.

Logistics Assistance Representatives

3-13. A LAR is a highly trained and experienced DOD civilian for a specific MDS aircraft, generally assigned to support aviation maintenance units in all operational environments.

3-14. A LAR is the direct representative of a MSC such as AMCOM or CECOM. The LAR can provide maintenance and safety messages from the MSC to the unit and assist with the completion of message requirements. The LAR is available to train unit personnel on new equipment or sustainment systems to include support and test equipment managed by the MSC.

3-15. The LAR can coordinate with systems engineers, as well as item managers, to authorize sustainment-level repairs and expedite the release and delivery of repair parts managed by the MSC.

Contract Plant Services

3-16. Trained and qualified engineers or technicians employed by the manufacturer provide these services in the plants and facilities of the manufacturer. Through contract plant services, Army personnel are taught to install, operate, and maintain the manufacturer equipment.

Contract Field Services

3-17. Qualified contractor personnel provide DA personnel with on-site support information on the installation, operation, and maintenance of new DA weapons, equipment, and systems.

Field Service Representatives

3-18. Field service representatives are employees of manufacturers of military equipment or components. They provide liaison or advisory service between their company and military users of their products. Known in the field as "tech reps," they provide information from the manufacturer to update the Army equipment capabilities. Field service representatives serve as technical communication channels between manufacturers and military users to help resolve technical problems.

ASSISTANCE REQUESTS

3-19. When requesting logistic assistance, aviation units should contact their local AMC/AMT LAO. Refer to AR 700-4 for LAO geographic areas of responsibility. Requests for assistance should include the following information:

- Name and location of the aviation maintenance unit requiring assistance.
- Specific types and quantity of materiel or weapons (make and model) of the systems for which assistance is needed and a general description of the problem.
- Reasons why organic resources are not available.
- Estimated length of time assistance is required, starting date, and POC.
- Type of logistic assistance personnel required.
- Specific requirements for security clearance.

ARMY OIL ANALYSIS PROGRAM

3-20. AOAP is a condition-monitoring program that improves equipment reliability and readiness by early detection of potential failures. The program applies to aircraft and ground equipment including GSE, MHE, power generation, and prime movers. Aircraft maintenance leaders must ensure the AOAP in each unit complies with all oil-sampling requirements. Units and levels of command will designate an AOAP monitor who is trained by the supporting lab or installation AOAP monitor. The AOAP monitor is a unit orders position. The QC section normally oversees day-to-day operations of the program.

3-21. AR 750-1 defines the AOAP objectives, policies, and responsibilities. TB 43-0211 identifies Army equipment enrolled in AOAP and sample intervals. Aircraft maintenance personnel must be familiar with these references as well as with the AOAP forms in DA PAM 738-751 governing oil samples. AOAP website is https://aoapserver.logsa.army.mil.

Note. To ensure SOF, an aircraft may be placed in a not mission capable (NMC) status before formal receipt of DD Form 2026 (Oil Analysis Request).

ARMY WARRANTY PROGRAM

3-22. The Army warranty program covers all items procured for Army use purchased with an accompanying warranty. The Army warranty program includes aircraft, aircraft weapon systems, and aircraft repair parts and components.

Note. Refer to AR 700-139 for additional guidance on the Army warranty program.

3-23. Aviation units receiving newly fielded equipment and components should check the type of warranty the Army purchased. When newly fielded equipment under warranty experiences malfunction, the unit should request assistance from the LAP office for answers to or resolution of warranty issues or questions.

3-24. Aviation equipment and components covered by the Army warranty program require special handling during the warranty period to keep the warranty valid. Details concerning warranty provisions are published in supply letters. The WARCOs or LAOs will have a copy of the warranty supply letter on items within their area of support. Warranties will increase the time required to perform maintenance.

3-25. The LAO or LARs will provide advice and assistance to the Army warranty control officer (WARCO) and aviation unit maintainers as part of the service interface established in AR 700-4. Representatives of the LAP will—

- Assist in establishing an Army electronic product support account to submit warranty action claims.
- Assist WARCOs in developing local procedures for warranty administration.

- Clarify warranty applications/exclusions and claim/report procedures upon user or WARCO request.
- Provide warranty information to users/WARCOs as a secondary source of information.
- Provide specific assistance as outlined in materiel fielding plans, technical and supply bulletins (SBs)/manuals, and related documents for warranty management.

3-26. After warranty issues are addressed and resolved, the unit shall submit a product quality deficiency report (PQDR). DA PAM 738-751 provides PQDR procedural guidance and information. DA PAM 738-751 provides the CECOM QDR action point addresses for submission of CECOM PQDRs. To submit AMCOM-managed equipment PQDRs, refer to DA PAM 738-751 for the AMCOM QDR action point address. DA PAM 738-751 also provides procedural guidance and instructions for completing DA Form 2407 and DA Form 2407-1 to file warranty claim actions.

FOREIGN OBJECT DAMAGE PROGRAM

3-27. Foreign object damage (FOD) program for maintenance operations is a basic requirement for all Army aviation units and will improve operational efficiency, provide for a safer operating environment, and reduce maintenance down time. Personnel who operate, maintain, or service aircraft or aviation GSE are responsible for adhering to the commander's FOD program. FOD accidents are an unacceptable impediment to Army operations. The FOD officer and NCOIC, placed on orders by the commander, ensure compliance with applicable regulations, SOPs, and manuals. Utilizing the ARMS checklist assists the FOD program leadership in validating each performance measure of the program.

Note. DA PAM 385-90 contains guidance on developing a FOD program and FOD prevention SOP.

CAUSES

3-28. FOD is damage to or malfunction of an aircraft caused by an object that is alien to an area or system or is ingested by or lodged in a mechanism of an aircraft. FOD may cause material damage, or it may cause a system or equipment to become unusable, unsafe, or less efficient. Some examples of FOD are—

- Ingestion of loose hardware or grass by an engine.
- Flight controls jammed by hardware or tools.
- Tires, skids, propellers, or tail rotors damaged by debris on the ramp or taxiway.

PREVENTION MEASURES

3-29. The objectives of a FOD prevention program are to find and correct potential hazards and to eliminate the causes of FOD. Training, work-site design, discipline, motivation, and follow-up on FOD incidents are essential factors of a sound program. All personnel must take an active role in FOD prevention. FOD prevention must be an essential part of each unit aviation accident prevention program.

3-30. The unit FOD prevention program is documented in writing and must be read by all unit personnel. FOD prevention countermeasures should also be integrated throughout the unit SOP.

RESPONSIBILITIES

3-31. FOD programs must be enforced, observed, and practiced daily. Commanders at all levels are responsible for enforcing FOD programs. They rely on their unit aviation safety officer (ASO) (when assigned), FOD officer/NCO, and unit personnel to make the FOD program effective.

Unit Commander

3-32. When establishing a FOD prevention program, commanders will appoint a FOD prevention officer/NCO to implement the unit FOD prevention program. This may be an additional duty for any unit officer/NCO other than the ASO/aviation safety noncommissioned officer or the aviation maintenance officer.

Unit Foreign Object Damage Officer/Noncommissioned Officer

3-33. The FOD officer/NCO will track scheduled FOD inspections and investigate all known and suspected FOD damage. He monitors the unit tool accountability program, maintains surveillance for unsatisfactory FOD conditions, and takes corrective action immediately. He will delegate specific areas of responsibility (such as a hangar or shop/maintenance work area) to appropriate unit personnel.

3-34. The FOD officer/NCO conducts surveys and documents results (minimum once per month) and inspects all unit areas. He notifies the unit ASO of hazards found during surveys for analysis and control option development. The FOD officer/NCO ensures FOD inspection checklists cover, as a minimum, procedures outlined in the unit FOD SOP. He uses the checklist for each inspection and submits the completed checklist to the unit ASO. Table 3-1 provides a sample unit FOD inspection checklist.

Table 3-1. Sample unit FOD inspection checklist

Biweekly FOD Inspection Checklist	SAT	UNSAT
1. Are maintenance personnel practicing FOD control procedures IAW unit SOP?		
2. Do maintenance personnel conduct a tool inventory after maintenance procedures are complete or at the end of the day?		
3. Do NCOs conduct regularly scheduled checks of work areas to ensure FOD prevention measures are observed?		
4. Are equipment and material not in use kept clear of maintenance areas?		
5. Is equipment available to keep runways, taxiways, hover lane, and parking areas clean?		
6. Are runways and other areas normally used for hover and ground operations inspected regularly?		
7. Where practical, are inspections made of all landing areas to determine FOD potential?		
8. Are all personnel periodically briefed on FOD and prevention techniques?		
9. Do aircrews and operating personnel report unsatisfactory conditions when first encountered?		
Biweekly FOD Inspection Checklist	SAT	UNSAT
10. Is the unit receiving United States Army Combat Readiness Center (USACRC) publications and posters on FOD?		
11. Do unit bulletin boards contain information on FOD?		
12. Do work areas have FOD posters displayed?		
13. Are FOD containers with locally manufactured "STAY SHUT" lids conveniently located around the hangar area?		
14. Are FOD containers prominently labeled?		
15. Are the tools accounted for after the work is completed?		
16. Are maintenance personnel familiar with the FOD prevention program in the unit?		
17. Are operational hazard reports (OHRs) being submitted on FOD problems when encountered?		
18. Are the inlet and outlet covers used when required?		
19. Are all crewmembers and maintenance personnel motivated and committed to FOD prevention?		
20. Are tool room personnel monitoring tool accountability and serviceability of tools?		
FOD Officer/NCO name	Unit	Date

Unit Aviation Safety Officer

3-35. The unit ASO (when assigned) will monitor and survey the FOD program to ensure effectiveness and adherence. Whenever possible, the unit safety officer attends unit safety meetings to address potential FOD problems, prevention, or investigations. The unit safety officer briefs new personnel on their responsibility for FOD prevention and keeps the commander and FOD officer/NCO informed on FOD issues.

Unit Maintenance Personnel

3-36. Unit personnel must take an active role in FOD prevention and be responsible and accountable for actions taken when performing aircraft maintenance. Unit personnel will use the "clean-as-you-go" approach to maintenance, making a thorough check of the area after each task is completed.

3-37. Maintainers will ensure aircraft openings (such as ports, lines, holes, and ducts) are properly protected to keep foreign objects from accidentally entering and ensure tools, hardware, and other equipment are accounted for at the end of each maintenance operation. Inspect equipment before use to ensure it will not cause damage. Ensure care is taken when installing any piece of test equipment.

3-38. Unit maintenance personnel will check engine inlet screens for loose, trapped, or broken objects that may produce FOD. When in doubt, they will immediately report FOD and potential FOD to the first-line supervisor. Unit personnel will place all residues and objects that may produce FOD in the proper container.

PROCEDURES

3-39. When an aircraft ingests foreign objects or fluids, FOD has occurred. Assigned personnel will ensure the following hazards are avoided during all aspects of aviation maintenance operations:

- Grease on work shoes/boots – FOD can lodge in the grease and transfer to the aircraft or GSE.
- Litter – police litter (such as nuts, bolts, cotter pins, safety wire, and rivets) in the work areas to minimize or eliminate the potential of damage to the aircraft, GSE, or personnel.
- Jewelry – ensure no jewelry (such as rings, watches, identification. tags, and pin-on rank) is worn during maintenance, inspections, and servicing of aircraft and GSE.

Investigation and Reporting

3-40. FOD hazards are reported through the OHR or accident investigation system. These data should be communicated to first-line supervisors, to the FOD officer/NCO, and ASO for immediate resolution. If there is a question about whether potential or suspected FOD hazards need to be reported, report it. The FOD officer/NCO/ASO will assist unit personnel in selecting an appropriate course of action.

Foreign Object Prevention in Maintenance Areas

3-41. Once the air inlet and compressor sections have been removed for maintenance, they are inspected before they are reinstalled. Unit TI will conduct inspections of the air inlet and compressor sections before installation of said components. Engine inlet covers are on all aircraft at all times unless the aircraft is being inspected or the engine inlet or exhaust area is being worked on.

3-42. Bolts, nuts, rivets, fasteners, screws, washers, safety wire, and other residue are disposed of in receptacles marked for FOD materials. These receptacles should be conspicuously placed on the flight line and in the hangar. Tools and supplies are accounted for upon completion of maintenance actions to prior to MOCs/MTFs.

3-43. Oil spills and grease spots are cleaned up immediately after they occur and reported to the spill response team for evaluation. Enforcing this policy will reduce accidents in maintenance areas.

Foreign Object Damage Walk Procedures

3-44. FOD walks are mandatory; maximum participation is encouraged to include all available crewmembers (aviators and crew chiefs). All FOD containers are emptied and FOD collected at the completion of the unit FOD walks.

AIRCRAFT CONDITION EVALUATION PROGRAM

3-45. Aircraft condition evaluation is an annual program that evaluates all Army rotary-wing aircraft. AMCOM, as the NMP, is assigned the mission according to AR 750-1 to develop overhaul programs based on data, funding, and sustainment capability. The aircraft condition evaluation program is used to evaluate and report the sustainment-level health of the airframe. The data are used to schedule aircraft for repairs and determine the location and depth of sustainment maintenance and repairs.

MAINTENANCE ASSISTANCE AND INSTRUCTION TEAM PROGRAM

3-46. The maintenance assistance and instruction team program upgrades Army materiel and units to a state of readiness consistent with assigned goals needed to carry out the Army missions. It will also ensure commanders at all levels are provided assistance in identifying and resolving maintenance, supply, and maintenance management problems within their units. The maintenance assistance and instruction team can also identify systemic problems in maintenance management and provide assistance to improve management of the maintenance workload at all levels of maintenance support.

Note. Refer to AR 750-1 for specific guidance on the maintenance assistance and instruction team program.

CORROSION PREVENTION AND CONTROL PROGRAM

3-47. Army TMs outlining procedures for the detection and treatment of corrosion for aircraft and associated equipment must be followed. A corrosion prevention and control (CPC) program will minimize aircraft and equipment damage, increase operational efficiency, provide for a safer operating environment, and reduce maintenance down time. Evaluation of CPC operations occur during the ARMS. Personnel who operate, maintain, or service aircraft or GSE are responsible for adhering to the commander published CPC program. Corrosion damage of aircraft or GSE is an unacceptable impediment to Army operations.

OBJECTIVES

3-48. Aviation units responsible for aircraft maintenance shall establish CPC programs. The type of program depends on the environment in which the aircraft and equipment may be exposed. At sea, conditions are considered the most severe. In this environment, aircraft and equipment are exposed to salt spray, ship stack gases, and aircraft engine exhausts. In other environments, land-based aircraft and systems may be exposed to industrial gases, salts, rain, mud, and mists containing sea salts.

3-49. A CPC program shall include trained maintenance personnel who are responsible for the prevention, early detection, reporting, and repair of corrosion damage. Such a program requires a dedicated effort by all maintenance personnel to prevent corrosion before it starts.

3-50. The maintenance leaders, with the assistance of QC personnel, will establish and implement inspections, procedures, and corrosion preventive measures. The maintenance leaders delineate individual and collective responsibilities for the conduct, management, and enforcement of the CPC program.

RESPONSIBILITIES

Unit Commander

3-51. Aviation commanders will integrate CPC awareness into all levels of maintenance to include support maintenance provided by aircraft maintenance contractors. CPC directives, guidelines, and procedures are published as an appendix to the unit aircraft maintenance SOP. The SOP will provide adequate instructions and awareness without reducing mission effectiveness. Commanders will ensure:

- Maintenance supervisors, TIs, aircraft crewmembers, and selected aviation maintenance unit personnel receive training in aircraft CPC programs according to AR 750-59, TM 1-1500-328-23, and TM 1-1500-344-23-series. Required entries for aircraft and equipment forms and records must be outlined and understood by all unit personnel.
- CPC directives and guidelines are followed.
- A CPC monitor is appointed on unit orders (additional duty), normally assigned to a TI or maintenance NCO.
- The CPC monitor receives complete training in corrosion prevention, treatment, and safety, if the monitor is not a graduate from an accredited corrosion course or program.
- Specific CPC responsibilities are delegated to appropriate maintenance officers/technicians, maintenance supervisors, and TIs.
- CPC SOPs are complete and revised when necessary. Maintenance personnel will familiarize themselves and comply with specified CPC procedures contained in the SOP.
- The CPC program is continuously reviewed. Recommendations for improvement must be reviewed and approved changes promptly implemented.

Unit Corrosion Prevention Control Program Noncommissioned Officer-In-Charge

3-52. The CPC program NCOIC will coordinate all actions affecting the CPC program and work with maintenance supervisors, TIs, and mechanics. The NCOIC will advise the commander on all CPC concerns and findings. The NCOIC implements and coordinates the commander's CPC program, ensuring all unit personnel are trained to conduct CPC procedures.

3-53. The NCOIC will monitor techniques and proficiency of maintenance personnel accomplishing corrosion inspections and aircraft washings, taking immediate corrective action when needed. Monitoring should include, but is not limited to, spot checks of chemicals used, dilution of cleaning compounds, and application of corrosion-preventive and water-displacing compounds.

PROCEDURES

3-54. An effective CPC program shall include thorough cleaning, inspection, preservation, and lubrication, at specified intervals, according to applicable aircraft and system maintenance TMs and TM 1-1500-344-23-series. Check for corrosion damage and integrity of protective finishes during all scheduled and unscheduled maintenance.

3-55. All identified corrosion shall be entered on the aircraft DA Form 2408-13-1 (Aircraft Inspection and Maintenance Record) or appropriate system fault record according to DA PAM 738-751. The status symbol will depend on the degree of corrosion, location, and allowable limits for the area as directed by the applicable aircraft maintenance TMs.

3-56. To prevent further deterioration, corrective action must be taken as soon as possible. When a corrosion defect/fault is assigned a "diagonal (/)" status symbol and corrective action is not initiated within 30 days from date of discovery, the aircraft or system status symbol is changed to an "X, grounding condition." The aircraft or system will remain NMC on readiness reports until corrective action has been taken.

3-57. Scheduled CPC inspections and actions shall be accomplished no later than the specified due date or hours as entered on the DA Form 2408-18 (Equipment Inspection List). When operational requirements preclude timely accomplishment of scheduled inspections and maintenance actions, the following guidelines are established:

- Corrosion inspections or actions prompted by a special occurrence or as required by airframe operating time according to the special inspections sections of the airframe and engine TMs are accomplished not later than the time specified in the manual.

- When the aircraft is away from the home station and facilities are unavailable, scheduled corrosion inspections and maintenance actions are deferred/delayed with higher headquarter commander approval.

- Once the aircraft has returned to home station or to a maintenance facility, it will not be flown until required corrosion inspections and corrective maintenance actions are completed according to applicable aircraft maintenance TMs.

Preventive Maintenance Procedures

3-58. A preventive maintenance program shall include—

- Regularly scheduled aircraft and system washing as specified by the maintenance unit SOP/TMs.
- Regularly scheduled cleaning or wiping down of all exposed unpainted surfaces, such as landing gear struts and actuating rods of hydraulic cylinders with a compatible fluid or lubricant.
- Keeping low-point drains open.
- Inspecting, removing, and reapplying preservative compounds on a scheduled basis.
- Earliest detecting and repairing of damaged protective coatings.
- Using clean water with low chloride content for aircraft and GSE washing and rinsing.
- Using padded panel racks to store panels/parts for aircraft and equipment during maintenance; using protective measures to prevent abrasions/scratches resulting from placement of such items as parts, tools, and toolboxes on wings, fuselage, or other aircraft surfaces.

Cleaning Procedures

3-59. Use only authorized cleaning compounds and solvents as described in TM l-1500-344-23-series or the appropriate TM. Dilution of materials will follow the recommendations in the aircraft-specific maintenance TMs or the label on the container. Comply with dilution instructions.

3-60. Exposure to chemical compounds can pose potential health hazards. Supervisors must ensure compliance with all product warning statements and placards. Maintenance personnel should avoid direct skin contact with solvents and breathing of vapors. Personnel will have access to material safety data sheets (MSDSs) (http://www.hazard.com/msds) to ensure compliance with required safety procedures.

3-61. The CPC program monitor will evaluate potential health problems and make sure the proper equipment is used and all cautions are observed. PCE/PPE is worn, to include goggles, gloves, aprons, and boots.

3-62. Aircraft cleaning is the first step in preventing aircraft corrosion. Aircraft should be cleaned regularly to—

- Prevent corrosion by removing salt deposits, other corrosive soils, and electrolytes.
- Allow a thorough inspection for corrosion and corrosion damage.
- Reduce fire hazards by removing accumulations of leaking fluids.

Frequency of Cleaning

3-63. Aircraft and systems shall be cleaned according to schedules required by applicable maintenance TMs. Under certain local conditions, depending on the type of system and usage, the normal wash cycle may not be sufficient. More frequent cleaning may be required for certain types of aircraft when—

- Excessive exhaust gases accumulate within impingement areas.

- Paint is peeling, flaking, or softening.
- Fluid leakage (such as coolant, hydraulic fluid, or oil) occurs.
- Exposure to salt spray, salt water, or other corrosive materials occurs.

Daily Cleaning

3-64. When an aircraft is deployed within 3 miles of salt water or flown below 3,000 feet over salt water, daily cleaning or wipe down is required on all exposed, unpainted surfaces such as landing gear struts and actuating rods of hydraulic cylinders.

Immediate Cleaning

3-65. Affected aircraft or system areas must be cleaned immediately if—

- Spilled electrolyte and corrosive deposits are found around battery terminals and battery area.
- Aircraft or systems are exposed to corrosive fire-extinguishing materials.
- Salt deposits, relief tube waste, or other contaminants are apparent.
- Aircraft or systems are exposed to significant amounts of salt water.
- Fungus growth is apparent.
- CBRN contaminants are detected.

Preservation Procedures

3-66. According to maintenance TMs, aircraft and systems are cleaned and treated with corrosion-preventive compounds after a wash. After corrosion is removed, if any finish is removed with the corrosion, pre-treat metal and apply new paint/coating.

Note. Sealant and corrosion-preventive compounds shall be used according to TM 55-1500-345-23, TM 1-1500-344-23-series, or aircraft maintenance TMs.

3-67. Corrosion is a major cause of avionics failure. Corrosion on avionics equipment is similar to airframe structure corrosion; however, small amounts of corrosion on avionics equipment can cause intermittent or complete system malfunctions. TM 1-1500-344-23-series and applicable maintenance TMs are used to mitigate these issues.

CORROSION PREVENTION AND CONTROL PROGRAM REFERENCES

3-68. Table 3-2 lists CPC program references.

Table 3-2. Corrosion prevention and control references

AR 750-1	Army Materiel Maintenance Policies
AR 750-59	Army Corrosion Prevention and Control Program
DA PAM 738-751	Functional User's Manual for The Army Maintenance Management System-Aviation (TAMMS-A)
TM 1-1500-204-23-(Series)	General Aircraft Maintenance Manuals
TM 1-1500-344-23-1	Cleaning and Corrosion Control Volume I Corrosion Program and Corrosion Theory
TM 1-1500-344-23-2	Cleaning and Corrosion Control Volume II Aircraft
TM 1-1500-344-23-3	Cleaning and Corrosion Control Volume III Avionics and Electronics
TM 1-1500-344-23-4	Cleaning and Corrosion Control Volume IV Consumable Materials and Equipment for Aircraft and Avionics
TM 55-1500-345-23	Painting and Marking of Army Aircraft

COMMAND SUPPLY DISCIPLINE PROGRAM

3-69. The CSDP is a compilation of regulatory requirements requiring implementation for standardizing supply activities throughout the Army (AR 710-2). The goal of this program is the proper care, use, replenishment, and safeguarding of Army property. The commander has command responsibility for this program. Likewise, platoon leader or section chief has supervisory responsibility for the program. Squad leaders, team chiefs, and staff officers-in-charge and NCOICs incur this same supervisory responsibility. Soldiers have direct responsibility if they have physical control of property or if they have signed for it on a hand receipt. Soldiers who sign a hand receipt are accountable for all components of items listed on the hand receipt unless they receive a valid shortage annex or shortage document listing components not available for issue. Without a valid shortage annex or document, an item is assumed complete. Supply sergeants, supply custodians, supply clerks, or warehouse personnel have custodial responsibility for property in storage awaiting issue or turn-in. Personal responsibility should be inherent in all members of the Army. These responsibilities are a cornerstone of sound leadership; they cannot be delegated, withdrawn, or ignored. These responsibilities are assumed with or without a written hand receipt. The CSDP allows commanders to set a climate in which supply policies are enforced. It establishes an environment in which Soldiers and leaders can manage property proactively and requisition supplies and equipment. Soldiers and leaders who are responsible for equipment must know their equipment, its whereabouts, and its status.

3-70. Commanders and leaders ensure physical resources to accomplish the unit mission remain present and serviceable. Commanders and leaders in maintenance organizations actively pursue elimination of any shortages and establish tracking of shortage reduction by quantity, type, and funding required to eliminate all unit shortages. This tracking will be reported to the battalion/squadron S-4 logistics officer to enable predictive budget activity. Unserviceable tools and equipment must be rapidly turned in to unit supply for incorporation in the replenishment process and not retained by hand receipt holders for accountability. Special tools purchased with unit funds or acquired by rapid fielding or other means will be entered into formal tracking by unit supply personnel and incorporated into PBUSE. Special tools must be included in unit 100 percent inventories and change of command or change of hand receipt holder inventories. Shortage reduction and special tool fill levels serve as quantifiable MOE for each maintenance unit.

CONFINED SPACE AND PROTECTIVE CLOTHING AND EQUIPMENT

3-71. A confined space is defined as a space large enough and configured for an individual to enter and perform work, has limited or restricted means for entry or exit, and is not designed for continuous employee occupancy.

3-72. Army personnel are prohibited from entering a permit-required confined space without an approved permit, personal protective clothing, monitoring equipment, or use of isolation/lockout/tagout procedures as stated in DA PAM 385-90.

3-73. Maintenance commanders will assign a PCE/PPE and confined space program coordinator to ensure compliance with DA PAM 385-90 requirements, if the unit anticipates the performance of any confined space operations. The coordinator will ensure compliance with all requirements, including personnel training, personnel certification, equipment assignment, maintenance, employment, and participation in the unit internal and external ARMS program.

3-74. Units will conduct a job hazard analysis to establish all PCE requirements. The PCE results will appear on all MSDS documents as PPE IAW Occupational Safety and Health Administration standards as required in support of the hazardous communication (HAZCOM) program.

TOOL BOXES

3-75. Toolboxes store hand receipt holder tools. Portable toolboxes enable carrying and storing a variety of hand tools. Canvas tool bags supplement these capabilities but provide little to no security. Paint, etch, tape, or mark all tools for easy identification during inventories. Each marked tool coincides with the associated toolbox identity (for example, each tool in toolbox B-1 is engraved with "B-1" to associate that tool with the corresponding toolbox.) Toolboxes must contain shadowed tool positions; if toolboxes/bags cannot be shadowed then an alternate, adequate, or practical means of tool accountability will be used.

Note. Tool containers for small tools such as hex wrenches may be marked instead of marking each individual tool.

3-76. Any time a tool is determined missing or broken on an aircraft, the mechanic will immediately inform their supervisor. The mechanic supervisor will immediately ground the affected aircraft and the aircraft will remain grounded until the missing tool or broken piece is found or "signed off" by the proper authority. The supervisor will notify their platoon or section leader, PC, and flight operations. A log to track missing or broken tools should be established. Recommended log information includes the serial number, calendar date, type of tool, Soldier name, action taken, and signature of the supervisor or maintenance officer.

3-77. Considerations for tool box use are:

- Toolboxes will be inventoried before any maintenance is conducted and re-inventoried at the completion of said maintenance.
- Toolboxes and work area are cleaned and maintained prior to departure from the work area or at the end of the workday IAW TM 1-1500-204-23-series.
- Toolboxes will not be laid on aircraft surfaces. Heavy tools will be properly secured when used on aircraft to prevent their falling and causing injury to personnel or damage to aircraft.
- All mechanics toolboxes are locked except when in actual use. The Soldier using the toolbox remains in the immediate area.
- Broken tools will not be stored in toolboxes or bags for accounting purposes. Broken tools must be turned in to unit supply immediately and an appropriate turn-in document placed in their shadow location until replaced.

Note. Units shall develop an SOP outlining tool accountability procedures (lost tools, marking of tools, required inventories, and replenishment procedures).

TOOL ROOM

3-78. The aviation maintenance tool room managed by ASES provides temporary utilization of tools to technicians for mission accomplishment without adding low density or bulky items to individual hand receipts. This consolidation facilitates 24-hour operations in tactical environments, allowing repairers to use robust hand, power, GSE, TMDE, and special tools when needed without the additional burden of maintaining and accounting for them on a full time basis. The tool room demands constant oversight and accountability reviews, including frequent inventories to ensure compliance with FOD and CSDP procedures, as well as PCE/PPE and CPC compliance. The ASES leader must ensure the highest level of tool and shelter maintenance rigor. The ASES leader also ensures replacement processing occurs in the tool room section, due to its multiple custodians for 24-hour operations and diverse customer base. The ASES tool room allows the ARP and the CRP to focus on work order completion instead of additional tool tracking. Assigned or attached aircraft maintenance personnel who manage, account for, or use special tools, calibrated tools, and common tools from the tool room to maintain aircraft or GSE must adhere to the commander published unit maintenance SOP with regard to tool room operations.

> *Note.* Refer to all applicable aircraft TMs and references listed at the end of this appendix for guidance on the management, accountability, use, and maintenance of all assigned tools.

RESPONSIBILITIES

3-79. Aviation maintenance tool rooms must fully support all ongoing aircraft maintenance operations. Responsible ASES personnel design a plan of support to provide required common and special tools to maintenance personnel when needed. Aviation maintenance commanders/leaders, maintenance officers/technicians, and NCOICs are responsible to draft and implement an SOP outlining tool room management and support responsibilities. In addition, this SOP will provide information and guidance to all personnel signing out tools.

Commander

3-80. The commander ensures PBUSE accountability of all special tools and GSE associated with the tool room according to AR 710-2 and AR 735-5. The commander approves policies and procedures for signing out tools from the tool room to support aircraft- and maintenance-related functions. The overarching goal of tool room support is to provide the required 24-hour support to increase OR of aircraft.

Section Sergeant/Maintenance Supervisor

3-81. The tool crib or tool room section sergeant or supervisor has direct oversight and responsibility of the tool room. He or she will ensure the tool room custodians remain in direct compliance with all procedures outlined in the tool room SOP. He or she has supervisory responsibility for all assigned tools in the tool room. He or she will ensure tool accountability by conducting, at a minimum, quarterly inventories of the tool room. The current and next inventory date will be posted in the tool room for easy reference.

3-82. He or she will prepare a report showing the results of the inventory. Any shortages noted are accounted for according to AR 710-2 and AR 735-5. Output from an automated system will satisfy this requirement. The section sergeant or maintenance supervisor will conduct random serviceability inspections of assigned tools in the tool room regularly. Additionally, he or she will ensure effective replenishment operations for unserviceable or lost items.

Tool Room Custodian

3-83. The tool room custodian is responsible for all tools contained within the tool room or tool crib, maintaining 100 percent accountability of the tool room. He or she will issue and receive tools according to procedures outlined in the unit SOP. Any tool from a tool room needed to complete a maintenance procedure is signed out before it can be removed from the tool room/tool crib.

3-84. The tool room custodian will maintain an updated roster of all assigned or attached unit personnel authorized to sign out tools. Tools issued from a tool room become the personal responsibility of the recipient (user). When not signed out, special/common-hand tools, tool sets, and kits are secured and controlled according to physical security standards of AR 190-51.

3-85. The tool room custodian will inspect all tools and equipment for completeness and serviceability before issue. He or she will conduct by-the-book preventive maintenance on all items assigned to the unit tool room on a continuing basis. An inventory sheet should be used to account for every tool/item that is part of a given SKOT. If a tool is issued out of a SKOT, it is accompanied by a copy of the inventory sheet. The inventory sheet is used every time the item is issued and returned to ensure continuous accountability.

3-86. The custodian performs a tool room inventory monthly using the current supply catalog and any associated PBUSE special tools documentation. A comprehensive tool room inventory is conducted before change of custodianship. Results, to include shortcomings or unserviceable/damaged tools or equipment, are reported to the responsible aviation section sergeant/maintenance supervisor. Unserviceable or damaged tools are turned in to the responsible aviation section sergeant/maintenance supervisor for immediate introduction into the replenishment process. The supervisor will ensure replacements are ordered through the unit supply room.

TOOL PROCEDURES AND PRACTICES

3-87. The tool room is a controlled access area ensuring safekeeping and accountability of property. Tools needed away from garrison are signed for on a temporary hand receipt. Personnel not assigned to the unit may sign out tools after coordination with the ASES OIC or NCOIC IAW the unit SOP. The tool sign-out register is sufficient for short-term use by unassigned personnel (typically less than 48 hours). Tools signed out to other units for extended periods will be hand-receipted on a DA Form 2062 (Hand Receipt/Annex Number).

3-88. Contact teams/personnel requiring tools in support of unit/element deployments are required to hand receipt tools for their respective maintenance support mission. In addition, they are responsible for turning in those tools once redeployed or at the completion of the rotation/mission unless other arrangements have been made with the tool room NCO/custodian.

3-89. The Army aircraft maintainer uses a variety of basic hand tools, measuring tools, power tools, special tools for aircraft, and torque tools. Aircraft maintainers must ensure familiarity with tool procedures and practices to guarantee availability and enhance unit and aircraft readiness.

Tool Care

3-90. The efficiency of an aircraft maintainer and the tools he or she uses are determined largely by the condition in which the tools are kept and maintained. Tools will be wiped clean and dry before being placed in a toolbox. If their use is not anticipated in the near future, they should be lubricated to prevent rust. This is especially true if tools are stored under conditions of extreme humidity or are continuously exposed to salt air. Remove all unserviceable tools from toolboxes and tool rooms and turn in for replenishment.

Tool Storage

3-91. Tools should always be kept in their appropriate storage place when not in use. A toolbox or case not only keeps the tool protected from dirt, but also ensures the tool can be found, as long as it is returned to its place after use. The toolbox should be locked and stored in a designated area and an inventory list maintained for that box.

Note. At the completion of a maintenance procedure, all aircraft maintainers should conduct an inventory of their toolbox when used. Complete accountability of assigned tools will reduce FOD accidents/incidents. All tools should be returned to their rightful place once maintenance is complete or at the end of the business day.

> **CAUTION**
>
> The use of cadmium- and zinc-plated tools on Army aircraft is prohibited. Use only chrome-plated steel or un-plated steel tools during disassembly or reassembly of aircraft components.

Tool Room References

3-92. Table 3-3 provides tool room references.

Table 3-3. Tool room references

AR 190-51	Security of Unclassified Army Property (Sensitive and Non-sensitive)
AR 710-2	Supply Policy Below the National Level
AR 735-5	Policies and Procedures for Property Accountability
DA PAM 710-2-1	Using Unit Supply System (Manual Procedures)
TM 1-1500-204-23-9	Manual for General Aircraft Maintenance (Tools and Ground Support Equipment)

SPECIAL TOOLS

3-93. Special tools are unique tools not assigned to aviation units by their MTOE or that appear in the MTOE in quantities insufficient to accomplish the volume of tasks associated with that tool. Many special tools may be depicted, described, and authorized by the repair parts and special tools list (RPSTL) located in proscribed TMs associated with each airframe or subsystem. Other items, either in the military supply system or commercially available, serve as special tools as well. Special tools are sometimes specified by the manufacturer for low-density repairs and procedures, or requested by Soldiers and technicians from the commander of the unit to reduce manhours, ease difficulties, or improve the efficiency of any unit operation. Special tools include everything from six-inch long #3 cross-tip screwdrivers and ratcheting wrenches to rotor head and engine stands, or borescopes. Special tools can account for millions of dollars in unit property for aviation maintenance organizations and must be tracked tenaciously.

3-94. The procurement and usage of special tools must receive approval and facilitation on a case-by-case basis by the unit commander through either unit supply or the technical supply section. Leveraging the government purchase card, military inter-departmental purchase request, local contracts, and GSA processes requires commander oversight to ensure new items appear on appropriate unit and individual hand receipts. Each hand receipt holder will have any associated or acquired special tools issued and added to their hand receipt IAW AR 710-2 and incorporated in the PBUSE accounting. Special tools and containers, regardless of cost or class of supply, receive formal tracking in the supply room on the hand receipt holder documentation. Organizing special tools into groups associated with each section having a hand receipt creates a section special tool kit and eases the transfer and accounting process. This ensures continual inventory as hand receipt holders and commanders change positions throughout the life of the unit, and prevents the loss and required re-purchasing of items not tracked by standard property book officer (PBO) and MTOE accounting procedures.

3-95. Special tools often carry a high price and bring with them unique considerations. Always create an accounting reference file with photographs in the supply filing system for special tools lacking TM or supply catalog inventories. Provide a copy of the accounting reference to PBO for archiving and utilization during change of command inventories or investigations. If the item is serial numbered, include the serial number on the hand receipts. Many special tools require calibration, and frequently this service is only available from the manufacturer. Ensure the unit TMDE coordinator makes contact with those manufacturers and establishes a procedure to obtain calibration. Include the procedures for special tools calibration in the accounting reference file and the TMDE SOP. The commander must ensure funding is secured to execute the calibration when the tool requires it. Additionally, a repair parts acquisition and training strategy for commercially obtained tools must accompany any new item. Again, the commander is responsible to resource these requirements and must consider them before approving any sophisticated new special tool.

3-96. Special tools that need to be fabricated or made from bulk materials frequently appear in the RPSTL. Special tools are not components of a SKOT and are not authorized in a supply catalog. Consequently, they require special accounting and tracking in PBUSE by unit supply, hand receipt holders, PBO, and the commander to prevent loss, pilferage, and the need to frequently repurchase or fabricate the same item. This tracking supports the CSDP.

> *Note.* If aviation maintenance units lack special tools outlined in the appendix of their respective RPSTL or demanded by operational needs, they must initiate the process to procure them.

TEST, MEASUREMENT, AND DIAGNOSTIC EQUIPMENT

3-97. TMDE includes torque wrenches, testers, test sets, and other test equipment used to verify whether aircraft systems are functioning or malfunctioning according to applicable regulatory policies and published aircraft TMs. Depending on the design, TMDE may be portable or fixed in place.

3-98. Whether a unit contains specific items of equipment depends on its category of maintenance (AMC/AMT or ASC/AST) and its prescribed TOE. TM 1-1500-204-23-series contain detailed descriptions and operating instructions for the most common test equipment.

> *Note.* Refer to applicable -23P aircraft RPSTL for a listing of aircraft-specific TMDE requirements. This list also grants authorization for unit maintenance personnel to procure TMDE.

3-99. AR 750-43 assigns Army-wide management of the Army TMDE calibration and repair support program to USAMC. In turn, the Army TMDE activity (through USAMC) is responsible for DA TMDE program execution and management. The National Guard Bureau is assigned management, command, and control over the ARNG maintenance companies and their assigned TMDE. It also controls calibration facilities at combined support maintenance shops. In addition, AR 750-43 prescribes policies and procedures, assigns responsibilities, and establishes goals and objectives applicable to the development, selection, acquisition, management, sustainment, and support of Army TMDE, associated test program sets, embedded diagnostics and prognostics, and interactive electronic TMs.

RESPONSIBILITIES

3-100. Unit commanders retain responsibility for all maintenance support programs to include TMDE. They must rely on a unit TMDE support coordinator to enforce policies contained in the unit maintenance SOP. The TMDE support coordinator is critical duty requiring unit orders. The TMDE support coordinator and assistant are assigned to the ASES. The TMDE SOP establishes the standard that must be met by all unit maintainers and TMDE users.

> *Note.* The goal of all unit calibration programs is for a delinquency rate (failure to submit for required support) of two percent or less according to AR 750-43 and an IMRF match against the unit TMDE inventory of 98 to 102 percent.

Commanders and Aviation Support Equipment Section Leaders

3-101. Commanders will designate, in writing, a unit TMDE support coordinator under the direct control of the ASES leader. Organizations with large quantities of TMDE (such as ASCs and ASTs) will assign the TMDE coordinator as a primary rated responsibility. The commander, ASES leader, and TMDE support coordinator are responsible for—

- Coordinating war, emergency, and contingency plans with the United States Army Test Measurement and Diagnostic Equipment Activity (USATA) when TMDE calibration and repair support is a requirement.
- Coordinating major changes affecting calibration and repair support requirements provided by USAMC elements with the USATA.

- Identifying TMDE support requirements to the USATA supporting organizations.
- Comparing the unit property books or TMDE inventory with TB 43-180 to initially determine the calibration and repair support requirements for the unit TMDE items; upon request, the supporting TMDE support activity can provide technical assistance to the TMDE owners/users in the identification of TMDE requiring support.
- Ensuring all TMDE is identified to include TMDE that may be embedded in sets, kits, outfits, special tools, or other assemblages.
- Turning in TMDE (to include all operator documentation and basic issue items (BIIs) in excess of authorizations, through appropriate channels) for redistribution.
- Developing and executing training programs that will attain and maintain the highest level of proficiency among personnel in the use, maintenance, and calibration of TMDE.
- Reporting TMDE problems affecting unit readiness.
- Taking appropriate actions to remove unnecessary/outdated TMDE from unit requirements and authorizations documents.

Test, Measurement, and Diagnostic Equipment and the Test, Measurement, and Diagnostic Equipment Support Coordinator

3-102. TMDE enables all levels of aircraft maintenance to occur with the highest regards for safety and maintenance standards. Maintenance cannot be performed on an aircraft to a specific TM standard unless calibrated items are calibrated and a valid calibration sticker is displayed. Refer to aircraft-specific RPSTL TMs for special TMDE requirements.

3-103. The TMDE support coordinator must enforce compliance with the unit TMDE SOP. He ensures TMDE users identify their calibration and repair needs and conducts regular follow-ups to adhere to the schedules and procedures for obtaining the required support. The TMDE support coordinator performs the following:

- Serves as the central POC for matters concerning TMDE calibration and repair support.
- Develops and implements the SOP for identification, turn-in, and control of TMDE requiring calibration and repair support.
- Ensures hand receipt holders update hand receipts when changes to TB 43-180 or supply catalogs occur.
- Ensures TMDE hand receipt holders receive accountability documentation when items enter the calibration process and are no longer in the possession of the hand receipt holder.
- Assures compliance with AR 750-43, DA PAM 750-8, TB 43-180, TB 750-25, command regulations, unit maintenance SOPs and appendices, and the supporting area test, measurement, and diagnostic equipment support team (ATST) external SOP.
- Reviews the IMRF monthly to ensure all authorized TMDE requiring calibration or repair support is contained therein and the listed information is correct, notifying ATST of any changes. The matching standard is 98 to 102 percent between the IMRF and the unit internal inventory list.
- Ensures the supporting ATST is advised when changes, additions, or deletions in the TMDE inventory occur to make sure the IMRF is maintained according to TB 750-25.
- Coordinates with supporting ATST and unit personnel to ensure the recording, scheduling, and reporting system is maintained as prescribed in AR 750-43 and TB 750-25.
- Monitors the projected item list to make certain TMDE is submitted for calibration service according to the published schedule; when necessary, arranges for unscheduled calibration support.
- Monitors the delinquent item list to determine causes of TMDE delinquency and initiates action to obtain calibration service for these delinquent items.
- Highlights the delinquent list, notifies the appropriate hand receipt holder, reports delinquencies to leaders IAW unit SOP, and provides the unit commander with a monthly update.

- Ensures the unit TMDE owner/user delinquency rate (failure to submit for required support) is two percent or less (commander MOE).
- Assures all organizational maintenance has been performed on TMDE submitted for support and the required accessories and manuals accompany the TMDE.
- Reviews all reports received from the support organization to—
  - Identify TMDE out-of-tolerance, repaired, or determined to be unserviceable when presented for calibration.
  - Determine if system maintenance checks previously performed using this out-of-tolerance TMDE must be repeated.
  - Advise TMDE owners/users who did not present their equipment for calibration, according to the schedule, that corrective action must be taken.
- Ensures new items of TMDE not listed in TB 43-180 are reported according to TB 43-180 and TB 750-25.
- Coordinates non-standard or OEM calibration procedures with command support.
- Tracks all TMDE deemed unserviceable until receipt of proper turn-in documentation before removal from the unit TMDE list (as well as the IMRF).
- Maintains a file of TMDE removal and addition documentation, delinquency reports, and IMRF match reviews for two years or the duration of the previous commander, whichever period is longer.
- Maintains a record of all items in temporary storage by nomenclature, model, and serial number; ensures this equipment is operational and the affixed DA Label 80 (U.S. Army Calibrated Instrument) has been over-stamped "calibrate before use" (CBU).
- Notifies the supporting ATST, in writing, that TMDE has been placed in storage so these items may be removed from the cyclic calibration schedule; ensures a designated temporary storage area is established for storing CBU/void items.
- Ensures calibration not required items possess appropriate labels and completion of all scheduled services.
- Constantly monitors the TMDE inventory to achieve maximum effectiveness; ensure items seldom used are placed in temporary storage.
- Turns unused items in to supply and initiates deletion actions to remove them from the TOE or TDA authorization.

3-104. The TMDE support coordinator ensures responsive TMDE calibration and repair support. These services may be rendered by an ATST, area calibration laboratory or support center, DOD support facility, or direct support (DS)/general support (GS)/ASC/AST support unit for the TMDE-support program.

3-105. The unit calibration program coordinator ensures TMDE identified for long deployments will not be due calibration while en route to a deployment site. TMDE due calibration while participating in a unit deployment, requires an out-of-cycle calibration request to the supporting installation calibration facility. As many as 250 items in the ASC and AST may be out of calibration upon arrival due to long gaps between load and receipt times. In instances of long dormancy between loading equipment and receiving items under the unit control once again, the TMDE coordinator will prepare a request for immediate support to the calibration support center servicing the unit upon arrival. Ideally, this request will be delivered to the future supporting calibration center prior to loading equipment for long transport to a theater or destination to allow adequate forecasting of surge requirements upon arrival.

3-106. The commander will appoint an alternate TMDE support coordinator and utilize several TMDE representatives in the platoons, shops, and sections as required. The overall responsibility for managing the TMDE support program is retained by the ASES OIC and the primary unit coordinator. However, the primary coordinator needs to ensure alternate TMDE coordinators are knowledgeable of the TMDE program objectives, policies, and procedures and of their inherent responsibilities.

User and Representative Responsibilities

3-107. The following checklist applies to unit TMDE users and representatives; additional checklists in applicable regulations also address compliance requirements and objectives that should be met by all TMDE users:

- Have the property book and hand receipts been reviewed to determine accountability requirements?
- Have TMDE calibration and repair requirements been identified?
- Does TMDE in use have a current DA Label 80 or DA Label 163 (U.S. Army Limited or Special Calibration) affixed and correctly annotated?
- Is TMDE (provided a limited calibration) identified with DA Label 163?
- Is physical inventory periodically conducted to verify the types and quantities of TMDE on-hand requiring calibration or repair?
- Are all TMDE changes, additions, and deletions identified to the supporting ATST as they occur?
- Is an operational check performed on items before they are placed in CBU status; is a correctly annotated DA Label 80 affixed; and has the supporting ATST been notified of the status change?
- When TMDE is removed from temporary storage (CBU), is it submitted for calibration before use?
- Is the storage area segregated from the work area?
- Are projected item lists provided by the supporting facility? Are they reviewed, and is corrective action taken?
- Are delinquent item lists (TMDE not presented for scheduled calibration) reviewed and corrective action taken by the affected hand receipt holder, and is the unit commander briefed?
- Are controls established to assure TMDE is not used after expiration of the calibration due date on the DA Label 80 or DA Label 163?
- When there is doubt about the accuracy of TMDE, is action taken to request unscheduled calibration?
- Has an operator or organizational maintenance program for TMDE been established?
- Is operator or organizational maintenance performed as prescribed by equipment maintenance manuals?
- Are preventive maintenance services performed on TMDE as listed in the appropriate technical publications, and are faults recorded on DA Form 2404 (Equipment Inspection and Maintenance Worksheet)?
- Is DD Form 314 (Preventive Maintenance Schedule and Record) maintained at unit level for all calibration not required items of TMDE requiring scheduled periodic preventive maintenance services other than calibration?

SUPPORT

3-108. Most calibration and repair support requirements of instruments used in support of Army materiel are listed in TB 43-180. The calibration procedures listed in TB 43-180 are DOD- or USATA-approved procedures and shall be used. The approved maintenance manual is also listed in TB 43-180. Unique special tools requiring civilian or OEM calibration must be addressed in the unit SOP and TMDE continuity guide.

Area Test, Measurement, and Diagnostic Equipment Support Team Capabilities

3-109. TMDE designated in TB 43-180 as requiring ATST support must be transported to the location where the ATST is slated to provide calibration and repair services. When justified by sufficient workload or when the size or configuration of the TMDE precludes movement, the ATST is dispatched to the TMDE owner/user site.

3-110. When a designated ATST is unable or not capable of providing calibration or repair service, the TMDE is evacuated as directed by the calibration and repair center. The ATST is responsible for providing the necessary service and returning the repaired and calibrated TMDE to the owner/user. When service external to the ATST is necessary, except for warranty TMDE, the ATST should arrange for the service and assure the return of the TMDE to the owner/user.

Area Calibration Laboratories/United States Army Primary Standards Laboratory Support

3-111. TMDE standards requiring the support of area calibration laboratories or United States Army primary standards laboratory may be transported to the ATSTs or shipped directly to the area calibration laboratories or United States Army primary standards laboratory.

Management Reports

3-112. IMRF is distributed quarterly to TMDE support coordinators. Units may request reports monthly. TB 750-25 requires TMDE calibration and repair support activities to establish and maintain an IMRF. The IMRF for TMDE-support program supported by DS/GS/ASC/AST units will also be maintained by the supporting ATST. The accuracy of these files rests, in part, with the TMDE owner/user that must initially provide accurate information and, thereafter, review master lists monthly for accuracy and take corrective action when necessary.

3-113. The TMDE owner/user must advise the supporting ATST/DS/GS/ASC/AST as changes, additions, or deletions in the TMDE inventory occur. The IMRF must contain all TMDE requiring support.

Forms and Labels

3-114. A DA Label 80 or DA Label 163 must be affixed to all calibration standards and TMDE identified in TB 43-180 as requiring calibration. This labeling certifies the instruments have been calibrated to required specifications and indicates support dates.

Note. Refer to TB 750-25 for detailed instructions on the preparation of these labels. Instructions for maintenance forms are in DA PAM 750-8.

3-115. Surveillance of the TMDE support program includes a review of forms and labels to ensure uniformity and proper annotation. Policies and questions pertaining to labels and forms used for instruments in storage are also specified in TB 750-25.

GROUND SUPPORT EQUIPMENT

3-116. GSE includes equipment and special tools required to maintain aircraft and associated system. The ASES is responsible for maintaining and accounting for common GSE in maintenance units. GSE supporting a single MDS is referred to as PGSE. The ARP and CRP maintain aircraft PGSE. Trained maintainers keep GSE and PGSE serviceable. Currently, there is no school MOS training specifically to support and maintain GSE or PGSE; this is a unit responsibility.

AUTHORIZATION DOCUMENTS

3-117. Authorization documents allocating GSE to aviation units are MTOEs, TDAs, and commercial off-the-shelf fielding documents. Additionally, command directed notification establishes a valid requirement for GSE. Authorization of GSE and PGSE is frequently contained in the repair parts TM for that specific aircraft. For a complete authorization of GSE and PGSE, maintainers must review the unit MTOE and all applicable supply catalogs for sets, kits, and outfits authorized as well as RPSTL manuals for their assigned aircraft.

INSPECTIONS

3-118. The most common types of inspections performed by using aviation maintenance units are daily and periodic inspections. The regularity of these inspections is determined by frequency of operation and conditions under which the equipment is operated. For more specific and detailed inspections of assigned GSE, refer to applicable references and publications.

MAINTENANCE

3-119. Most GSE failures can be prevented with standardized maintenance practices. Establishing a unit GSE maintenance SOP is the responsibility of the ASES leader. The ASES leader will designate the GSE NCOIC as an NCO trained and qualified to inspect and maintain all pieces of GSE (AGPUs, compressors, heaters, towing vehicles, fueling vehicles, test stands, and electronic test equipment). TM 1-1500-204-23-9 provides criteria and technical data for serviceability inspections, storage and shipment, and general maintenance procedures. Specific TMs contain operator and support maintenance procedures. Maintenance beyond the operator level will depend on the agency or proponent for the item and on the availability of maintenance capability.

3-120. To ensure GSE availability, the ASES OIC and NCOIC will—

- Evaluate the operational status of GSE.
- Ensure CPC program compliance for all GSE.
- Emphasize individual responsibility and verify all operators are trained and licensed before using GSE maintained by the ASES.
- Ensure all appropriate publications are current, on-hand, and used.
- Ensure pre-operation and post-operation checks and services are continuously done and documented.
- Allot time for preventive maintenance checks and services (PMCS) and scheduled maintenance.
- Conduct periodic inspections and inventories.
- Ensure GSE operation and maintenance standards are detailed in the unit SOP.
- Ensure status of applicable GSE (AGPU and generic aircraft nitrogen generator) is reported during regularly scheduled unit status report meetings.

REPAIR PARTS

3-121. Units must maintain PLL for GSE as specified in the applicable TMs. Each unit is responsible for listing its GSE PLL requirements and providing a copy to technical supply and the SSA.

3-122. Aviation units typically possess little or no GSE PLL. As a result, some manufacturers have halted production of outdated equipment and its repair parts. The numerous makes and models of one type of equipment further complicate the problem of identifying repair parts.

Note. If an aviation unit is having a difficult time obtaining repair parts for its assigned GSE, input the GSE NSN into FEDLOG to obtain the source of supply (SOS) and commercial and government entity code. Once the SOS and the commercial and government entity code are identified, contact the inventory control point or the manufacturer directly to obtain needed repair parts. The support operations section in the ASB or SAMO in the ACS can assist in rapid acquisition of difficult to find parts.

STORAGE

3-123. Equipment, specifically GSE, shall be stored under cover, in buildings, or as required IAW AR 740-1. The equipment shall be stored to permit access for inspection and servicing during the storage period. Adequate security measures and fire protection shall be provided.

3-124. GSE in storage does not require periodic calibration. Enter "CBU" on the DA label 80 either at the time the equipment is placed in storage or on the date indicated on the label as the calibrated due date.

3-125. GSE preserved for long-term storage is unpreserved, exercised, and preserved again within 12 months of the preservation date. Equipment preserved according to TM 1-1500-204-23-9 is inspected at 90-day intervals.

REQUESTS FOR ADDITIONAL AVIATION GROUND SUPPORT EQUIPMENT

3-126. Sometimes, aviation units need GSE other than that authorized or required by MTOE or TDA. Tropic, desert, or arctic environments often create the need for additional equipment to supplement authorized equipment listed in the unit MTOE. The unit in need of additional equipment should submit a request through command channels to the program manager-aviation GSE. The request should include the following information:

- Identification of the specific requesting unit.
- Number of applicable TOE, MTOE, or TDA.
- Complete nomenclature, stock number, and quantity of needed items.
- Justification for each item, including a statement that the item can be maintained.
- If the item is nonstandard, the reason for not using a standard item.
- Statement as to whether the additional equipment should be included in the TOE, MTOE, or TDA.

3-127. The RPSTL contained in applicable TMs shows GSE needed to support assigned aircraft. If an item is listed, it can be requested, even if it is not included in the unit TOE, MTOE, or TDA.

ACCOUNTABILITY

3-128. AR 710-2 states that, as a minimum, all property is inventoried annually. Accountability compliance of assigned GSE is according to AR 735-5. Commanders will add all non-MTOE GSE to the unit PBUSE data file.

FORMS AND PUBLICATIONS

3-129. DA PAM 750-8 lists required DA forms on which data is to be recorded and maintained. The following DA and DD forms are used in support of GSE in accordance with DA PAM 750-8:

- DA Form 5988 (Equipment Inspection and Maintenance Worksheet) or DA Form 2404-used to list equipment faults that create an NMCS equipment status.
- DA Label 80-used for equipment requiring calibration.
- DD Form 314.
- DD Form 1577 (Unserviceable [Condemned] Tag-Materiel).
- DD Form 1577-2 (Unserviceable [Reparable] Tag-Materiel).

3-130. A reference library must be established with required publications on-hand to ensure GSE is properly operated and maintained. The reference library will contain technical publications, lubrication orders, MWOs, TBs, TMs, and supply catalogs.

Note. DA PAM 25-30 lists publications required to support GSE.

This page intentionally left blank.

Chapter 4

Automated Management Systems

This chapter provides aviation maintenance commanders, maintenance officers/technicians, and maintainers with an explanation of the Army automated management systems. Leaders and maintainers are required to anticipate, analyze, and tailor available automated systems for effective and timely support of complex weapon systems and aircraft. The measure of maintenance success on the battlefield will continue to be the availability of aircraft that are FMC and ready-to-fight (RTF).

SECTION I – STANDARD ARMY MANAGEMENT INFORMATION SYSTEM

4-1. STAMIS is a functional information management system designed to provide the logistics support infrastructure required for military ground and aviation operations. The technical goal is to establish a seamless and interoperable network. The STAMIS network facilitates the vertical and horizontal flow of sustainment and maintenance status information to units Army-wide.

Contents

4-2. Components of the system primarily include ULLS-A (E), Unit Level Logistics System-Ground (ULLS-G), PBUSE, Standard Army Retail Supply System (SARSS), Standard Army Maintenance System (SAMS), integrated logistics analysis program (ILAP), and Global Combat Support System-Army (GCSS-A).

UNIT LEVEL LOGISTICS SYSTEM-AVIATION (ENHANCED)

4-3. ULLS-A (E) provides aviation commanders, maintenance officers/technicians, and maintainers with the ability to track maintenance and materiel readiness management operations and prepare maintenance management forms and records. It also enables technical supply personnel to process requests and initiate procedures that provide maintenance personnel with aircraft repair parts and components.

Note. Access the AKO ULLS-A (E) website at https://www.us.army.mil/suite/page/604562.

4-4. ULLS-A (E) enhances the tracking and control of aviation maintenance, sustainment, and aircraft forms and records. ULLS-A (E) can also process aircraft transfers, maintain operational and historical records, process Class IX (air) repair parts, and enhance maintenance operations overall.

4-5. ULLS-A (E) automates bench stock listings (stocked and maintained manually with an automated reordering process), PLL, reportable component management, and maintenance management process performed by PC. ULLS-A (E) is the current system of record for all PLL/bench stock and the TAMMS-A operations at the unit level. ULLS-A (E) enhances and supports those tasks associated with controlled exchange of reportable components listed in TB 1-1500-341-01.

4-6. ULLS-A (E), at the AMC/AMT, is configured into a network operation. An ULLS-A (E) notebook computer assigned to each aircraft facilitates those tasks previously performed on the manual logbook.

Army aviation units are normally supported by three workstation computers (PC, QC, and technical supply) and a file server (database) positioned in the PC office. Maintenance tasks performed by crew members and maintenance personnel are entered into the ULLS-A (E) notebook and transferred daily onto the unit data base. Tasks and activities performed by PC and QC are transferred to the ULLS-A (E) unit database. These procedures will ensure the ULLS-A (E) workstations and notebooks are current and reflect the latest maintenance status assigned to the airframe.

4-7.   The PC office will provide procedural guidance on the functional aspects and operations of the ULLS-A (E). The PC OIC/NCOIC coordinates all actions taken when an aircraft becomes partial mission capable (PMC) or NMC. Actions include, but are not limited to, aircraft systems and subsystems troubleshooting, aircraft component repair/replacement, requisition of a serviceable aircraft repair part/component, or controlled exchange of an aircraft repair part/component. Once a course of action has been determined, the ULLS-A (E) database should be updated.

4-8.   The PC office receives and coordinates daily data transfers from/to maneuver companies/troops according to established schedules. The PC office performs data transfer functions to higher STAMIS for maintenance and supply support. It also prepares and provides required daily, weekly, and monthly reports to the BAMO or battalion/squadron AMO according to established policies and procedures.

4-9.   The TIs are the principal operators in the QC section. The TIs will review the ULLS-A (E) database on the maneuver company/troop's computers to ensure all appropriate information (such as new and corrected faults, man-hours, when discovered, how recognized, and flight time) is entered correctly into the corresponding aircraft ULLS-A (E) notebook.

4-10. TIs will also review closed faults for completeness and correctness. They will keep all aircraft historical records (to include configuration control and weight and balance) current in the ULLS-A (E) database. TIs archive completed records and forms according to established procedures. Records are archived according to DA PAM 738-751.

4-11. Technical supply personnel will perform automated logistics functions affecting requests, receipt, storage, issue, and accountability of the aviation maintenance unit assigned PLL. When an airframe is down for parts, the PC OIC will direct technical supply personnel to initiate automated aircraft repair parts and component requests. NMCS aircraft will carry the highest priority designator (PD) allowed for the unit. The PC office will report NMCS aircraft status to the BAMO or battalion/squadron AMO.

4-12. The crew chief/maintenance personnel are responsible for daily data entries to ensure ULLS-A (E) accurately reflects status and condition. To maintain up-to-date automated records, maintenance personnel must promptly and accurately input all faults identified and inspections performed into the ULLS-A (E) notebook. Maintenance personnel will enter related maintenance actions affecting the status of the original write-up into the ULLS-A (E) notebook as they occur or at the earliest opportunity.

4-13. If a maintenance fault (other than the initial entry) with a grounding condition "X" is found, maintenance personnel will immediately transfer the ULLS-A (E) notebook faults into the PC ULLS-A (E). After PC is notified and maintenance information is transferred into the ULLS-A (E), maintenance actions to correct the grounding condition "X" fault will begin immediately.

4-14. If routine maintenance is being conducted to clear an entry from a DA Form 2408-13-1, the PC section is notified that the affected airframe is NMC until the maintenance actions are complete.

Note. According to DA PAM 738-751, flight packs may be used for seven mission days while an aircraft is away from homestation. Printed electronic forms from the flight pack (DA Forms 2408-13-1 [Aircraft Inspection and Maintenance Record], 2408-13-2 [Related Maintenance Actions Record], and 2408-13-3 [Aircraft Technical Inspection Worksheet]) may be used when the ULLS-A (E) is down. As soon as the system is operational, maintenance personnel will transfer entered information from the printed electronic forms into ULLS-A (E) as soon as possible.

4-15. A single ULLS-A (E) notebook can be used as a record-keeping tool for several aircraft; however, the logbook data card must be changed to switch between aircraft. The user should use only one data card per laptop to avoid possible data loss or corruption. Automated logbook entries are entered on the notebook and saved to the logbook data card. Logbook entries are performed according to DA PAM 738-751 using the ULLS-A (E) automated logbook program.

4-16. Aircraft data is entered into the ULLS-A (E) notebook on a real-time or near real-time basis. Pilots, maintenance personnel, and crew chiefs enter data and events into the logbook as required. Platoon sergeants/section chiefs monitor all daily data-entry operations by subordinate crew chiefs and review all ULLS-A (E) closed faults for completeness and correctness.

Note. Crew chiefs and maintenance personnel should transfer their data frequently. Frequent transfers to/from the server provide timely recognition of any problem areas and allow for easier resolution.

4-17. ASCs/ASTs are provided with an ULLS-A (E) to support field maintenance activities for customers and operational readiness float (ORF)/RTF aircraft. The assigned logbook and ULLS-A (E) notebook will accompany the aircraft to the ASC/AST in order to track and record all performed maintenance actions. ULLS-A (E) allows the PC to generate and manage ASC/AST-level work orders and post statuses to the maintenance request register. It also provides the means to produce and manage internal work orders (intra-shop), which are printed and supplied to the ASC/AST ARP and CRP.

4-18. SOF messages and TBs are disseminated and updates to the user logbook data are transferred back to the logbook from the server.

UNIT LEVEL LOGISTICS SYSTEM-GROUND

4-19. ULLS-G facilitates supply and maintenance operations at the unit level while eliminating the potential for errors that can occur under a manual system. ULLS-G also provides motor pool operations with dispatch capability. The ULLS-G alert dispatch option allows multiple dispatches to be printed. ULLS-G operation does not change between garrison and field environments.

PROPERTY BOOK UNIT SUPPLY ENHANCED

4-20. PBUSE is the Army sustainment property accountability system. PBUSE gives the commander a real-time view of assets, allows him to access the system for queries without the PBO and also provides—

- Real-time total AV throughout all levels of Army management.
- Automatic logistics Army authorization document system updates. Logistics Army authorization document system is an electronic version of the MTOE that updates PBUSE and other property book accounting systems.
- Elimination of unique item-tracking reporting through automatic serial number tracking.
- Automated catalog changes.
- Unit transfer/task force/split operations.

4-21. When direct connection to the web is not possible, the system operates in a disconnected stand-alone mode. Upon completion of a stand-alone operation, the system is reconnected to the web for resynchronization of the user data to the central database.

STANDARD ARMY MAINTENANCE SYSTEM

4-22. SAMS provides commanders and maintenance managers with accurate and timely maintenance management and sustainment information at the ASC/AST. It provides visibility of inoperative equipment and required repair parts, selected maintenance, equipment readiness, and equipment performance reports. It also provides completed work order data to the LOGSA for equipment performance and other analysis.

SAMS is comprised of Standard Army Maintenance System-Level 1 (SAMS-1) and Standard Army Maintenance System-Level 2 (SAMS-2). When fielded, Standard Army Maintenance System-Enhanced (SAMS-E) replaces SAMS-1, SAMS-2, and ULLS-G.

STANDARD ARMY MAINTENANCE SYSTEM-1

4-23. SAMS-1 automates work order registration and document registers. It automates inventory control and reorder of shop and bench stock as well as automating work order parts and requisitioning. SAMS-1 is assigned to ASCs/ASTs and forward support companies/forward support troops.

4-24. SAMS-1—

* Automates maintenance documentation and information gathering and transmittal.
* Provides management of work orders and work order tasks.
* Allows transfer of repair parts/due-ins between work orders and shop stock.
* Accounts for direct, indirect, and nonproductive manhours.
* Simplifies and standardizes the collection and use of maintenance data.
* Improves readiness management and visibility by providing equipment status and asset data.
* Raises the quality and accuracy of performance, cost, backlog, manhour, and parts data through improved maintenance management.

4-25. SAMS-1 conducts logistics and maintenance interfaces with the following systems:

* Technical.
* SAMS-2.
* Standard Army Retail Supply System-Level 1 (SARSS-1).
* Standard Army Retail Supply System-Gateway (SARSS-Gateway).

STANDARD ARMY MAINTENANCE SYSTEM-2

4-26. SAMS-2 is an automated maintenance management system used at the ASB, CAB/ACS, theater sustainment command (TSC), and sustainment brigade support operations.

4-27. SAMS-2 provides maintenance and management information to each level of command, from the user to DA-levels. SAMS-2 collects, stores, and retrieves maintenance information from SAMS-1 sites and allows managers to coordinate maintenance workloads. SAMS-2 passes significant maintenance and supply information to higher commands for the purpose of maintenance engineering and readiness reporting.

4-28. SAMS-2 conducts interfaces with the following systems:

* Technical.
* SAMS-1.
* SAMS-2.
* LOGSA.

STANDARD ARMY MAINTENANCE SYSTEM-ENHANCED

4-29. SAMS-E replaces SAMS-1, SAMS-2, and ULLS-G functionality, and ensures rapid supply and maintenance operations at unit level. SAMS-E provides motor pool operations with an alert dispatch option allowing multiple dispatches to be printed. SAMS-E also provides the ability to track requisitions, deadline faults, FMC and NMC status, job order status, equipment availability, mileage of rolling stock, hours of operation, and operational pace/tempo funding.

STANDARD ARMY RETAIL SUPPLY SYSTEM

4-30. SARSS is a multi-echelon supply management and stock control system. SARSS is comprised of SARSS-1 at the DS-level, Standard Army Retail Supply System-Level 2A/C (SARSS-2A/C) or

Corps/Theater Automated Data Processing Service Center (CTASC), and SARSS-Gateway. SARSS provides supply-related data to the ILAP system at various functional levels.

4-31. SARSS supports technical, SAMS, PBUSE, non-automated customers, and the dual-based operations concept. SARSS is fully integrated from the user through theater Army-level. It can support worldwide deployment of forces to contemporary operating environments, including stability or civil support operations.

STANDARD ARMY RETAIL SUPPLY SYSTEM-1

4-32. SARSS-1 is the standard supply system used for receipt, issue, replenishment, and storage operations. It operates at the ASB and support battalions. SARSS-1 in each supply echelon is capable of sustaining prime support responsibilities for each customer unit. Each customer unit can interact directly with any SARSS-1.

4-33. SARSS-1 is the system of record. It maintains accountable balances and is supported by a SARSS-2A activity. It depends on Standard Army Retail Supply System-Level 2B (SARSS-2B) for catalog support and computation of stockage levels. SARSS-1 determines replenishment based on stockage levels furnished by the supporting SARSS-2B. It provides information data to SARSS-2A and SARSS-2B for stock management.

STANDARD ARMY RETAIL SUPPLY SYSTEM-2A/C

4-34. SARSS-2A/C performs time-sensitive supply functions. These include management of controlled items, lateral search of stocks to fulfill unsatisfied customer requirements from subordinate SARSS-1 activities, and redistribution of excess.

4-35. SARSS-2A/C operates on CTASC hardware. SARSS2-AC/CTASC performs time-sensitive supply management functions for referral; excess disposition; and management for Classes II, III (P), IV, VII, and IX (air). It manages redistribution of supplies. SARSS-2A/C/CTASC also maintains a custodial availability balance file that provides visibility of SARSS-1 assets to include divisional and non-divisional functions. SARSS-2A/C processes include the SARSS-2A functions.

STANDARD ARMY RETAIL SUPPLY SYSTEM-2B

4-36. SARSS-2B performs management functions that **are not** time sensitive. These include document history, demand analysis, and catalog updates at the installation and United States property and fiscal office. It supports subordinate SARSS-1 and SARSS-2A by performing stockage-level computations, tailoring catalog files, and maintaining active and inactive document history data.

STANDARD ARMY RETAIL SUPPLY SYSTEM-GATEWAY

4-37. SARSS-Gateway is an interactive/batch-oriented transaction processor that routes transactions to and from each interfacing STAMIS. It provides a communications network and the capability to send transactions to the defense automatic addressing system. It provides the appearance of a seamless, near real-time supply system to unit-level supply and maintenance activities.

4-38. SARSS-Gateway provides customer access to all assets available within a specified geographical area. Requests are electronically transmitted from customers to a gateway computer, where lateral search/issue decisions are made based on the availability balance file residing there. If assets are not available, the gateway forwards the request to the wholesale SOS and provides the status to customers on the actions taken.

INTEGRATED LOGISTICS ANALYSIS PROGRAM

INTEGRATED DATABASES

4-39. ILAP is the standard management tools used by the Army to collect, integrate, and display sustainment and financial data. Register at the following site, https://liw.logsa.army.mil, to gain access to ILAP and the multiple reports it generates.

REPORTS

4-40. ILAP has been fielded and operates at all echelons of the active Army, Army Reserve, and ARNG. Management reports in ILAP are developed with input from the customer in a rapid development process that shows the customer a management report; solicits the customer reaction to the report; and modifies the report to begin another cycle. This process is repeated until the customer requirement is met. Reports generated by ILAP support supply, maintenance, and finance management functions. The following **is not** an all-encompassing list but represents a common set of routine management reports that ILAP can provide:

- Stock number analysis.
- Document number analysis.
- Document history.
- Recoverable management.
- ASL management.
- ASL review.
- Equipment status.
- Workorder and parts research.
- Man-hour summary.
- Army working capital fund credit data.
- Credit details by document number.
- Army credit table.

Note. To interpret ILAP reports, the user must know the codes inside the ILAP report. The "codes" tab provides most of the codes used in ILAP reports. The "codes" tab is also available inside each of the ILAP reports to use as a reference.

4-41. Once a given report has been retrieved by ILAP, the results of all reports must be saved to the unit local drives. Users should not save data on the ILAP servers. These reports can be printed to facilitate tracking and reconciliation of management reports.

GLOBAL COMBAT SUPPORT SYSTEM-ARMY

4-42. The Army is transitioning its sustainment processes from an echeloned, mass-inventory approach to a more efficient and responsive distribution system based on the availability and use of accurate information. As a key enabler of this process transformation, the Army is moving away from multiple, stand-alone custom software applications to an integrated, commercial enterprise resource planning solution. The Army will connect the national and tactical sustainment domains using the Global Combat Support System-Army (GCSS-A). GCSS-A consists of two components:

- Field/tactical (F/T).
- Product lifecycle management plus (PLM+).

4-43. GCSS-A (F/T) will provide a single, real-time, common operating picture of the Army tactical sustainment requirements, assets, capabilities, and shortfalls. GCSS-A (F/T) is the tactical-level building block of the transformation to a single Army logistics enterprise (SALE) that will provide information superiority through real-time visibility of personnel, equipment, and supplies anywhere in the distribution pipeline and within the operational environment. GCSS-A (F/T) will provide field and sustainment personnel with logistical readiness information and allow the Army to reengineer tactical sustainment business processes to be consistent with commercial best business practices.

> *Note.* The GCSS-A website is located at https://www.gcss-army.lee.army.mil/index.html.

4-44. At the operational level, GCSS-A (PLM+) is the hub providing data management and SALE-related product data. It will act as the data warehouse for the exchange of tactical and strategic information with Army battle command, joint systems, and DLA and Army national level logistical and procurement systems. GCSS-A (PLM+) is the critical link for integrating the current logistics modernization program, GCSS-A (F/T), and the future implementation of SALE. GCSS-A (PLM+) is the organizational and technical framework necessary for a fully-integrated logistics enterprise as envisioned in the SALE. By emphasizing a single solution, the Army will minimize the long-term changes that might have been required within the national and tactical domains if development of those programs had continued in separate development environments.

BATTLE COMMAND SUSTAINMENT AND SUPPORT SYSTEM

4-45. The Battle Command Sustainment and Support System (BCS3) (formerly combat service support control system) collects and processes selected sustainment data in a seamless manner from STAMIS and manual systems/processes, and other related source data and hierarchical automated C2 systems (such as, Force XXI Battle Command Brigade and Below [FBCB2] and GCCS-A). Based on these inputs, the BCS3 supports of the Army Battle Command System (ABCS) common operational picture (COP) by—

- Generating and disseminating near-real time sustainment C2 reports.
- Responding to sustainment related ad hoc queries.
- Updating the database an average of every three hours.
- Providing sustainment warfighting function information.

4-46. The system displays a three-dimensional picture using topographic details selected by the user from a menu of audible mapping features. BCS3 provides the logistics portion of the COP on the maneuver control system. It also provides the maneuver sustainment commander with enhanced briefings and data-management capabilities. The current logistical data is augmented with analytical and decision support tools that enable the commander to make well-informed decisions rapidly and effectively.

4-47. BCS3 provides commanders with current and future combat power estimates in what is called the running estimate. BCS3 fuses data from satellites, radio frequency identification (RFID) tags, interrogators, and transponders enabling BCS3 to track and display locations of vehicles and cargo as they move within an AO. BCS3 obtains data and files from the maneuver control system and incorporates operational data with sustainment data providing commanders with a comprehensive and robust view of the AO. Tactical units providing electronic feeds to FBCB2 are displayed on BCS3. The display provides an aggregated view of icons representing unit locations derived from Blue Force Trackers.

SECTION II – LOGISTICS SUPPORT ACTIVITY

LOGISTICS INTEGRATED DATABASE

4-48. The logistic support activity (LOGSA) is a leveraging technology that provides immediate access to many logistics web-based tools including the logistics integrated database (LIDB), the parts tracker, and other capabilities. LOGSA products and services include sustainment tools in support of equipment readiness for users, maintainers, and managers of the Army aircraft systems, subsystems, and weapon systems. LOGSA tools independently and collectively contribute to the Army transformation goals in reducing the logistics support footprint.

4-49. The LIDB stores national and tactical historical information and provides real-time status of Army readiness, requisition, supply, and maintenance and asset information to customers worldwide. The information needed to equip, arm, move, and sustain Soldiers and fix and fuel their equipment and corresponding systems can be accessed from one central source using one log-on identification and password. A LOGSA system access request (SAR) form must be completed to gain access to LIDB support functions. This form can be located at https://www.logsa.army mil/index.cfm?fuseaction=home.startSite. The logistics portal to access web sites from DOD, DLA, GSA, Army, Navy, Air Force, and Marine Corps is located at http://www.dtc.dla mil/logport/index.htm.

4-50. LIDB uses modules (or file folders) to segregate the volumes of data into user-friendly packages. Primary modules are located on the main menu screen under the headings "Query Database" and "Decision Support."

4-51. From the main menu, double click on the "Query Database" menu icon. Once the "Query Database" menu is opened, the user can access modules and maintenance and logistics support management information critical to all aviation maintenance commanders/leaders, maintenance officers/technicians, and maintainers.

PUBLICATIONS MODULE

4-52. The publications module identifies all equipment publications required to maintain each Army end item. This module provides aviation maintainers with the critical references needed to conduct by-the-book maintenance. This module also allows access to the following:

- A list of TMs, technical manuals, SBs, MWOs, and supply catalogs.
- A list of publications for the major components appearing in the equipment component of end items, BIIs, and RPSTL.
- Information found in DA PAM 25-30, as well as command-authenticated publications (sustainment maintenance work requirements).
- A two-section list, one listed by line item number and NSN sequence and the other by publication number.

MAINTENANCE MODULE

4-53. The LIDB maintenance module contains data on completed maintenance actions reported from DS and GS units and activities from the total Army. SAMS is the field maintenance system that feeds closed work orders.

4-54. The LIDB maintenance module includes a history of each maintenance action as it progressed through the maintenance process. This history allows maintenance managers to determine time spent in a particular status such as awaiting parts, in shop, awaiting pickup, or in initial inspection. This maintenance history is useful in determining what affects downtime in the maintenance system. It also provides a listing of all parts used during a maintenance action. The LIDB maintenance module can generate reports on an entire item for a particular owning/support unit identification code (UIC) or Army command or to a specific serially numbered end item.

RETAIL DEMANDS MODULE

4-55. The retail demands module contains all demands from units throughout the Army. Customers have access to data depicting repair parts' consumption rates and demands and costs for specific end items/repair parts. This information can be tailored for an individual unit-assigned Department of Defense Activity Address Code (DODAAC).

4-56. The module provides historical retail demand data generated from requesting units throughout the Army. The database is the Army central repository for all individual requests of issue generated at the organizational level.

4-57. The field systems that feed LIDB are the technical, SARSS, Army Materiel Command Installation Supply System, and SAMS. Customers can query by end item code, DODAAC, NIIN, installation, geographic area, and Army command/division.

ITEM INFORMATION MODULE

4-58. The item information module is the official Army catalog of Army-managed and Army-used items. These data provide information about all classes of inventory items critical to requisitioning, maintenance, and disposal of aircraft repair parts and components.

Note. Information about an aircraft repair part or component interchangeability/substitutability can also be accessed from this module.

4-59. The line item number report, NIIN report, reference number report, and Army master data file (AMDF) report can be retrieved from the item information module. The AMDF reports include the item data, NIIN detail, interchangeability and substitutable data, component data, equivalent item data, order-of-use data, freight data, packaging data, medical user data, special Army data, and automatic return item list data.

SUPPORT ITEM REQUIREMENTS DATA

4-60. The support item requirements module provides data for parts used on end items, compares end-item part applications, and develops repair part requirements for support of end items in peacetime and contingency. Related program information on supply-related products and services follows. These products and services include repair parts to end item application, peculiar item and reverse support list allowance computation, and recommended ASL/PLL.

4-61. The support item requirements module offers "the spare/repair parts to end item application," in addition to some new capabilities in an online environment. Current data are provided because the LIDB is continuously updated as new information is received.

4-62. Another helpful feature for aviation maintainers conducting lateral and vertical searches of aircraft repair parts is a report that compares two end items and identifies parts peculiar to each and parts found on both. This information is useful for identifying common or individual repair part applications.

4-63. The module also allows the user to compare an end item to a list of end items (for example, the TOE). This comparison is known as a reverse support list allowance card. The user can also compare an end item to a list of end items and the ASL to identify candidates for deletion or stock-level reduction that result from the loss of a supported end item. This comparison is known as a tailored reverse support list allowance card. These reports can be printed or saved in word-processing, spreadsheet, or database formats for local use.

PIPELINE MODULE

4-64. The "pipeline" is the area within the LIDB where the user can find information regarding customer and requisition wait time, velocity management, and retrograde in-transit visibility (ITV). The pipeline is a centralized database providing visibility of supply and transportation actions for requisitions placed by aviation units that are unfillable by the supporting ASB SSA and, ultimately, passed to the wholesale system to be filled.

4-65. As materiel moves through the pipeline worldwide, automated supply and transportation systems feed the current status on the requested materiel's location to the pipeline. The pipeline provides a quick reference to requisition status, shipping information, and receipt of materiel requisitioned by the requesting unit.

4-66. A pipeline inquiry is available via WebLIDB and web logistics (WebLOG). It may also be accessed through other DLA web links. The pipeline serves as the Army's single database for supply and transportation actions according to military standard requisitioning and issue procedures, AR 725-50, and applicable DOD transportation regulations.

ELECTRONIC TECHNICAL MANUALS

4-67. LOGSA maintains the Army technical publications repository. Sustainment of the electronic technical manual (ETM) disks is cyclical, occurring either quarterly or semiannually as necessary. ETMs on disk are on the LOGSA webpage at https://liw.logsa.army.mil/index.cfm?fuseaction=home.main. Disks must be ordered like any other publication; as a result, the unit publication account should be updated to automatically receive the latest release. When ETMs are used with the ETM-interface software, ordering repair parts through technical and SAMS is a quicker and more accurate parts request.

SUPPLY-RELATED PRODUCTS AND SERVICES

FEDERAL LOGISTICS DATA

4-68. Federal logistics (FEDLOG) is an interactive product available on disk or the world-wide-web. It contains logistical information for the Army, Navy, Air Force, and Marines and the Federal Logistics Information System. FEDLOG is the primary source of AMDF information for Army customers worldwide.

Note. Refer to chapter 8 for additional information on FEDLOG.

ARMY PRE-POSITIONED STOCK

4-69. LOGSA provides visibility of war-reserve authorization and asset data via the Army pre-positioned stocks module in LIDB. This visibility includes the pre-positioned brigade sets, sustainment material, and operational project stocks across all five Army pre-positioned stockpiles to include CONUS, Europe, Southwest Asia, Korea, and afloat. LOGSA also maintains the Army war-reserve stockage list in this module.

ROUTING IDENTIFIER CODE

4-70. LOGSA is the single responsible organization within DA that assigns, changes, and issues routing identifier codes. The routing identifier code helps the Soldier get the requested item needed for his unit quickly and efficiently by routing the transaction to the corresponding SOS. The routing identifier code routes the request to all inter-service and intra-service agencies interested in the supply transaction on that item.

4-71. The routing identifier code contains the proper history of the requisition and can be accessed by all interested agencies. This code indicates a document's creator and recipient, whether it be a requisition follow-up or other transaction. Primarily, the routing identifier code tells units who will supply the equipment needed to execute their missions (for example, aircraft repair part requisition routing identifier code B17-AMCOM).

CONTINGENCY STOCKAGE CUSTOMER SUPPORT REQUIREMENTS LIST

4-72. LOGSA is the Army focal point for contingency stockage customer support requirement products to be used to support ASLs and PLLs. These are lists of combat repair parts for use at unit and DS levels.

4-73. The listings can be used as a planning tool to determine Class IX (air) requirements in a combat or contingency environment. The listing includes the recommended support item NSN, quantity, cost, weight, cube, and SOS. The support item requirements module, added to LOGSA LIDB, allows users to develop their own product in an online environment. If users do not have access to the LIDB, LOGSA will prepare the desired reports for them. The reports are the organizational PLL and DS ASL.

4-74. LOGSA is the source for recommended peacetime ASL/PLL/bench stock lists. It computes parts recommendations to support all equipment except Class VIII (medical) used in a peacetime (garrison) environment. The support item requirements module, added to LOGSA LIDB, allows the user to develop ASL/PLL/bench stock candidate lists in an online environment.

4-75. These reports assist field units with planning maintenance support and estimating ASL/PLL operating costs. To obtain a recommended ASL or PLL, use the LIDB support item requirements module or, if LIDB access is not available, contact LOGSA via email at amxsmlb@logsa.army.mil. Include the following information in the email:

- UIC.
- Level of maintenance performed (for example, unit, DS, or GS).
- Days of supply required in 15-day increments.
- End item NIINs and on-hand quantities.
- Unit POC.
- Telephone number, mailing address, and email address.

WEB LOGISTICS PARTS TRACKER

4-76. Parts tracker provides status of a requisition as it navigates the supply process. This status provides visibility of the requisition as it moves through the military or commercial transportation systems. The WebLOG parts tracker can be accessed at https://liw.logsa.army.mil/index.cfm?fuseaction=home.main. Access to radio frequency tag information pinpoints the location of parts traveling through the defense transportation system.

4-77. The parts tracker also provides exact location information from commercial shippers by entering a document number. The parts tracker module demonstrates how, by integrating with other modules of the LIDB, it provides the Army with a single tool that performs analysis across maintenance, readiness, and supply business processes.

4-78. The parts tracker relates readiness, maintenance, and supply issues to specific spare/repair parts and locates those parts within the Army or joint supply chain or in transit within the sustainment pipeline. The parts tracker will aid in successful Army transformation by serving as a single analysis tool for Soldiers and logisticians at the joint, strategic, national, or tactical levels.

4-79. The WebLOG parts tracker resides within the WebLOG materiel track module to track spare/repair parts and major end items in the Army supply and transportation pipeline. WebLOG parts tracker can assist aviation maintenance units by tracking unit-generated aircraft repair parts requisitions by—

- NIINs.
- DODAAC and NIINs (maximum of five NIINs).
- Radio frequency tags.
- Document numbers (maximum of five).
- Transportation control numbers.
- Commercial transportation carrier tracking numbers.

LOGISTICS-911

4-80. LOGSA logistics-911 (LOG911) can assist users with readiness, maintenance, SSA, transportation catalog, and logistic data. The goal of the LOG911 team is to resolve problems within 48 hours. LOG911 offers solutions to complex sustainment issues such as—

- Providing sustainment information, feedback, and assistance to garrison and deployed forces.
- Resolving deployment sustainment issues affecting equipment readiness.
- Expediting requisitions and tracking movement of items affecting equipment readiness.

- Passing requisitions from deployed units during contingences to wholesale supply agencies.
- Providing critical supply, maintenance, and transportation information.

4-81. For assistance with logistic issues affecting equipment readiness, contact the LOG911 team and access LOG911 information at https://weblog.logsa.army.mil/log911/index.cfm.

SECTION III – DEFENSE LOGISTICS AGENCY AUTOMATED SYSTEMS

ASSET VISIBILITY

4-82. Asset visibility (AV) replaced the DESX system. DESX provided an automated computer system for tracking DOD supply requisitions and inventory items, and for placing or modifying DOD requisitions.

4-83. AV provides the unit with end-to-end AV in the DOD logistics operational pipeline and accurate information on the location, movement, status, and identity of units, personnel, equipment, and supplies. AV provides the ability to act upon that information through access to integrated operational views of wholesale and retail stocks, requisitions, and transportation information to facilitate overall performance of DOD joint logistics practices in support of unit requirements.

Note. AV information is accessed at https://www.av.dla.mil/welcome/.

4-84. AV data comes from many source systems throughout the military. Most sources are updated on a daily basis using a 'behind-the-scenes' process called extract, translate, load (referred to as ETL for short). The assets tracked in AV are broken down into these functional areas:

- Bulk fuel: Information on the on-hand stock levels of the various types of bulk fuel (such as, jet fuel and diesel fuel) to include DLA/Defense Energy Support Center (wholesale) locations and service (retail) locations. This also includes bulk fuel onboard Army and Marine Corps prepositioned ships.
- Wholesale/retail inventory: Information on wholesale and retail assets. This functional area is associated with the asset category of in-storage and includes all classes of supply.
- Blood inventory: Information on blood and blood-related products in DOD medical facilities.
- Ammunition: Information on wholesale and retail inventory status levels for Army, Air Force, Navy, and Marine Corps ammunitions.
- Prepositioned stock/war reserves: Information on Navy and Marine Corps maritime prepositioned ships, Army prepositioned stocks, and Air Force war reserve material amassed in peacetime to sustain wartime operations.
- Reference data: Cross-referencing information to enable users to get more information on pre-defined query data for materiel and facilities.
- Requisition status–information on the status of requisitions.
- Transportation: Information on assets in-transit via land, sea, or air moving within the defense transportation system and tracked via the global transportation network through RFID tags.
- Unit equipment: Equipment accounted for and maintained by organizational units within the various military services, which is based upon an authorized allowance. This type of equipment consists of Class VII principal end items and Class II clothing and equipment.

4-85. AV provides views of assets based upon their status and physical location. These views are not mutually-exclusive, for example, an afloat prepositioned item may be considered in-storage and in-theater:

- In-storage: In-storage assets are those assets stored (on the shelf) at retail consumer sites, retail intermediate storage sites, disposal activities, or in wholesale inventories, to include ashore and afloat prepositioned assets. In-storage assets encompass all classes of supply.

- In-process: In-process assets are those assets on order from the SOS. These types of assets are at some stage of the procurement process; however, because of potential near-term delivery, they are of great interest to war planners and fighters.
- In-transit: In-transit focuses on the movement of assets (materiel and personnel) from origin to destination. DOD identifies the contents of a shipment and monitors movement throughout the asset pipeline. In addition, DOD can reconstitute and re-direct shipments. In-transit personnel queries provide visibility into the status and location of personnel traveling on military aircraft.
- In-theater: In-theater focuses upon those assets immediately associated with unit activities. These items may be in-process, in-storage, and/or in-transit and be within one or more theaters.

WEB VISUAL LOGISTICS INFORMATION PROCESSING SYSTEM

4-86. Web visual logistics information processing system is a web-based, access controlled query system usable from any internet-attached computer. It accesses the logistics on-line tracking system, a defense automatic addressing system center relational data base system, which portrays the life cycle of a sustainment (request for issue) action.

Note. To gain access to the defense automatic addressing system center automated logistics systems, aviation maintenance unit personnel must have a request log-on identification and password, which can be obtained at https://www.daas.dla.mil.

4-87. ASC/AST customers can use the web visual logistics information processing system to track requisitions for aircraft repair parts or components from their release into the DOD pipeline, until the materiel is posted to the accountable records at the ASB SSA. The web visual logistics information processing system also can track reports of excess and movement of those excesses to the destination sustainment facility or disposal.

4-88. The web visual logistics information processing system integrates information on SOS, DOD project code, transaction status code, unit of issue code, signal code, hold code, advice code, and condition code, among others, to assist the user in tracking a request for issue through its life cycle.

4-89. The web visual logistics information processing system—

- Allows the defense automatic addressing system center customer to track requisitions with a simple user interface.
- Provides a quick response time to subscriber inquiries.
- Processes inquiries by document number, unit activity, project code, transportation control number, or NSN.
- Allows the defense automatic addressing system center customer to process queries regarding life cycle of specific request-for-issue transactions.
- Receives information regarding materiel management actions such as requisitions, supply/shipment status, and customer confirmations.

SECTION IV – SINGLE STOCK FUND

4-90. Single stock fund extends down to the divisional and non-divisional ASL level. USAMC, as the national manager, capitalized stocks previously maintained in installation retail stock fund and operations and maintenance accounts. The main single stock fund (SSF) characteristics are a single point of sale, a single credit process, and a NM management process.

SINGLE POINT OF SALE

4-91. The single point of sale is the point at which a consumer-funded requisition is satisfied by a nationally-controlled Army working capital fund-supply maintenance Army account. The current retail stock fund and wholesale stock fund points of sale were merged to create a single point of sale. Aviation maintenance unit requisitions for aircraft repair parts and components are obligated upon submission to the Army working capital fund, SARSS-1. Billing occurs after an Army working capital fund-supply maintenance Army account issues the item.

4-92. The single point of sale may be in one of two places. If the item is stocked locally, the supporting Army working capital fund-supply maintenance Army SARSS-1 account fills the request and issues it to the aviation maintenance unit. If the item is not stocked locally, the request is passed to a higher SOS, and then the wholesale SOS fills the request and issues the item.

SINGLE CREDIT PROCESS

4-93. Credit from the Army working capital fund-supply maintenance Army to the consumer-funded activity is based on the Army credit policy. Serviceable and unserviceable credit values are computed and corresponding "credit value indicator codes" are assigned annually. Computation of serviceable and unserviceable credit values are performed with the annual price update. Credit is granted at the point of materiel turn-in (serviceable and unserviceable) from the consumer-funded activity to the supporting Army working capital fund-supply maintenance Army activity. These credit rates are stabilized, annualized in the year of execution, and predictable.

NATIONAL MAINTENANCE MANAGEMENT PROCESS

4-94. The NM management process is a strategy to move to a centrally coordinated and controlled repair-based sustainment system. Under SSF, repair is performed for return to stock rather than repair and return to the owning organization. Under the NMP, items repaired and returned to stock are repaired by an approved NM provider to a national standard.

4-95. USAMC participates with the tactical community in review/update of below sustainment-level requisitioning objectives and retention levels during ASL reviews. The tactical commander, based on local readiness and training considerations, identifies DS/RX items. DS/RX items are funded with operation and maintenance, Army dollars and will not be capitalized. Therefore, the national-level manager will not own, or have visibility, of these assets. Aircraft maintainers have transitioned to two categories of maintenance; national- and field-category. The overall objective of NM management is to increase fleet readiness at the weapon system level while reducing operation and sustainment costs by accomplishing repairs to a higher standard.

4-96. The national category consists of organic sustainment facilities, the industrial base, and qualified below-sustainment activities:
- The overall focus is sustainment readiness.
- Items repaired are returned to the supply system.
- The source of funding is Army working capital fund-supply maintenance.

4-97. The field category consists of organizational, DS, and GS maintenance units/activities:
- The overall focus is near-term readiness to maintain and generate combat power.
- Items are repaired and returned to the user.
- The source of funding is operation and maintenance, Army dollars.

SECTION V – COMMON LOGISTICS OPERATING ENVIRONMENT

COMMON LOGISTICS OPERATING ENVIRONMENT

4-98. The common logistics operating environment is a process to achieve a technology-enabled force equipped with self-diagnosing equipment platforms that interact with a network sustainment infrastructure supporting condition-based maintenance plus (CBM+). Common logistics operating environment provides real-time, integrated health management and platform/Soldier status data to optimize equipment readiness and improve battlefield distribution (https://lss.lta.army.mil/ako_pwd/ml/cloe/cloe.htm).

CONDITION-BASED MAINTENANCE PLUS

4-99. CBM+ is a set of maintenance processes and capabilities derived primarily from real-time assessment of weapon system condition through embedded diagnostics and prognostics that obtain data from embedded sensors, and external tests and measurements using portable equipment (AR 750-1). The goal of CBM+ is to perform maintenance only upon evidence of need. CBM+ capabilities include:

- Enhanced prognostic and diagnostic techniques.
- Failure trend analysis.
- Electronic portable or point-of-maintenance aids.
- Serial item management.
- Automatic identification technology.
- Data-driven interactive maintenance training.

EMBEDDED DIAGNOSTICS

4-100. Embedded diagnostics determines and reports the cause of a failure by detection of failure symptoms through the use of sensors, central processing unit, and a user interface integrated (or embedded) into the design of the system (AR 700-127) (see AR 750-43 for additional information).

Note. Diagnostics: after the failure.

EMBEDDED PROGNOSTICS

4-101. Embedded prognostics detects and reports component degradation prior to failure through the use of sensors, central processing unit, and a user interface integrated (or embedded) into the design of the system (AR 700-127) (see AR 750-43 for additional information).

Note. Prognostics: prior to failure.

DATA COLLECTION

4-102. To the Soldier, CBM+ converts aircraft condition data into proactive maintenance action. Scheduled inspections are supplemented or replaced based on analytical data defining the condition of the aircraft and its components.

4-103. At the tactical level, CBM+ provides tools, test equipment, embedded on-board, embedded diagnostics, and embedded prognostics for monitoring aircraft condition data (temperature, vibration, and cycle time) and environmental factors (desert, arctic, high humidity, and usage profiles). CBM+ also presents recommended proactive maintenance actions based on actual component wear. CBM+ embedded diagnostics and embedded prognostics present logisticians with an increased ability to predict equipment parts requirements, significantly decreasing the time a Soldier waits for a part.

4-104. At the strategic level, CBM+ data collected from embedded sensors, such as health and usage monitoring systems, translates into predictive trends and metrics that anticipate component failure based on the actual operating environment. This predictive approach allows for proactive acquisition and delivery of requisite spare parts to perform maintenance before imminent component failure and adjustment of scheduled maintenance tasks based on actual equipment condition.

4-105. At the national level, CBM+ is a data-centric, platform-operating environment within the SALE. Aviation maintainers from the flight line through the logisticians in AMCOM's Integrated Materiel

Management Center to the Corpus Christi Army Depot will have visibility of component failures and availability across the common logistics-operating environment and via the end-to-end logistics data warehouse. Using algorithms jointly developed by the Aviation Engineering Directorate, industry leaders, academia, and the OEMs, CBM+ information systems will monitor critical maintenance data elements and determine component and system health. The result will be better data elements that help Army aviation evaluate the way it designs, builds, and supports future systems with new and dynamic maintenance programs.

4-106.   CBM+ enabling technologies include but are not limited to—

- Real-time data migration within the common logistics-operating environment.
- Closed-loop information systems that receive and transmit maintenance actions/instructions from the data warehouse down to the platform level and incorporate all automated systems.
- A common tactical STAMIS, such as the ULLS-A (E) and GCSS-A, that gather and integrate information obtained from the platform maintenance environment.
- Enterprise data warehouse, capable of recording condition, usage, maintenance, parts tracking, environmental conditions, and intelligent prognostics; this data warehouse must provide detailed data to Aviation Engineering Directorate and OEM engineers while also providing summary programmatic information to program and materiel managers.
- Portable maintenance aids such as automated historical records, cockpit voice recorders, and flight data recorders.
- Health and usage monitoring systems that monitor, transmit, and record operating parameters.
- In-line oil sensor technology and reporting.
- Components with integrated smart, self-diagnosing, repair technologies.
- Lightweight multipurpose modular test kits and built-in automatic test equipment.
- Survivability enhancements (active and passive systems) and redundant systems.
- Embedded command, control, and communications for transmitting/data bursting embedded diagnostics and embedded prognostics data from the platform through the common logistics operating environment infrastructure to maintainers, decision-makers, and logisticians.
- Total AV of the sustainment pipeline.

Chapter 5

Brigade/Squadron Aviation Materiel Officer and Support Operations

The combination of the BAMO/SAMO and support operations efforts in support of the CAB or ACS mission ensures synchronized mission goals and reduced duplicity of resource commitments. By applying the advice of the brigade/squadron's most senior maintenance warrant officer to the support operations focus on supporting subordinate units, every aviation maintenance and sustainment challenge receives the most skilled level of attention. These experts work to improve resource allocation within the CAB and ACS.

SECTION I – BRIGADE/SQUADRON AVIATION MATERIEL OFFICER

DUTIES AND RESPONSIBILITIES

5-1. The BAMO/SAMO fills positions assigned by MTOE/TDA. Refer to DA PAM 611-21 to determine who is authorized to fill BAMO/SAMO positions. The BAMO assigned to the CAB and the SAMO in the ACS should work hand-in-hand with AMC/AMT/ASC/AST PC and support operations personnel (if applicable) as a key supporting member of the maintenance team.

5-2. The BAMO/SAMO advises the brigade/squadron commander on maintenance personnel management, supply, equipment, and facility assets to maintain and repair Army rotary, fixed-wing, and unmanned aircraft. He may help organize maintenance elements in support of CAB/ACS operations. He provides expertise in preparing, implementing, and maintaining SOPs for management of maintenance activities. Additionally, the BAMO/SAMO participates in internal maintenance evaluations organized by the support operations section and conducted by subordinate commands.

5-3. The BAMO/SAMO interprets regulations, TMs, and orders pertaining to maintenance and sustainment actions of Army aircraft for commanders and subordinates. The BAMO/SAMO normally works alone; however, depending on the unit and the MTOE structure, additional personnel may be assigned to the section to assist. The BAMO/SAMO office provides continuous maintenance and logistical information to the brigade commander and staff on aviation and aviation-related systems matters. The BAMO/SAMO keeps the command informed of current and future capabilities based on the current maintenance posture. He or she also assists maintenance companies and troops in planning maintenance actions based on operational necessities. The BAMO/SAMO consolidates the MOE reports as necessary to ensure maintenance situational awareness to the brigade commander and staff.

5-4. In coordination with the entire aviation maintenance leadership team, the duties and responsibilities of the BAMO/SAMO include the following:

- Provides aircraft maintenance and related activity reporting.
- Collects, combines, and presents MOE reports to the commander and maintains an MOE archive.
- Coordinates and submits a monthly aircraft readiness report.

- Informs the commander of the unit maintenance posture and current capabilities.
- Responds to all levels of staff concerns regarding aviation maintenance (P4T3) and execution of the maintenance plan.
- Coordinates recurring aviation maintenance resource management meetings at the brigade level.
- Serves as principal staff advisor to develop and maintain aircraft maintenance and logistics deployment plans.
- Assists in determining composition of the deployment or redeployment team.
- Assists in determining resources required to execute the deployment and redeployment.
- Monitors the deployment execution and provides procedural guidance when necessary.
- Monitors and advises commanders at all levels on—
  - AMC/AMT operations (TM 1-1500-328-23 and this manual).
  - ASC/AST operations.
  - Sustainment maintenance and combat retrograde MWOs.
  - Nonstandard equipment applications; for example, airworthiness release (AWR), interim statement of airworthiness qualification (ISAQ), or LOA.
  - Organizing for BDAR and DART missions (FM 3-04.513).
  - TMDE compliance (AR 750-43).
  - AOAP compliance (AR 750-1).
- Facilitates effective scheduled maintenance forecasting and planning with all units for brigade assets in support of mission requirements, the flying-hour program, and the MOE bank time goals.
- Tracks, advises, and reports on performance goals in Classes III, III (packaged), V, and IX (air).
- Assists in SOP development.
- Supports maintenance policy development and adherence, including the following actions:
  - Monitors aviation life support equipment (ALSE) (TC 1-508) resource issues.
  - Organizes routine aviation maintenance readiness councils, conferences, or meetings.
  - Monitors maintainer utilization and effectiveness.
  - Monitors automation execution and information technology discipline.
  - Ensures adherence to applicable references, publications, and maintenance information messages (MIMs).
- Serves as an evaluator during internal maintenance unit ARMS inspections.
- Reviews, assesses, and assists submission of brigade/squadron aviation maintenance excellence awards at least semi-annually.
- When required, coordinates with the unit commanders and maintenance leaders to meet P4T3 needs for each airframe.
- Assists units in coordinating maintenance procedures for nonstandard repair applications between LARs, OEM, and the applicable project management office. BAMO/SAMO may discuss issues with contracting officials on aviation contract performance affecting brigade/battalion assets.
- If appointed as COR or ACOR, he or she—
  - Participates in Army command contractor staffing missions.
  - Helps project contractor staffing levels to meet additional maintenance requirements.
- Monitors brigade aviation resource management, to include:
  - Flying-hour program execution and effect on the allocated Class IX (air) budget.
  - Contracting resources.

- GSE maintenance.
- ALSE resources.
- Nonstandard equipment acquisition and sustainment funding.
- BAMO/SAMO equipment purchase and sustainment.

GOVERNMENT FLIGHT REPRESENTATIVE

5-5. The BAMO/SAMO is trained to become the government flight representative, project officer/COR, or the ACOR. If not retained by the ASB or other command, these duties may become the responsibility of the BAMO/SAMO when the aircraft, equipment, or property is maintained by contractors, to include MTF of aircraft.

5-6. Performance of these duties is essential when the primary providers of the contract are not collocated with the unit receiving maintenance support. The performance of these duties can take place in garrison or while aviation units are deployed from home station.

5-7. In addition, life support and system support for these contractors will typically fall to the government flight representative, COR, or ACOR assigned to a CAB or ACS. The BAMO/SAMO performing any of these roles remains responsible for managing those related contractors and providing for their overall welfare.

Note. Refer to FM 3-100.21 for further guidance on assigned contractors tasked with providing aviation maintenance and logistics support.

COORDINATING ACTIONS

AVIATION READINESS REPORTING CAPABILITIES

5-8. The BAMO/SAMO is required by AR 700-138 to forward a roll-up report to LOGSA. The following steps are necessary:
- Generation of the daily readiness report.
- Automated roll up of the reporting unit at the brigade/battalion maintenance office to the division.
- Automated transmission of reports from the BAMO/SAMO to the division or higher HQ.
- Generation of the monthly readiness report.
- Automated transmission, via knowledge asset management network, to the Utility/Cargo/Attack Helicopters Project Office, Redstone Arsenal, Alabama.

MANAGING AIRCRAFT AND WEAPONS SYSTEMS

5-9. When aircraft are identified for aircraft or weapons systems modifications, improvements, or upgrades, the BAMO/SAMO has unique responsibilities. The BAMO will outline the brigade responsibilities and manage all coordination efforts to ensure smooth maintenance and logistics support between unit personnel and personnel responsible for aircraft or weapons system modifications, improvements, and upgrades. These responsibilities include—
- Scheduling new equipment training for maintainers and operators when required.
- Assisting commanders in determining how equipment and weapons system improvements are going to affect the unit assigned mission.
- Assisting units with coordinating and arranging a systematic flow of aircraft into maintenance for scheduled modifications, upgrades, and improvements.
- Tracking all completed aircraft and weapons system improvements.

- Ensuring availability of up-to-date technical information to maintain improved and upgraded systems.
- In concert with support operations, ensuring all required parts for systems upgrades are on-hand before maintenance actions begin.
- Monitoring that brigade/battalion personnel follow policies and procedures to ensure pertinent forms and records are updated to reflect the addition of new items and deletion of replaced items.
- Facilitating the completion of multiple MWOs on the same piece of equipment at the same time.

COORDINATING AUTOMATED ACTIONS

5-10. The BAMO/SAMO retrieves reports from the ULLS-A (E) box. These reports provide the BAMO/SAMO with the flexibility to go into the automated system and retrieve any reports needed to support the brigade mission. He or she will coordinate with the Combat Service Support Automation Management Office for evaluation and maintenance support of the BAMO/SAMO.

5-11. With ULLS-A (E), the BAMO/SAMO monitors maintenance manhours, aircraft repair parts and components, maintenance work orders, and aircraft historical data. Chapter 4 addresses specific functions and reports of the ULLS-A (E).

Note. LIDB stores national and tactical historical information and provides real-time status of Army readiness, requisition, supply, maintenance, and asset information to customers worldwide. The information needed to man, arm, fix, fuel, move, and sustain Soldiers and their systems can be accessed from one central source, using one log-on identification and password. To gain access to LIDB support functions, the user needs to complete the LOGSA SAR form and request access to LIDB. The SAR can be completed online at the LOGSA website (www.logsa.redstone.army.mil).

SECTION II – SUPPORT OPERATIONS

DUTIES AND RESPONSIBILITIES

5-12. The support operations section coordinates with the brigade and battalion S-4 and the BAMO to establish maintenance priorities and resolve maintenance and logistics support issues. The support operations section is organized to coordinate logistics support and provide distribution management to the CAB. It is also staffed to accomplish contracting, petroleum, ammunition, movement control, and transportation and to assist in tracking and expediting release of supplies (repair parts).

Note. In the ACS, there is no support operations section; therefore, the SAMO may use this manual as a menu to integrate support operations. With fewer aircraft than the CABs, the support operations requirements for aviation maintenance are reduced in the ACS. This does not mean the SAMO will not require augmentation to perform both SAMO and support operations functions together but frames the quantity of support operations in relationship to the size of the organization. The squadron S-4 and supply platoon in the AST may provide unique logistical assistance to the SAMO as he or she simultaneously performs both roles.

5-13. Under the direction of the support operations officer, this section provides centralized, integrated, and automated C2 and planning for distribution management operations within the battalion. It coordinates with logistics operators in the fields of supply, maintenance, and movement management for the support of units assigned or attached in the brigade area. The primary concern of the support operations section is customer support and increasing the responsiveness of support provided by subordinate units. This section continually monitors the support and advises the battalion commander on the ability to support future tactical operations.

5-14. The support operations section coordinates required annual internal ARMS inspections for aviation support and maintenance companies and troops. It also collects, consolidates, and archives tri-annual maintenance unit ARMS progress reports for command review. Along with this function, the support operations section will conduct a semi-annual logistics award recommendation council for logistics unit commanders and representatives to advise in logistics award preparation and submission processing.

5-15. With ITV/total AV, BCS3, FBCB2, and the maneuver control system, the support operations section has access to significant, useful information and receives such information in near-real time. This access allows support operations personnel to identify problems quickly and allocate resources efficiently. BCS3 provides support operations with the visibility of the logistics status from the ASB back to theater level. This staff section serves as the POC for supported units. It directs problems to appropriate technical experts within subordinate branches. The support operations section—

- Conducts continuous logistics support analysis.
- Plans and coordinates aerial resupply and plans for landing zones in the vicinity of the BSA.
- Develops the sustainment synchronization matrix.
- Submits sustainment forecasts to the sustainment brigade support operations/distribution management center (DMC).
- Manages all flat-racks throughput to and retrograding from the BSA.
- Coordinates and provides technical supervision for the ASB sustainment mission, which includes supply activities, maintenance support, and coordination of transportation assets.
- Identifies tentative force structure and size to be supported.
- Coordinates the preparation of the support operations estimate on external support.
- Provides support posture and planning recommendations to the ASB commander.
- Sets up and supervises the logistics operations center.
- Provides centralized coordination for units providing external support to the brigade.
- Coordinates with the CAB S-3 for air routes for supply and medical support.
- Analyzes the effect of BCS3 reports.
- Advises the battalion commander on the status of logistics support.
- Coordinates logistics support for units passing through the brigade area.
- Analyzes contingency mission support requirements.
- Revises customer lists (as required by changing requirements, workloads, and priorities) for support of tactical operations.
- Coordinates external logistics support provided by subordinate units.
- Advises the battalion commander on the supportability of ASB missions and of shortfalls that may affect mission accomplishment.
- Serves as the single point of coordination for supported units to resolve logistics support problems.
- Plans and coordinates contingency support.
- Develops supply, service, ground maintenance, and transportation policies.

5-16. The support operations officer will perform functions as the BCS3 manager. The support operations officer must work with the S-2, S-3, S-4, and signal staff officer (S-6) to establish and manage the BCS3 network and database. The support operations officer must maintain DS supply point and maintenance data entered into the system. Specific tasks for the support operations officer are the following:

- Gathers, inputs, and maintains supply point sustainment data in the system; he or she must also conduct the - and SARSS download to BCS3 to capture support maintenance data.
- Develops the commander's tracked item list to track supply point items of interest.
- Sets message handling tables to correctly route supply logistics messages.

- Sets status thresholds for supply point items.
- Establishes reporting times for subordinate DS units.
- Sets support to supported relationships to reflect which supply points support which units.
- Establishes and sets continuity operations pairing according to guidance from the CAB S-4.
- Support operations assist supported units in locating needed parts.

5-17. If an aircraft is NMCS for a minimum number of aircraft repair parts, a requisition PD of AOG may be used. AOG parts requests are typically approved by the owning company commander or battalion commander. Once an AOG parts request is approved, the technical supply section processes the request through the SSA. AOG requests are processed directly to an SSA. The requesting unit will then immediately notify the support operations section and BAMO. AOG requests are transmitted by the most expeditious means.

5-18. The support operations section will conduct sustainment horizontal and vertical searches for critical serviceable parts in support of the unit maintenance mission. Once a part is located, steps and actions covering procurement of aircraft repair parts and/or the requisition process must be followed as outlined in the unit maintenance SOP. If a SSA is not collocated with the supported unit, request information must be transmitted to the SSA. The BAMO will monitor AOG requisitions until the unit receives the AOG components.

5-19. The DESX is another avenue that can track parts and requisitions. DESX is an automated computer system for tracking DOD supply requisitions and inventory items and for placing or modifying DOD requisitions. DESX allows queries by telephone or email messages or from World Wide Web forms. DESX systems are located at all 19 DOD inventory control points, and are available for aviation maintenance customers 24 hours a day, seven days a week.

5-20. Five basic supply support options are available through DESX:
- Status checks.
- Stock availability checks.
- Ability to submit new requisitions.
- Ability to modify existing requisitions.
- Ability to talk with a customer service representative at certain sites.

Note. The DESX Web option can be reached at https://www.dlis.dla mil/desx. To gain access to this site, the user must register and receive a log-in identification and password. Questions regarding registration forms for log in identification and passwords can be sent to desx@dlis.dla.mil. To use this option, the user must have a mil or .gov domain address.

INTEGRATED LOGISTICS ANALYSIS PROGRAM

5-21. The support operations section leverages ILAP to effect rapid acquisition of assets and provide positive tracking. ILAP is available to brigade logisticians and leaders to retrieve logistics and financial data while tracking Class IX (air) budget matters. ILAP operates at all echelons of the Army to provide management capability to unit, corps, installations, component, and theater levels.

5-22. Financial data is pulled from defense finance and accounting service data sites. Logistics data is obtained from appropriate supply and maintenance sites. These cross-functional data are integrated and aggregated to upper echelons to provide summary decision support views and detailed information drill-down capabilities to the document detail level. This process of assembly and aggregation affords Army departmental users the opportunity to do Army-level analysis and data query.

5-23. The traditional tools imbedded in the current STAMIS (SAMS and SARSS) and financial systems do not provide managers the detailed report needed in today's fluid environment. Thus, managers must gather data from various sources to perform their jobs. The process of gathering data consumes a great deal of time and makes it difficult for managers to share information, which generally leads to incomplete and untimely answers. ILAP provides a computer-based tool that integrates the data. To learn how to access ILAP go to https://liw.logsa.army.mil/help/general/mergedProjects/ILAP/whnjs.htm.

SUPPLY SUPPORT ACTIVITY INTERACTION

5-24. The relationship of the support operations officer, the SSA accountable officer, and the BAMO is crucial to the sustainment of serviceable aircraft systems and subsystems, as well as GSE. To foster a professional relationship, the support operations officer and BAMO should—

- Conduct a face-to-face meeting with the AO to ensure aviation needs, including shortages of critical aircraft repair parts, receive documentation, and discuss resolution planning.
- Ensure the responsible AO is aware of ever-changing aircraft repair parts requirements and priorities.
- Request the AO provide timely information of logistical issues to include STAMIS shortcomings.
- Allow the AO to serve as a POC for tracking aircraft repair parts/components off the installation.
- Allow the AO to provide guidance on turn-ins, credits, excesses, forms and records, and reports.
- Obtain assistance from the AO on all sustainment issues (such as ASL, bench stock, and shop stock).
- Obtain tracking numbers for brigade/battalion/unit-generated document numbers on and off the installation.

This page intentionally left blank.

Chapter 6

Production Control

This chapter provides PC personnel with a "how-to" guide for effectively managing maintenance operations. This chapter also provides aviation maintenance management principles required to maintain, repair, overhaul, and apply modification work orders, safety-of-flight messages, and other mandated maintenance functions. Judiciously applying these principles will ensure the airworthiness of all assigned/attached aircraft.

SECTION I – DUTIES AND RESPONSIBILITIES

PRODUCTION CONTROL OFFICER-IN-CHARGE

6-1. The aviation maintenance unit commander selects the PC OIC based on skills, qualifications, experience, and leadership abilities. In the AMC/AMT, the PC officer is a warrant officer graduate of the aviation maintenance officer course and a qualified MP. In the ASC/AST, the PC OIC is a captain and should be a graduate of the aviation maintenance officer or MP course.

Contents

6-2. The PC OIC is the principal maintenance manager-coordinator in the AMC/AMT or ASC/AST and coordinates maintenance and sustainment actions at the company/troop and battalion/squadron level. The PC OIC is the AMC/AMT or ASC/AST commander's primary maintenance advisor for all internal production and maintenance activities.

6-3. In the absence of the maintenance commander, the PC OIC can act as the battalion/squadron primary maintenance advisor at battalion/squadron level. The PC OIC controls daily maintenance operations and workflow within the maintenance or support company/troop. The PC OIC must assist the commander in balancing unit maintenance priorities with unit mission requirements. The PC OIC orchestrates maintenance efforts and priorities by coordinating with commanders, BAMO/SAMO, and the support operations officer on maintenance issues requiring command-level attention.

COMMAND RELATIONSHIPS

6-4. The AMC/AMT or ASC/AST commander has overall responsibility for aviation maintenance activities. The PC OIC is responsible for controlling aviation maintenance production matters according to command guidance and acts as the direct link between the unit commanders and the maintenance or support company/troop platoons, and sections for internal and external production issues.

6-5. The AMC/AMT PC OIC is the main POC between AMC/AMT, aviation operational companies and troops, and the ASC/AST. The ASC/AST PC OIC is the primary POC to the supported units. The commander and staff must be kept informed of critical maintenance issues and the operational status of battalion/squadron equipment.

6-6. The PC OIC establishes, coordinates, and directs priorities of work with the maintenance leadership, to include QC, ARP, CRP, ASES, technical supply section, and maneuver companies/troops. Responsibilities include but are not limited to—

- Analyzing, planning, and coordinating required support for all maintenance activities.
- Supervising preparation of reports and records.
- Coordinating with the AMC/AMT and/or ASC/AST as required.
- Establishing maintenance priorities based on command guidance.
- Facilitating appropriate DART capability and responsiveness IAW FM 3-04.513.

PRODUCTION CONTROL OFFICER RELATIONSHIPS

6-7. The PC OICs and the BAMO/SAMO must interact and closely coordinate all sustainment activities, which aides in mutually achieving high rates on the maintenance MOE. The support operations officer is responsible for sustainment support management. The support operations officer, with the BAMO, facilitates sustainment support to all AMC/AMT and ASC PC officers. In the case of the ACS, the SAMO performs this function for the AST and AMT PC officers.

6-8. When airframes are experiencing longer-than-normal NMCS times, the PC OIC will coordinate logistic actions with the support operations officer or SAMO to expedite release of high-priority repair parts. To further assist the PC OIC, the support operations officer or SAMO will coordinate with logistics support representatives in the fields of supply, maintenance, and movement management to track or expedite release of high-priority repair parts.

OFFICE ADMINISTRATION

6-9. The PC OIC is responsible for the internal management and administration of the PC section. The PC OIC provides oversight and supervision to ensure all administrative duties are performed on a timely basis and all reports/processes are executed and delivered on or before the required suspense.

ASSISTANT PRODUCTION CONTROL OFFICER

6-10. In the ASC/AST, the PC office consists of an assistant PC officer and a 151A aviation maintenance officer/technician. The assistant PC officer provides depth to the ASC/AST by managing the larger quantities of work orders. Additionally, the assistant PC officer enables 24-hour PC operations when required. The assistant PC officer reinforces the PC officer in the execution of his duties and serves as the PC officer in his absence.

PRODUCTION CONTROL NONCOMMISSIONED OFFICER-IN-CHARGE

6-11. The commander and PC OIC select the PC NCOIC based on skills, qualifications, experience, and leadership abilities. The PC NCOIC is usually one of the most senior and experienced maintenance NCOs assigned to the unit. The PC NCOIC should be an advanced noncommissioned officer course graduate.

6-12. The PC NCOIC will coordinate all maintenance actions in the absence of the PC OIC and assistant PC OIC, and will act on his or her behalf when required. The PC OIC, assistant PC OIC, and PC NCOIC must function as a team. When one acts, the other must be aware of all decisions and priorities. The PC NCOIC will assist the PC OIC and assistant PC OIC, and, in their absence, coordinate and establish priorities of work.

PRODUCTION CONTROL CLERK

6-13. In AMC/AMTs, the commander, PC OIC, and first sergeant will select the PC clerk based on skills, qualifications, and experience. The PC clerk should be a senior-grade specialist with knowledge of supported aircraft systems and subsystems. He requires a working knowledge of automated systems

(ULLS-A [E]) and related software. The PC clerk should demonstrate sufficient knowledge to assist the PC NCOIC in managing the battalion/squadron ULLS-A (E) server. In ASC/ASTs, the flight operations specialist in the PC section also serves as the PC clerk. The PC OIC, assistant OIC, and NCOIC will train this Soldier to support their mission and the MOE.

6-14. The PC clerk is responsible to the PC OIC, assistant PC OIC, PC NCOIC, and ultimately, the commander for—

- Execution of administrative PC functions, processing, and updating of ULLS-A (E) information.
- Updating and processing forms, records, and work orders pertaining to aircraft systems and subsystems according to appropriate regulatory guidance, manuals, and the ULLS-A (E) end-users guide.
- Distribution and evacuation of work-ordered unserviceable aircraft repair parts and components to the ASC/AST or sustainment-level support agencies.
- Generation of internal work orders for maintenance support from assigned shops and maintenance sections.
- Reconciliation of work orders with the supporting and supported units according to the SOP.
- Reconciliation of work orders within the maintenance unit.
- Reconciliation of evacuation work-order from external maintenance activities and agencies as required.
- Distribution of forms and records to QC and flight operations for inspection IAW AR 25-400-2 and DA PAM 738-751.

SECTION II – OPERATIONS

MEETINGS

6-15. The PC meeting allows for consolidation, coordination, and synchronization of internal and external maintenance and sustainment actions. Unscheduled maintenance from previous day/night operations may be discussed to prioritize or shift workflow from the previous plan. This meeting ensures all leaders and maintenance managers have a clear picture of current and projected aircraft availability and work order and scheduled maintenance status. A formal PC meeting is not always necessary. For example, a detachment may be small enough that the PC OIC is able to monitor and coordinate all maintenance activities without a meeting.

AGENDA

6-16. The agenda of each PC meeting should follow a specific and well-defined format. The PC meeting agenda should facilitate the organization of workflow, priorities, and coordination among sections, platoons, and companies. The agenda can be built as the duty day progresses so information is not forgotten at the following PC meeting.

6-17. The PC meeting is a team-building event that should not exceed one hour. The PC meeting provides essential personnel/leaders with situational awareness, not only in and around their areas of responsibility but of the overall maintenance posture.

6-18. PC personnel in the meeting must be immediately notified of any maintenance support performed in their absence. When these maintenance actions take place, they are the exception rather than the rule. Periodic follow-ups and updates throughout the day to PC are made to ensure an accurate and current picture of aircraft readiness. Table 6-1 (page 6-4) and table 6-2 (page 6-5) are examples of an agenda shell and may be tailored as required.

Table 6-1. Typical AMC/AMT PC meeting agenda

Roll call		
	PC OIC	
	PC NCOIC	
	PC clerk/PC ULLS-A (E) administrative	
	QC	
	Technical Supply	
	ARP	
	CRP	
	ASES	
	Maneuver Units	
Administrative data/notes		
	PC OIC/NCOIC	
	PC/ULLS-A (E) clerk	
		ULSS-A (E) send/receive update and production index
		Forms/records
	QC–trends, policy changes, and/or issues	
	Technical supply NMCS report brief/zero lines PLL/recoverable items report status	
	ARP	
	CRP	
	ASES	
Maneuver company/troop (each company/troop briefs major changes and support requirements)		
	Maneuver company/troop status brief (changes)	
	Flight schedule	
	Scheduled maintenance	
	Unscheduled maintenance	
CFSRs		
	Aircraft manufacture representative	
	Specific aircraft component representative	
	Support contract team leader	
	AMCOM LAR	
PC resource prioritization plan		
Section confirmation briefs		
PC outsourcing requirements brief		
Alibis		
PC back brief		
Commanders closing comments		

Table 6-2. Typical ASC/AST PC meeting agenda

Roll call	
	PC OIC and assistant PC OIC
	PC NCOIC
	PC clerk/PC ULLS-A (E) admin
	QC
	Technical supply
	ARP
	CRP
	ASES
	MTF Section
Administrative data/notes	
	PC OIC, assistant PC OIC, and NCOIC
	PC/ULLS-A (E) clerk
	ULSS-A (E) update and production index
	Forms/records
	QC–trends, policy changes, and/or issues
	Technical supply NMCS report brief and zero balance PLL/recoverable items report status
	ARP
	CRP
	ASES
	MTF Section
CFSRs	
	Aircraft manufacture representative
	Subcomponent representative
	Support contract team leader
	AMCOM LAR
Scheduled maintenance status	
Evacuated work order status	
PC resource prioritization plan	
Section confirmation briefs	
Alibis	
PC back brief	
Commanders closing comments	

ATTENDEES

6-19. Commanders will ensure junior leaders attend the PC meeting as an opportunity to observe and develop an understanding of maintenance operations and management, which is an essential building block of leader development. The following personnel should frequently attend PC meetings:

- AMC/AMT or ASC/AST commanders/first sergeants.
- Flight company/troop commanders/first sergeants (aviation operational units only).
- Platoon leaders/sergeants (maneuver platoon, ARP, and CRP).
- Support operations officer and NCOIC.

- PC OIC/assistant PC OIC/NCOIC (meeting facilitator).
- ASO or unit safety manager.
- PC clerk.
- ULLS-A (E) administrator/clerk.
- Technical supply officer/NCOIC.
- QC OIC/NCOIC.
- Shops officer/NCOIC.
- Maintenance officers/NCOIC.
- MPs.
- Armament officer/NCOIC.
- Contract support maintenance team lead.
- CFSR.
- LAR.

6-20. Senior leadership is critical to the success of any maintenance program; therefore, weekly attendance is highly encouraged by the following individuals:
- Battalion/squadron commander.
- Battalion/squadron executive officer.
- Battalion/squadron assistant S-3.
- Support operations officer.
- BAMO/SAMO.
- Battalion/squadron command sergeant major.

EVALUATING AND ESTABLISHING PRIORITIES OF WORK

6-21. The PC OIC is responsible for evaluating and establishing work priorities. The company/troop commander sets the goals for the MOE, but the ultimate work prioritization responsibility to achieve these MOE falls on the PC OIC. When conflicts arise between supported units and the PC OIC, the PC OIC should establish work priorities in the best interest of the overall battalion/squadron maintenance program with the support of the maintenance leadership team.

6-22. This continuous evaluation of work priorities requires close supervision and follow-up at all levels. Effective communication skills are required to best determine and relay the priorities of the day or week. The establishment of work priorities by the PC OIC results in a balance of workload.

APPLICATION

6-23. Using P4T3 will result in a smoother, more predictable environment for the supported and supporting elements in the performance of inspections or services. Outlined below is an example of the P4T3 process that can be used in the PC meeting to increase communications and establish professional working conditions between the supported and supporting team elements:
- Maintenance leader: Identifies service (problem).
- Maintenance leader: Briefs PC of the intended day to perform the service (plan).
- PC OIC and assistant OIC: Inquires if required parts to perform the service are available (parts).
- PC OIC/assistant OIC: Coordinates with the supporting element (internal or external) (people).
- Maintenance leader: Updates the PC OIC/assistant OIC/NCOIC concerning the progress of the aircraft nearing the service window, time line, and expected service date (people).
- PC OIC/assistant OIC/NCOIC: Coordinates with appropriate shop/platoon supervisor (people).
- Shop supervisor: Validates necessary tools and parts are on-hand (tools/parts).
- Shop supervisor: Validates training of individual assigned to perform service (training).
- Maintenance leader: Once the aircraft has entered the service window, notifies PC (plan).

- Maintenance leader: Allocates time to perform the service; back briefs command and PC of the estimated time of completion (time).
- ULLS-A (E) is used to track all maintenance and sustainment actions (technology).
- PC OIC/assistant PC OIC: Orders execution of the service to shop supervisor (plan).

Note. The service may have to be rescheduled if unscheduled maintenance interrupts the aircraft scheduling and the required number of hours cannot be flown into the service window.

Aircraft Maintenance Status Processing

6-24. The aircraft daily status report is based on data migration via the send disks, local area network, or wireless from the maneuver companies. PC will continually update the aircraft status. The ULLS-A (E) server is automatically updated once data migration is complete. The PC clerk is responsible for informing the PC OIC, assistant PC OIC, and NCOIC of any changes.

Production Control Status Board

6-25. The PC board (table 6-3) is a depiction of displayed data on aircraft status, shop operations, or unique issues. Accurate and prompt information recorded on the board is used to control current operations, plan anticipated work, and measure work performed. Although maintenance managers have quick access to information through ULLS-A (E), a well-planned and informative PC board (equipment status board) can serve as a handy, quick-look source of information for the commander and other personnel (such as platoon leaders and section chiefs). The status board serves as a good source of information on the progress of non-standard goals or missions associated with the MOE.

Table 6-3. Example PC board layout

(Unit) PC Status Board			
Aircraft/System	**Status**	**Fault/Issue**	**Remarks**
037	/		
954	X	Hard landing	Awaiting tool - Bell (ASC/AST)
Special tool fabrication	In progress	Spanner wrench out of round	TASMG accepted fabrication work order on 10 Feb 09

6-26. The design of the PC board should be simple and easy. The organization of the board is left to the individual. Some suggested entries are:

- Current aircraft/system status (updated throughout the day as the status changes).
- Priority of work.
- Status of special tools and equipment (such as hoists, tugs, AGPUs, and test sets).
- Reasons for stopped work.
- Work awaiting receipt of parts (can be used to track status of parts for NMCS aircraft).
- Document number and status.
- Significant evacuation work order tracking.
- Phase status (for example, "75 percent" [estimated percentage complete]).

Maintenance Man-Hour Estimates

6-27. MACs provide a baseline estimate of manhours required to accomplish a given repair or task. Maintenance managers start with the MAC baseline and apply unit specific variables to arrive at a reasonably accurate estimate of the time necessary to accomplish a repair or task. Variables include but are not limited to number of personnel, individual Soldier experience and time in service/MOS, availability and condition of tools and equipment, and work environment (such as arctic, desert, in a hanger, outside, day, or night). Some variables are easier to assess than others; however, as the maintenance manager gains experience, his estimates will become more refined and accurate. The goal is accurate and timely reporting of manhour estimates to the commander to assist in managing the unit and meeting operational requirements.

WORK ORDER TRACKING AND FILING SYSTEM

6-28. ULLS-A (E) provides an efficient tracking mechanism for maintenance and supply actions. This automated system provides maintenance section and shop personnel with a snapshot in time of maintenance actions taking place within their areas of responsibility.

6-29. Tracking work order status within ULLS-A (E) is the preferred method. There are methods for tracking the status of work orders outside of ULLS-A (E) in the event ULLS-A (E) is not working or available. PC personnel can track assigned work orders through files created under the "My Documents" folder or within an Excel spreadsheet. PC shops will track work orders using the following categories:

- Inspection.
- Parts required.
- Waiting parts.
- Shop.
- Maintenance in progress.
- Inspection.
- Test flight.
- Delivery/pick-up.

COMPONENT EXCHANGE

REPARABLE EXCHANGE

6-30. RX stock is maintained at the ASB distribution company or support troop SSA. The SSA provides on-hand recoverable repair items for issue on a one-for-one basis. IAW DA PAM 710-2-1, DA Form 2765-1 (Request for Issue or Turn-in) is prepared and hand-carried with the unserviceable item to the ASB/AST SSA RX section to exchange for a serviceable item.

6-31. RX items are normally repaired by the ASC/AST component repair section and then placed back into stockage at the SSA. If the component or LRU cannot be repaired, it is retrograded through supply channels.

6-32. An RX listing (containing the NSN, item description, end-item application, and authorization) is distributed to all units supported by the ASB/AST. RX items are not normally authorized on the unit PLL.

CONTROLLED EXCHANGE

6-33. Controlled exchange is the removal of serviceable components from unserviceable, economically reparable end items for immediate reuse in restoring a like item or weapon system to a mission capable condition. AR 750-1 sets forth the following criteria:

- Approval authority remains with the commander of the organization in formal control of the system.
- Controlled exchange by field- and sustainment-levels of maintenance is authorized only when—
    - It is the only means of providing an FMC end item or weapon system to a supported unit within the period indicated by the initial PD on the maintenance request.
    - Approved by the field or sustainment maintenance commander, installation materiel maintenance officer, or a designated representative.

6-34. In all cases, the individual owning aircraft unit commanders will be notified when controlled exchange actions are to be conducted and documentation will be furnished to the unit responsible for reporting aircraft status on DA Form 1352 (Army Aircraft Inventory, Status and Flying Time). Approval authorities stated above are IAW approvals as directed in AR 750-1 and TM 1-1500-328-23.

6-35. The controlled exchange recommendation presented to the commander should be a consolidated maintenance team decision involving PC, QC, and technical supply. Each unit commander will be notified and must concur before the controlled exchange recommendation proceeds to approval if the recommended controlled exchange occurs between aircraft of different companies/troops in the same battalion/squadron. Controlled exchange documentation will be furnished to the units as stated above.

6-36. Controlled exchange is an Army maintenance management tool. Aviation maintenance SOPs must contain controlled exchange policies and procedures. Controlled exchange actions require stringent and meticulous record-keeping procedures, particularly when transferring historical data between aircraft records. There must be a continuous dialogue between PC, QC, technical supply, and maintenance personnel before, during, and immediately after the controlled exchange.

6-37. Control exchange documents and logs are locally produced and maintained IAW AR 25-400-2. Controlled exchange maintenance procedures should not be considered complete until all forms and records are closed out and filed. Upon controlled exchange action approval, an authorization form is initiated in four copies and distributed as follows:

- A copy is used by the PC office for DA Form 1352 reporting purposes; this copy is filed in the PC office controlled-exchange logbook. Controlled-exchange sheets for each reporting period are filed with the DA Form 1352 as supporting documentation IAW AR 700-138.

- A copy is given to QC for its controlled exchange files.

- A copy is filed in the donor aircraft logbook; aircraft records are annotated to reflect item controlled exchanged to aircraft serial number. If the component is a serial-numbered item, the serial number of the component is annotated.

- A copy is filed in the gaining aircraft logbook; aircraft records are annotated to reflect item controlled exchanged to aircraft serial number. If the component is a serial-numbered item, the serial number of the component is annotated.

Note. Refer to chapter 4 for information on SSF procedures and chapter 7 for information on RX and controlled exchange procedures.

Note. The ULLS-A (E) database lists only reportable items for the controlled exchange process. Non-listed reportable items must be manually input into the controlled exchanges process. For example, a wheel and tire are not reportable items in the ULLS-A (E) database; therefore, a manual input is required when completing the commanders comments.

UNSCHEDULED MAINTENANCE MANAGEMENT PROCEDURES

MANAGING UNSCHEDULED MAINTENANCE

6-38. An unscheduled maintenance requirement occurs when an aircraft experiences an unexpected malfunction, premature component breakdown, or battle damage. The PC OIC/assistant PC OIC/NCOIC prioritizes, coordinates, manages, and tracks unscheduled repairs.

SCHEDULED MAINTENANCE MANAGEMENT PROCEDURES

SCHEDULING SYSTEM

6-39. A scheduling system promoting efficient workflow is needed to ensure customers receive their aircraft with the least possible delay. Many factors must be considered when developing a scheduling system. These factors may include the current workloads and priorities of the supported units, the availability of tools, and the supply of major components, parts, and hardware.

6-40. A PC operation requires a scheduling system and preplanned workflow. The PC element must track the following information to establish maintenance workweek priorities compatible with the unit mission:

- Mission requirements and priorities of supported commanders, to include numbers of aircraft and scheduled systems, and specific capabilities required for those aircraft and systems.
- Aircraft maintenance flow, by flying hours remaining for each assigned aircraft until upcoming scheduled maintenance inspections.
- Current total number of flight hours, status of avionics and armament, and the operational status of each assigned aircraft.
- Work in progress and work deferred/delayed.
- ASC/AST work in progress and work deferred/delayed.
- Time-change requirements for components, by individual assigned aircraft tail number.
- Non-flying enabling systems scheduled maintenance intervals.

MANAGING SCHEDULED MAINTENANCE

6-41. Scheduled maintenance takes place anytime an aircraft phase, progressive phase maintenance, preventive maintenance service, scheduled component replacement or non-flying system service (such as night vision goggles or GSE) is conducted. Scheduled maintenance actions and procedures can suffer from a lack of coordination and communication. Poorly coordinated scheduled maintenance events will have a negative effect on the battalion/squadron aircraft readiness.

6-42. To ensure minimum disruption to the supported unit mission (training/tactical) and aircraft/system readiness, PC personnel will ensure a suitable maintenance program is in place to coordinate all maintenance and sustainment actions. Contents of the maintenance program must be fully communicated, by way of a maintenance SOP, to all levels of command within the battalion/squadron. Battalion/squadron leadership must accept responsibility and provide command emphasis in support of the maintenance program.

6-43. Maintenance functions are designed to maintain the fleet and systems to a standard allowing the operational commander to accomplish the mission on time, every time. The PC office should have visibility on all major scheduled maintenance requiring internal and external support. The visibility of maintenance actions allows the PC OIC/assistant PC OIC/NCOIC to coordinate and forecast support, allowing for reaction time.

MANAGING DEFERRED/DELAYED MAINTENANCE

6-44. The PC OIC/assistant PC OIC/NCOIC prioritizes maintenance actions daily. Occasionally, insufficient personnel, equipment, and/or time may exist and the PC OIC/assistant PC OIC/NCOIC decides which aircraft/components are repaired or deferred/delayed.

6-45. The commander is the approval authority for all deferred maintenance actions (DA Form 2408-14-1 [Uncorrected Fault Record (Aircraft)]). Deferred/delayed maintenance actions cannot be postponed indefinitely, they must be coordinated and scheduled to be performed at the earliest opportunity. Deferred/delayed maintenance actions should be completed when an aircraft experiences an unscheduled maintenance requirement or is scheduled for a preventive maintenance service or phase. If a deferred/delayed maintenance procedure is not corrected during an unscheduled repair, PMCS, PPM, or phase, then the owning unit commander will sign or validate the explanation in the logbook extending the deferral/delay beyond the repair opportunity. The PC section ensures all follow-on deferrals/delays receive command review and signature.

6-46. Deferred/delayed maintenance should be monitored and minimized by PC and maneuver platoons/companies. In monitoring deferred/delayed maintenance work orders, PC evaluates the open fault status for each aircraft during mandatory monthly, or more frequent, recurring logbook reviews for excessive deferred/delayed maintenance. The trending of deferred/delayed maintenance should be tracked for faults and work orders of less than 30 days, 31 to 60 days, and more than 60 days. Faults or work orders deferred/delayed for 31 to 60 days should receive PC office and maneuver platoon/company/troop emphasis and those more than 60 days should receive command review to determine the validity and reasons for the deferral/delay. PC sections resource as necessary to eliminate work order backlogs. These work orders are associated with a system requirement and indicate an area where combat power can be generated. The backlog report, as part of the production index, is part of the unit MOE.

COORDINATING INTERNAL MAINTENANCE SUPPORT

6-47. Internal maintenance support is coordinated at the daily PC meeting by the PC OIC/assistant PC OIC/NCOIC. Internal maintenance support, whenever possible, is aligned with the daily operations of the maneuver companies to ensure a matched and responsive support effort. Internal maintenance support not only conducts work-order requests for maintenance, but the PC section will also assist the maneuver units by reviewing aircraft logbooks during each reporting period to identify open faults for coordination with PC.

COORDINATING EXTERNAL MAINTENANCE SUPPORT

6-48. The AMC/AMT PC OIC/NCOIC plans and coordinates all external maintenance requests with the ASC/AST PC office and conducts daily transmittals of STAMIS information as necessary to track ongoing maintenance actions. The ASC/AST PC officer will coordinate for all evacuation work orders outside the brigade or ACS. The PC OIC/assistant PC OIC/NCOIC should plan and allow for as much lead-time as possible to maximize the P4T3 process.

BATTLE DAMAGE ASSESSMENT AND REPAIR

6-49. The purpose of BDAR is to rapidly return disabled equipment to combat or enable the equipment to self-recover. BDAR is the responsibility of the commander (based on mission, enemy, terrain and weather, troops and support available, time available, and civil considerations) and is accomplished by the operator/crew and field maintenance personnel. The commander is responsible for the training and resourcing of BDAR and DART operations and delegates those missions to an OIC. See FM 3-04.513 for more information.

6-50. The assigned OIC is responsible for training, coordinating, organizing, assembling, and assigning the appropriate DART package to affect aircraft recovery. The AMC/AMT OIC will coordinate with the ASC/AST if recovery is beyond the capability of the AMC/AMT. If assigned to the ASC/AST, the OIC will coordinate with the AMC/AMT to effect recovery of the downed aircraft.

COORDINATING MAINTENANCE OPERATIONAL CHECKS AND MAINTENANCE TEST FLIGHTS

6-51. The PC OIC will coordinate all MOCs and MTFs at the PC meeting with the supported company/troop and, on case-by-case basis, throughout the duty day as required. The ASC/AST will coordinate MOCs and MTFs at PC meetings with the MTF section representative. After a successful MOC or MTF, the aircraft status is changed according to TM 1-1500-328-23, AR 700-138, and appropriate aircraft TMs.

MANAGING AN AIRCRAFT PHASE AND PERIODIC MAINTENANCE PROGRAM

6-52. Each maneuver company/troop is individually responsible for managing the flow of aircraft into phase by hours or days (figure 6-1). The companies work with one another and the AMC/AMT PC OIC/NCOIC to sequence major inspections that reduce lag times created by limited assets for performing inspections.

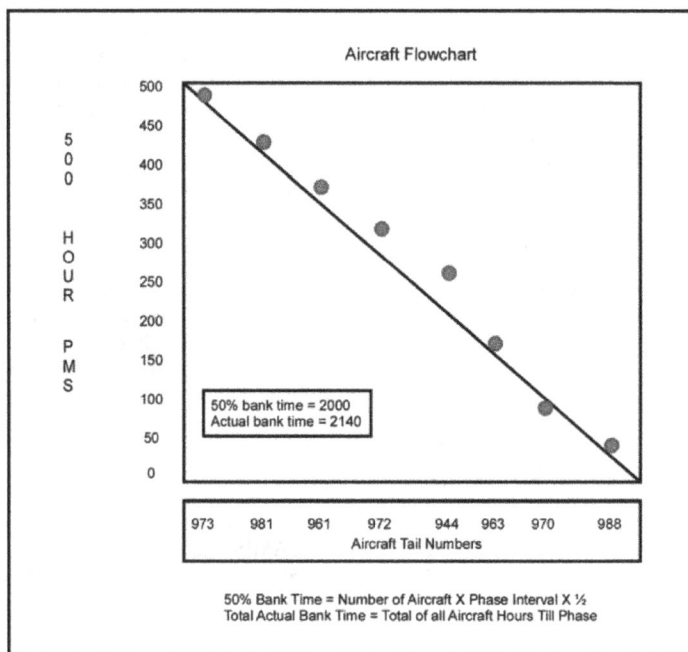

Figure 6-1. Bank time flowchart

6-53. Maintenance units can support a predetermined number of aircraft in phase at any time (capacity), and aviation maneuver units want to avoid a large percentage of assets in scheduled maintenance simultaneously. This multi-phase condition reduces operational flexibility and limits training opportunities. When managing the scheduled maintenance program, predetermined hourly intervals generally determine approximate induction dates for a phase or progressive maintenance scheduled inspection. This process places some limits on predictability but maximizes the hours flown between scheduled maintenance. To enhance predictability when using the hourly method, units either fly or rest aircraft to support the sequential flow of systems into the program, as phase capacity becomes available.

6-54. In operations with high or very predictable tempos, predetermining a date of induction, regardless of hours flown on the aircraft, can yield a predetermined amount of bank time sufficient to support foreseeable operations. This method will sometimes induct aircraft into scheduled maintenance early, sacrificing short-term bank hours for overall program sustainment. This date generated predictability can ease pre-maintenance supply and verification operations challenges such as phase kit ordering, time between overhaul (TBO) acquisition, MTF scheduling and logbook pre-inspection, while producing the required available aircraft hours between scheduled events.

6-55. The AMC/AMT PC OIC will assist the maneuver companies in their flow management and manage the overall battalion/squadron phase flow to ensure multiple company/troop aircraft are not in phase at the same time. The PC OIC/NCOIC monitors and manages spacing between major scheduled maintenance events and phase maintenance inspections.

6-56. The coordinated scheduled maintenance effort includes consultation with the BAMO/SAMO and ASC/AST PC to ensure adequate phase and periodic maintenance work orders reach the ASC/AST to maintain proficiency. This percentage of phases and PPMs will never drop below 20 percent without brigade or air cavalry squadron commander documented approval.

COORDINATING PHASE AND PERIODIC MAINTENANCE PROCEDURES

6-57. PC should coordinate closely with QC personnel when preparing inter-shop maintenance requests and accompanying forms and records. DA Forms 2408-13-1, 2408-13-2, 2408-13-3, and 2407 should specify, in detail, all work required or inspections to be performed. The following sequence applies to a typical phase and periodic maintenance (TM 1-1500-328-23):

- Logbook review and phase parts requisition.
- Prephase MTF.
- Aircraft arrival.
- Forms and records flow.
- Final inspection.
- Postphase MTF inspection.
- Release of aircraft.

Logbook Review and Phase Parts Requisition

6-58. Prior to induction and near the five-percent system hours remaining point, the accepting unit will conduct a thorough logbook review of entries, deferrals/delayed entries, and historical data to prepare for induction. This allows supply and management anticipation for components, parts, stock, and special tools.

Prephase Maintenance Test Flight Inspection

6-59. During the prephase test flight inspection, maintenance personnel should conduct the following actions:

- Whenever practical, MPs should perform a prephase test flight on aircraft scheduled for phase or periodic maintenance.
- The maintenance and PC officers should review the results to determine the platoon and/or section work assignments.
- Faults noted become part of the phase inspection.
- The assigned TI should participate in the test flight when possible.

Aircraft Arrival

6-60. Upon aircraft arrival at the maintenance facility, the—

- PC accepts the aircraft and logs it on DA Form 2405 (Maintenance Request Register).
- PC , along with QC, receives and reviews aircraft forms and records to include DA Form 2407, the aircraft equipment logbook, historical files, and ULLS-A (E) computer.
- QC personnel conduct a joint aircraft inventory with the supported unit before acceptance is considered complete.

Note. Units under the ULLS-A (E) or SAMS-1 system will follow the procedures outlined in the appropriate end-user manual.

Forms and Records

6-61. When evaluating forms and records, PC and QC personnel will conduct the following:

- PC personnel will complete block 24 of DA Form 2407; a copy of the receipt and inventory sheet go to the supported unit representative.
- PC assigns and directs the workflow through the various platoons and/or shops, entering all maintenance requirements on the PC board and ULLS-A (E).
- As work progresses through the platoons, shops, and sections, QC personnel conduct in-progress inspections.
- QC personnel conduct inspections on inter-shop maintenance requests as they are completed, routing them to the PC shop.
- PC personnel extract the necessary information from the completed inter-shop maintenance requests and DA Forms 2408-13-1, 2408-13-2, and 2408-13-3 to enter appropriate information on DA Form 2407.

6-62. Maintenance personnel will record faults on DA Forms 2408-13-1, 2408-13-2, and 2408-13-3. If the unit is assigned the ULLS-A (E), authorized personnel will make appropriate entries.

Final Inspection

Before- and During-the-Final Inspection

6-63. Before and during final inspection,—

- PC personnel receive and consolidate all documents relating to the aircraft maintenance performed to ensure all required maintenance was completed.
- The phase team NCOIC notifies QC the aircraft is ready for final inspection; the phase team NCOIC provides necessary forms and records. This inspection—
  - In addition to recorded in-progress inspections, ensures thorough, quality maintenance has occurred and an airworthy aircraft is presented to the owning unit.
  - Verifies inspection plates and panels have been correctly reinstalled and the aircraft has been properly serviced and cleaned.
- QC personnel check forms and records in the aircraft equipment log assembly (records) to ensure all entries are neat, correct, and up-to-date.

After-the-Final Inspection

6-64. After final inspection,—

- The TI signs or initials and enters the Julian date in block 26 of DA Form 2407. His signature or initials indicate he has inspected the aircraft and verified all services and repairs have been done.
- The TI must sign in the correcting information block if the maintenance or repairs requested are recorded in the faults or remarks block of DA Form 2408-13-1 as an "X" grounding condition.
- The TI determines whether an MOC or MTF is required according to TM 1-1500-328-23 or appropriate aircraft manuals; if an MOC or MTF is required, PC is notified.
- Maintenance personnel remove the BII list gear and loose equipment required for test flight purposes from the loose equipment storage area and reinstalls it in the aircraft.
- Maintenance personnel will annotate in the aircraft logbook if an MOC or MTF is required.
- Authorized maintenance personnel will make appropriate entries in the ULLS-A (E) computer.

Postphase Maintenance Test Flight Inspection

6-65. After phase inspection completion, a MTF inspection will be conducted:

- When the test flight is performed, a qualified MP will perform the postphase test flight inspection of the aircraft.

- If the MP does not release the aircraft after the test flight, he makes the required entry on DA Form 2408-13-1. The deficiency or fault is corrected and another test flight is conducted. This cycle continues until the aircraft test flight is acceptable.
- Maintenance personnel ensure all inventoried equipment is inside and properly stored in the aircraft after the test flight, and then the aircraft is ready for release.
- QC personnel return the completed paperwork, forms, and records to the PC shop.
- PC personnel notify the owning unit the aircraft is ready for delivery.

Release of Aircraft

6-66. When releasing the aircraft to the owning unit,—

- QC personnel and the owning unit crew chief or representative perform a joint DA Form 2408-17 (Aircraft Inventory Record) inventory.
- The PC clerk enters the Julian date on form when aircraft maintenance was completed.
- The owning unit representative completes DA Form 2407, signifying acceptance and delivery of the aircraft.
- Authorized maintenance personnel will make appropriate entries in the ULLS-A (E) computer.

ARMY MAINTENANCE REGENERATION ENABLERS

6-67. According to AR 750-1, the authorized Army maintenance regeneration enablers are RTF and ORF.

READY-TO-FIGHT

6-68. RTF is a strategic asset deployed to the theater of operations consisting of an authorized quantity of assets providing rapid weapon system replacement. These assets are maintained by USAMC activities with a sustainment maintenance mission to exchange aircraft with supported units when repairs cannot be accomplished.

OPERATIONAL READINESS FLOAT

6-69. ORF is a strategic asset deployed to an installation consisting of an authorized quantity of assets used to maintain established readiness levels or meet training availability requirements during peacetime. These assets are maintained by TDA and MTOE maintenance activities with a field or sustainment maintenance mission to exchange with supported units when repairs cannot be accomplished within Army command-established guidelines. ORF assets awaiting issue are maintained at the Army maintenance standard defined in AR 750-1.

SECTION III – UNIT LEVEL LOGISTICS SYSTEM-AVIATION (ENHANCED) FUNCTIONS

6-70. PC, with assistance from QC personnel, commissions and decommissions the deployed server. The ULLS-A (E) deployed server allows a unit the flexibility to "push" aircraft away from the primary database to support area operations. The deployed server enables maintenance personnel, including TIs, to migrate maintenance-related data back to PC for flight hours and readiness reporting purposes.

6-71. When conducting split-based operations, the deployed server function provides a unit with the capability of deploying aircraft to support operations away from the unit primary database. The deployed server allows maintenance managers access to management functions, except program administrator functions, while tracking maintenance actions.

Note. If the server is down for any reason, PC will manually process maintenance-related functions. Once connectivity is restored, manual entries are uploaded into ULLS-A (E).

6-72. The PC functions for ULLS-A (E) software are innovative and assist the PC user with various tools to enhance the following:

- Tracking aircraft status, reporting, and flying hours according to AR 700-138.
- Maintaining a work-order log.
- Initializing and processing work-order requests.
- Facilitating aircraft transfers.
- Initiating and tracking parts requisitions.
- Monitoring overall maintenance operations and generating required reports.

DEPARTMENT OF THE ARMY FORM 1352-1

6-73. The DA Form 1352-1 (Daily Aircraft Status Report) provides an accurate reporting of aircraft inventories, maintenance status, and flying time. The 1352-1 daily screen is displayed, providing access to the authorized user for making desired individual entries onto the form.

DEPARTMENT OF THE ARMY FORM 1352

6-74. DA Form 1352 provides PC personnel with an updated account of the following:

- Total aircraft hours flown.
- Total FMC time.
- PMC supply time.
- PMC maintenance time.
- Total NMCS.
- Total sustainment maintenance time.
- Total field-level maintenance (ASC/AST) time.
- Total AMC/AMT time.
- Daily aircraft hours flown.
- Total number of landings.
- Total number of autorotations.

6-75. Other than the authorized PC user, only authorized QC users are able to view and print the DA Form 1352. Only authorized PC users are able to enter, modify, and save DA Form 1352 data.

6-76. When the "parts" button on the DA Form 1352 menu screen is used, the authorized user can access the following screens:

- Pending parts requisitions.
- Parts currently on-order.
- Creating parts requests.
- Updating requests (this will pull the document numbers to the parts screen from technical supply).

6-77. Once the "parts" button is clicked, the "parts view" screen will appear. The "parts view" screen provides the PC authorized user with the following options:

- Accept/reject parts requested.
- View pending parts request.
- Create parts request.
- View DA Forms 2408-13-1 and 2408-13-2.
- View DA Form 2407.

6-78. The DA Form 1352 can be accessed through the "utilities" menu. This menu provides the following options and printing capabilities:

- Daily status report.

- Hoist status report.
- DA Form 1352 front-side report.
- Feeder report.

6-79. From this location, the user has access to the following data entry options of the 1352 back-side comments blocks A to M; enter remarks/comments as deemed appropriate:

- FMC is five-percent or more below goal.
- NMCS exceeds goal.
- NMC maintenance exceeds goal.
- PMC exceeds five-percent.
- Aircraft involved in sustainment maintenance.

6-80. From the same location, the user has access to the following data-entry options on the backside of the 1352, blocks N-1. Enter remarks/comments on the back side of the 1352 as deemed appropriate:

- Commander overall assessment.
- Comments by item of equipment.
- Comments: MOS or skill level shortage.
- Comments: TMDE.
- Comments: Maintenance facilities.
- Comments: Maintenance workload.
- Comments: Automated logistics system(s).
- Comments: Transportation or order ship times.
- Comments: operational pace/tempo.

6-81. From the same location, the user, after migrations are complete, will press the "update flight hours" button. Once pressed, all flight hours previously entered on DA Form 2408-12 (Army Aviator's Flight Record) will transfer, updating the DA Form 1352-1 and flight hour reports.

6-82. The PC OIC/assistant PC OIC/NCOIC monitors and reviews the DA Form 2405 for high-priority work orders daily and all other priorities at least weekly. The PC OIC/NCOIC confirms aircraft status and parts requirements whenever aircraft go down.

6-83. The PC OIC/assistant PC OIC/NCOIC prioritizes the workflow against the backlog of each shop to monitor and minimize the number of work orders. Each shop NCOIC should be able to brief the backlog on a daily basis and explain reasons for a delay (for example, a back order of repair parts or lack of personnel). The PC OIC/assistant PC OIC/NCOIC assesses each reason for delay and makes every effort/arrangement to mitigate them(such as, investigating the details of a back ordered part or seeking out temporary utilization of qualified personnel from other units).

DEPARTMENT OF THE ARMY FORM 2407

6-84. Authorized users have three options to access the work order menu: from the PC menu, at the initial start screen, or in the back-shops login screen. From any of these options, authorized users can select the work order button to enter the DA Form 2407 work order main page.

6-85. From the DA Form 2407 work order main page, the user can choose from the following options:

- DA Form 2407 –enables the user to view the current highlighted DA Form 2407.
- DA Forms 2408-13-1 and 2408-13-2 –brings the user to the current write-up on the DA Form 2407.
- New DA Form 2407 –enables the user to create a new DA Form 2407.
- Reports –enables the user to view, print, or electronically transfer the following reports:
    - Accepted work orders.
    - Work orders by shop.

- Work orders by age.
- Rejected work orders.
- Pending work orders.
- Work orders by status.

MONITORING NOT MISSION CAPABLE SUPPLY DOCUMENT NUMBER STATUS

6-86. The PC OIC/assistant PC OIC/NCOIC monitors the daily status of Class IX (air) repair parts affecting the status of a work order or the overall mission readiness of an aircraft.

6-87. Technical supply reports the status of all AOG and NMCS parts requests during the daily PC meeting. Any changes in the status of these repair parts are briefed as soon as possible to the PC OIC/assistant PC OIC/NCOIC.

6-88. The PC OIC/assistant PC OIC tracks the weekly expenditures on bench stock and unscheduled repair part requests, as well as turn-in credit. This information is provided by the technical supply OIC to the PC section and the maintenance unit commander to track the unit overall aviation funding financial fitness. The BAMO, SAMO, and support operations officer must be notified if prolonged maintenance downtime results from the lack of AOG and high PD requested repair parts.

6-89. The SOS item manager is the source for tracking information on a given high PD and/or AOG repair part request. He or she focuses on processing high PD/AOG requests and the release and shipment of critical repair parts. Through ULLS-A (E), PC personnel can track high PD information, financial transactions, and open the document register.

AIRCRAFT TRANSFERS

6-90. TM 1-1500-328-23 identifies the standards of serviceability for aircraft transfers. A transfer is defined as a change of property accountability from one organization to another. The cost of transfer, inspections, and maintenance is the responsibility of the transferring activity.

6-91. Historical forms and records provide commanders and maintenance managers with information on aircraft transfers (gains/losses). These records must be controlled and kept safe from loss or damage and are sent to the gaining unit separate from the aircraft.

6-92. The aircraft transfer option is accessed from the main menu and the user can transfer aircraft in two ways: transfer aircraft or transfer unit. With the transfer aircraft option, any single aircraft is transferred. With the transfer unit option, an entire UIC is transferred.

Note. Before any type of aircraft transfer, DA Form 1352 must be completed with a gain/loss code and the gain/loss comments on the back of the form.

Chapter 7

Technical Supply

This chapter provides technical supply personnel and aircraft maintainers with a "how-to" on technical supply procedures. Technical supply management involves identifying, procuring, and maintaining the minimum assets required to meet operational requirements. AR 710-2, DA PAM 710-2-1, DA PAM 710-2-2, and DA PAM 738-751 address aviation sustainment procedures and policies.

SECTION I – DUTIES AND RESPONSIBILITIES

TECHNICAL SUPPLY OFFICER

7-1. The battalion or squadron CW3 AMO is the technical supply officer. In the ASC/AST, the technical supply officer is typically an aviator from the MTF section. The position of the technical supply officer is a primary rated duty and commanders will appoint these officers on orders. Additionally, the technical supply officer may perform MTF duties for the maintenance unit. He is responsible for and has oversight of the technical supply section's internal management and daily operations. This includes requesting, processing, issuing, stocking, and turning in aircraft repair parts and components. He will coordinate high-priority UND A and B parts requests with the unit PC OIC. If authorized by the commander, the technical supply officer will certify and authorize all high-priority requisitions and review the Commander's Exception Report. The technical supply officer balances the unit aviation budget and prepares a periodic report for the S-4 and maintenance unit commander to review.

Contents

TECHNICAL SUPPLY NONCOMMISSIONED OFFICER-IN-CHARGE

7-2. The technical supply NCOIC is directly responsible for the training and operational management of the technical supply section to include the request, issue, stockage, and turn-in of all Class IX (air) repair parts, special tools, and components. He will coordinate high-priority (UND A and B) requests with the technical supply officer. The technical supply NCOIC directs the work and supervises all technical supply actions assigned to the logistics clerks.

7-3. Technical supply personnel require a working knowledge and understanding of supply publications, FEDLOG, and NSN breakdown. Refer to DA PAM 710-2-2 for more information on cataloging and NSN breakdown.

TECHNICAL SUPPLY CLERK

7-4. Automated supply specialists assigned to technical supply sections process all high-priority (UND A and B) and routine priority (UND C) aircraft requisitions. They request, issue, stock, and turn-in all Class IX (air) repair parts, special tools, and components. Technical supply clerks maintain logs and files for manually prepared forms.

SECTION II – PRINCIPLES

CLASSES OF SUPPLY

7-5. AR 710-2 identifies and defines the classes of supply. The most commonly used by aviation maintenance are Classes II, III, V, and IX (air):

- **Class I** – Subsistence, including free health and welfare items.
- **Class II** – Clothing, individual equipment, tentage, tool sets and tool kits, hand tools, and administrative and housekeeping supplies and equipment (to include maps). Class II items include items of equipment, other than major items, prescribed in authorization/allowance tables and items of supply (not including repair parts).
- **Class III** – POL, petroleum and solid fuels, to include bulk and packaged fuels, lubricating oils and lubricants, petroleum specialty products; solid fuels, coal, and related products.
- **Class IV** – Construction materials, to include installed equipment and all fortification/barrier materials.
- **Class V** – Ammunition of all types (to include chemical, radiological, and special weapons), bombs, explosives, mines, fuses, detonators, pyrotechnics, missiles, rockets, propellants, and other associated items.
- **Class VI** – Personal-demand items (nonmilitary sales items).
- **Class VII** –Major end items are equipment that is ready for its intended use: (principal items); for example, helicopters, launchers, tanks, mobile machine shops, and vehicles.
- **Class VIII** – Medical material, to include medical-peculiar repair parts.
- **Class IX** – Repair parts and components (to include kits, assemblies and subassemblies, and reparable and nonreparable) needed to provide maintenance support of all equipment to include aviation-specific repair parts categorized as Class IX (air).
- **Class X** – Material to support nonmilitary programs, such as agricultural and economic development, not included in Classes I through IX.

CATEGORIES OF SUPPLY

7-6. Supplies are requested and issued using three categories of supply; scheduled, demanded, and regulated.

SCHEDULED

7-7. Scheduled supplies may be reasonably predicted and usually do not require a requisition for replenishment. Requirements are based primarily on troop strength, equipment density, mission demands, forecasts, daily usage, or any combination. Scheduled supplies normally are shipped to users based on preplanned distribution schemes.

7-8. Classes I, III (bulk), V, and VI are typically scheduled supplies. Classes I and VI are based on troop strength. Class III (bulk) is based on long-range forecasts, equipment densities, and historic usage factors. Class V is based on densities of weapons and the unit assigned mission. Class IX (air) is based on aircraft flight hour demands to ascertain predictable repair parts and kits required that support the established scheduled supplies.

DEMANDED

7-9. A requisition must be submitted for demanded supplies. Classes II, III (packaged), IV, V, and IX (air) are considered demanded supplies. Aviation repair parts fall into this category and must be requisitioned through organizational STAMIS. Unit STAMIS automatically records a demand with every processed request. Unit equipment work ordered to higher maintenance support, such as radios and LRUs, requires a manual demand entry into the unit STAMIS.

REGULATED

7-10. Regulated supplies may be scheduled or demanded. The commander controls these supplies by marking them as regulated because of scarcity, high cost, or mission needs. Any item or group of items may be designated as regulated but the commander usually identifies select items from Classes II, III (bulk), IV, V, and VII as regulated. If an item is regulated, the commander must approve its release before it is issued. Items designated as command–regulated are identified in operation plans and orders.

TYPES OF SUPPLIES

7-11. Refer to AR 735-5 for regulatory policies and procedural guidance. For accountability purposes, all Army property (except real property) is classified as expendable, nonexpendable, or durable. An ARC is assigned to each item of supply to identify its specific classification and the degree of accounting and control that must be applied at the user level.

EXPENDABLE

7-12. Expendable items are identified by an "X" found in the ARC column of the AMDF contained on FEDLOG. Supplies that lose their identity when used to repair or complete other items are considered expendable such as assemblies, repair parts, and accessories. All Class IX (air) repair parts and items consumed in use, regardless of price, are expendable. Some items, although classified as expendable, require additional supply and issue controls such as items identified as recoverable or pilferable. Many special tools are labeled as ARC "X"; however, their frequently high costs demand accounting IAW AR 710-2. Citing the ARC as "X" does not relieve the user from responsibility and accountability requirements.

NONEXPENDABLE

7-13. Nonexpendable items are identified by an "N" found in the ARC column of the AMDF contained on FEDLOG. Class VII items are nonexpendable supplies and assigned a line-item number. The AMDF contains pertinent data, to include line-item numbers.

DURABLE

7-14. Durable items are identified by a "D" found in the ARC column of the AMDF contained on FEDLOG. The PBO at the appropriate level of command designates organizations authorized to request supplies and maintain the durable document register for all supply actions. Durables require no formal accounting after issue except hand tools requiring hand-receipt control. Citing the ARC as "D" does not relieve the user from responsibility and accountability requirements.

METHODS OF DISTRIBUTION

7-15. The three distribution methods of resupply are supply point distribution, unit distribution, and throughput distribution.

SUPPLY POINT DISTRIBUTION

7-16. The supplying unit issues supplies from an established supply point. Technical supply personnel pick-up their supplies using organic transportation. This is the typical method used to distribute supplies to requesting units.

UNIT DISTRIBUTION

7-17. Unit distribution is identified as delivery of supplies directly to the unit. A unit representative meets the resupply package at the logistics resupply point and guides the package to the unit position.

THROUGHPUT DISTRIBUTION

7-18. Throughput distribution delivers supplies from the operational level directly to the requesting or DS unit. Shipments bypass one or more echelons in the supply chain to speed delivery forward. Throughput is the most responsive distribution method and efficient use of transportation assets.

SECTION III – GUIDELINES

REQUISITION MANAGEMENT

7-19. The Class IX (air) repair parts appendix/annex to the AMC/AMT and the ASC/AST unit SOP, written and updated by technical supply, outlines procedures and requirements within the unit. Technical supply outlines ULLS-A (E) or SARSS automated procedures for all assigned/attached unit Soldiers. Appendix A identifies the basic content of an internal and external SOP.

7-20. The SOP will reflect the automated system the command uses. The procedures specified in the SOP must conform to all applicable guidance in governing regulations, directives, and policies. The SOP should be a day-to-day management tool used by all unit personnel. AR 710-2, DA PAM 710-2-1, and DA PAM 710-2-2 are essential references for maintenance officers or technicians when writing an SOP.

REFERENCE PUBLICATIONS AND DOCUMENTS

7-21. These publications and documents must be available in the unit's technical supply section:
- AR 25-400-2.
- AR 710-2.
- AR 725-50.
- AR 750-1.
- AR 750-10.
- DA PAM 710-2-1.
- DA PAM 710-2-2.
- MWOs.
- SBs.
- TBs.
- TMs or commercial equivalent for supported equipment.
- AMDF contained in FEDLOG.
- Automatic return item list.
- Identification lists.
- Master cross-reference lists.
- Supply catalogs.

FEDERAL LOGISTICS INFORMATION

7-22. The FEDLOG database provides aircraft maintainers and aviation logisticians with the ability to identify items in the inventory and order the correct aircraft part/component.

7-23. FEDLOG is for official use only products. Cataloging for all services has been consolidated under the Defense Logistics Information Service. FEDLOG information is contained on disk. Aircraft maintainers and logisticians can query FEDLOG, using the CDs, to obtain management data, part and reference number data, freight data, supplier data, characteristics data, and representative drawing data. FEDLOG is also available on a digital video disk and the internet. Aviation unit personnel contact the unit publications officer or NCOIC to request a subscription to FEDLOG. Disks must be rendered unreadable before disposal or recycling.

7-24. With data obtained from FEDLOG, technical supply personnel can—

- Process and edit customer requests.
- Ensure NSN and part number accuracy of repair parts received.
- Update stock records.
- Ensure accuracy of inventories.
- Process receipt of aircraft repair parts/components.
- Facilitate Class IX (air) budget reconciliations by verifying dollar-cost value of newly processed aircraft repair requests as well as verifying dollar credits received for unserviceable turn-ins.

7-25. Subscription information or questions regarding FEDLOG should be direct to USAMC, Logistics Support Activity, ATTN: AMXLS-MLA Building 5307, Redstone Arsenal, AL 35797-7466 or email fedlog@logsa.redstone.army.mil.

SECTION IV – PROCEDURES

MANAGEMENT BY TYPE OF LOADS

7-26. AR 710-2 states that loads are a quantity of expendable/durable supplies kept by units to sustain their operations. Loads of Classes VI, VII, and X will not be kept. The Army Command, Army Service Component Command, or direct reporting unit will designate the units required to keep one or more of the four types of loads: basic, operational, ammunition basic, and prescribed.

BASIC LOADS

7-27. Basic loads are quantities of Classes I through V (to include maps) and VIII (except medical equipment repair parts) supplies. Basic loads must be capable of being moved into a combat environment using organic transportation in a single lift. Basic load quantities are used to support peacetime operations only when no supporting operational loads are available. Basic load items subject to deterioration or having a shelf life are replaced as required. Excesses in basic loads caused by unit pack may be kept and used.

OPERATIONAL LOADS

7-28. Operational loads are quantities of Classes I through V (to include maps) and VIII (except medical equipment repair parts) supplies that sustain peacetime operations for a specific time. These supplies may be moved into a combat environment if transportation is available after essential lift requirements have been met. Expendable Class II, III (packaged), IV, and VIII supplies are authorized up to a 15-day stockage based on the allowance in common table of allowances (CTA) 50-970. Electronic access to expendable/durable items is at https://webtaads.belvoir.army.mil/usafmsa/.

AMMUNITION BASIC LOADS

7-29. Ammunition basic load assets, including CTA 50-909 items, on-hand at the unit level are accounted for on property book records; listed by DOD identification code, quantity, lot number, and serial number. Units not designated to have an ammunition basic load on-hand will have a properly prepared and authenticated DA Form 581 (Request for Issue and Turn-in of Ammunition) on-hand. This DA Form 581 provides the authorization for the ammunition basic load to be on-hand or on-order. The PBO provides an information copy of the DA Form 581 to the supporting ASP who will ensure, depending on mission need and storage capability, the ammunition is stocked or a pre-positioned requisition is in place for the ammunition required. The PBO will maintain the basic load authorization data on the property book to expedite deployment.

PRESCRIBED LOADS

7-30. Prescribed loads of significant Classes II, IV, and IX (air) organizational maintenance repair parts support the daily maintenance operations. Stockage of PLL line items are demand supported. AMC/AMT and ASC/AST commanders must approve and sign the PLL list. Once the PLL is approved and signed, aircraft repair parts and components listed in the PLL are stocked IAW AR 710-2. Stockage of nondemand-supported repair parts is limited IAW AR 710-2.

DEVELOPING STOCKAGE LISTS

7-31. The LIDB assists users in determining the Class IX (repair parts) stockage requirements that support their organic equipment. LIDB users can compute peacetime and contingency stockage lists when needed. After logging in and moving to the support item requirements module, a user selects the peacetime model or contingency model from the report criteria tab. The peacetime model allows the user to select limited parameters (location, level, and number of days of the operation). The contingency model permits the user to select and vary other parameters (such as resupply or no resupply, availability goals to be met by the model, average customer wait time, percentage of equipment in use each day, equipment survivability in combat, optimization preference, and scenario horizon). Changes to these variables let the user complete "what if" drills to match different potential operating conditions. After developing the product, the user saves the results in text files to include the stockage list, end item applications of each support item, and summary information about the product.

7-32. In the LIDB, the user can determine the support items for an end item or all end items associated with a specific support item. The user also can extract on-hand equipment densities from the LIDB asset module for use in many of the support item requirements processes. Finally, the user can compare the support items on two or more end items and determine the support items considered common or unique to those end items. An ASL can be added to the mix for identification of possible repair part turn-ins determined to be excess. LIDB access can be obtained at https://weblidb.logsa.army.mil/arf/index.jsp. Needed products can be obtained quickly by contacting amxlsmlb@logsa.redstone.army.mil.

STOCKAGE LIST MANAGEMENT

7-33. AR 710-2 provides management guidance for PLL, bench stock, and shop stock stockage items. Aviation maintenance units establish internal SOPs to manage their own PLL, bench stock, and shop stock.

7-34. Based on accumulation of demand history, SARSS generates a PLL change list for each customer. This list shows proposed additions, changes, and deletions to a unit PLL.

7-35. PLL stock add-and-retain criteria are controlled by manager parameters. Each proposed addition, deletion, and stockage-level change requires subsequent action by the customer and the ASB SSA.

7-36. The customer annotates the list to show desired action on proposed changes and sends the annotated list to the SSA. Using the annotated lists, the SSA sends change cards for processing in the PLL update process. An updated PLL is provided to each customer.

FORMS AND RECORDS

7-37. DA PAM 710-2-1 provides guidance on the use of forms. DA Form 2064 (Document Register for Supply Actions) must be maintained manually if the unit document register is not automated or the ULLS-A (E) is down.

7-38. The ULLS-A (E) supply management module tracks demands for unit-generated requests. Demands recorded and tracked by ULLS-A (E) are reviewed by technical supply personnel on a recurring basis. PLL lines failing to meet the established demand criteria as outlined in regulatory policies are evaluated by the maintenance officer or technician for deletion from the PLL. Refer to the ULLS-A (E) end users manual (EUM) for user information and procedural guidance.

7-39. SARSS-1 provides the unit demand summary list, product control number AGL-C39, monthly to each unit. The list shows unit demands for PLL and non-PLL items. It also provides detailed demand data for review of the unit demand history when technical supply personnel consider changes to the PLL.

7-40. Each quarter, the PLL computation subprocess of the demand analysis process generates a PLL change list for each unit. This list identifies all items recommended for additions, deletions, or changes in authorized stockage levels. NSN and management control number lists are printed in NIIN sequence. MCNs are in full stock number sequence.

7-41. The aviation maintenance officer/technician and technical supply officer must review the demand analysis list for accuracy. The review consists of analyzing the list and considering whether to add, delete, or recommend changes to stockage levels. Once the review is complete, recommendations are given to the aviation maintenance commander. Commanders have three choices prior to submitting the list to the SSA: approve, disapprove, or modify the recommendations.

BENCH STOCK ITEMS

Management Procedures

7-42. Bench stock items are authorized for all aviation maintenance units. Aviation maintenance officers/technicians, based on experience, should recommend additions, deletions, or stockage-level adjustments to ensure maintenance procedures are not halted due to a shortage of bench stock items.

7-43. The customer work request priority may be used to request the quantity required to complete the job when stock is at zero balance. Bench stock items are not demand supported. The authorized stockage level is 30 days for all units not collocated with a higher-level SSA; if collocated with an SSA, the authorized stockage level is 15 days. SSA bench stock procedures are outlined in DA PAM 710-2-2.

> *Note.* Refer to appendix G for compliance guidance on management, request procedures, and computation and stockage requirements of all bench stock items assigned to aviation maintenance units.

7-44. According to AR 710-2, bench stocks are authorized at all aviation maintenance units. Bench stocks are composed of low-cost, high-use consumable Classes II, III (packaged), IV, and IX (Air-not including components) items used by maintenance personnel at an unpredictable rate. Examples of these items are common hardware, resistors, transistors, wire, tubing, hose, thread, welding rods, sandpaper, sheet metal, rivets, seals, oils, grease, and repair kits.

7-45. The commander or designated representative will conduct a semiannual review of the bench stock IAW AR 710-2. No specified demand criteria exist that units must meet to add line items to the bench stock list.

Management in Support of Split-Based Operations

7-46. At the AMC/AMT, bench stock management can be centralized, collocated with other aircraft repair parts, and internally managed by technical supply personnel. The technical supply section is responsible for coordinating and overseeing accountability procedures, to include regularly scheduled inventories, as outlined in AR 710-2. Aviation operational unit bench stock items can be stored in flyaway containers, or similar containers, to facilitate deployment in support of split-based operations and internal daily use.

7-47. At the ASC/AST, bench stock management and accountability is the responsibility of the individual platoon, section, or shop authorized to carry and store bench stock and the company/troop consolidated technical supply. Trained technical supply clerks will comply with all accountability and inventory requirements for their assigned bench stock in their platoon, section, or shops.

7-48. ASC/AST units also consolidate a select number of assigned technical supply clerks and bench stock from each section or shop at the company/troop level. The company/troop technical supply OIC, consolidated clerks, and bench stock operation of this section report directly to the PC officer, assistant PC OIC, and NCOIC. An ASC/AST consolidated bench stock section will standardize the unit bench stock management procedures. The consolidation of personnel and bench stock provides—

- A centralized, single point of issue.
- A combination of the same item held in multiple sections/shops allowing a lower total quantity.
- The most efficient use of personnel to provide split-based and continuous operations.

SHOP STOCK ITEMS

7-49. Shop stocks are demand-supported repair parts and consumables stocked within a maintenance activity (ASB with a support-level maintenance mission authorized by an MTOE, TDA, or joint table of allowances). SSA shop stock procedures are outlined in DA PAM 710-2-2.

7-50. Shop stock repair parts are used internally to accomplish maintenance requests or programmed repair. Criteria for the number of demands required and the items authorized for stockage are outlined in AR 710-2.

7-51. ASL items are maintained by the ASB or AST SSA to support and complement aviation maintenance unit PLL. The ASL is the SSA authority to stock the item and is controlled and flexible. It shows items proven, by experience, to be sufficiently active at an SSA to warrant stockage. The ASL also contains other items with a projected need.

AUTHORIZED STOCKAGE LIST

7-52. The ASL is a list of all items authorized to be stocked at a specific level of supply to meet the needs of the aviation customers they support. The supporting SSA ASL becomes the SOS from which aviation units can replenish their stockage of parts and components to authorized levels.

7-53. To support decisions to stock items, demand history files are maintained to reflect the most recent 12-month period. At the ASB or AST SSA, demand frequency files are maintained for each item issued to aviation units for Classes II, III (packaged), IV, and IX. Items selected for stockage will make up the ASL.

7-54. Essentiality of a repair part or component is a primary consideration when technical supply personnel determine the range of items for the ASL. The essentiality code for each NSN can be found in the AMDF. Repair parts selected for stockage are restricted to the following essentiality codes: C, D, E, and J.

7-55. The ASL identifies authorized items to be stocked in the SSA to support customer demands. Although an item may qualify as an ASL item, the manager may or may not add the item to the ASL because of stockage and funding constraints of the SSA. SARSS considers an item qualified for stockage when it is demand-supported, an ORF item specifically authorized for incorporation, an initial provisioning item, or a mission-essential or mandatory stockage item.

7-56. SARSS automatically considers ASL items receiving insufficient demand during a 180-day period for a stockage list code change or deletion from the ASL. The SSA manager is responsible for managing the ASL and implementing demand analysis corrections within three days.

REPARABLE MANAGEMENT

STOCKAGE CRITERIA

7-57. According to DA PAM 710-2-2, reparable management includes reparable assets having a maintenance reparability code of D, F, H, or L. These assets are job ordered by the SSA to a maintenance unit or activity, repaired or washed out, and returned to the SSA for stock or disposition. Reparables are part of the SSA ASL. SSAs receive, store, and issue these assets from a specific RX activity. The stock records officer at the SSA and maintenance shop officer at the ASC/AST jointly select DS repair items based on demand history and maintenance data.

7-58. Reparables may be selected for stockage if these items are—

- Authorized for removal or replacement at the support maintenance level or lower according to technical publications.
- Authorized for repair at the DS level and the maintenance unit is authorized the personnel and tools to do the repair.

REPARABLE EXCHANGE

7-59. ASB (distribution company) and AST (supply platoon) SSAs maintain a selected list of aircraft RX parts. When alerted by the PC OIC or maintenance officer/technician, technical supply personnel will scrub internal repair parts lists to see if the aircraft parts needed are aircraft RX parts. If needed repair parts are RX items, technical supply personnel will initiate the required forms to request serviceable RX aircraft repair parts or components. Request for turn-in forms must also be initiated to accompany unserviceable repair parts. DA Form 2765-1, request for issue or turn-in, is prepared IAW DA PAM 710-2-1 and hand-carried, along with the unserviceable component, to the ASB (distribution company)/AST (supply platoon) RX section for exchange with a serviceable item. Ensure demands for components are logged into the STAMIS of record by the technical supply clerk.

7-60. Applicable references and publications must be complied with when processing requests for issue/turn-in. In addition, technical supply personnel must comply with guidance outlined in the external SOP distributed by the ASB (distribution company) or AST (supply platoon) SSA. Chapter 6, section III, outlines RX procedures.

7-61. RX procedures exchange serviceable aircraft repair parts, components, and assemblies for unserviceable items using standard issue and turn-in documents and procedures. Normally, items being exchanged must be reparable or recoverable. However, RX is sometimes used for other types of items for which issue must be controlled.

INSTALLATION SUPPLY SUPPORT ACTIVITY

7-62. The installation SSA will not maintain stockage levels, except for reparables repaired by the installation for DS SSAs or installation activities identified as DS system customers. Requisitions for those classes of supply under the DS system will flow through the installation SSA for editing, funding, and screening of excesses before being sent to the DMC. SSA procedures are outlined in DA PAM 710-2-2.

SECTION V – AIRCRAFT REPAIR PARTS MANAGEMENT

7-63. Supply and maintenance activities consume 10 percent of the Army's annual budget. Maintenance leaders should conduct a daily review of maintenance activities to ensure effective and efficient practices are utilized that aid in keeping costs to a minimum and possibly lead to cost reductions. A reduction in maintenance costs means an increase in available resources to support force structure, training, and other high-priority needs. One method of minimizing costs is ensuring the use of all available diagnostic equipment to troubleshoot and repair a system versus multiple component replacement as a troubleshooting method.

STORAGE OF AIRCRAFT REPAIR PARTS OR COMPONENTS

7-64. Storage of aircraft repair parts or components are a continuation of receiving and preliminary to issuing. Accuracy of records and operations are critical to ensuring stored repair parts are quickly located and made ready for issue. The storage activity provides physical receipt, storage, maintenance-in-storage, and safeguarding of items and records. Supplies received and signed for from an SSA are processed and document registers reconciled.

7-65. After NMCS aircraft repair parts (high-priority requisitions UND A) are received, processed, and document registers reconciled, these repair parts will not be stored. Unit technical supply personnel will contact owning units for immediate pick up of all high-priority requested parts. Aircraft repair parts received and processed but not released to owning units are stored according to guidance outlined in this section.

7-66. PLL line items are stored, secured, and protected according to the control inventory item code. This code is listed in the AMDF contained on FEDLOG. Care of aircraft repair parts or components in storage are managed and inspected IAW AR 740–3 and DOD 4145.19-R-1. Bench stock and PLL line items are stored in an area convenient to maintenance personnel, shops, and work sites. Units must emphasize proper storage of aircraft repair parts during field operations. Unprotected repair parts, components, and assemblies can quickly deteriorate if exposed to the elements.

7-67. An inspection schedule must be established for items in storage. Unpackaged and unpreserved items must be inspected for rust, corrosion, and broken packs. Particular emphasis must be placed on items with an established shelf life (such as rubber gaskets, neoprene seals, and batteries) to ensure expired-date packages are not issued. Storage practices should comply with safety and environmental laws and regulations. Technical supply supervisors must have a rotational plan, outlined in their SOP, for personnel to follow when issuing stocks with an established shelf life.

DETERMINING NEED AND PRIORITY OF REQUISITIONS

7-68. The maintenance status of an airframe will determine the UND for a specific requisition. The UND for a specific repair parts request is determined by the PC OIC or maintenance officer/technician. Refer to section VII and the ULLS-A (E) EUM for procedural guidance on using the technical supply module.

7-69. If an airframe is at work stoppage because of the lack of parts (NMCS), parts requested against that particular airframe are ordered using a UND of "A" high priority. UND of "A," combined with the aviation unit force activity designator, will determine the highest priority to be used. Refer to DA PAM 710-2-1 for further guidance.

7-70. If maintenance actions continue on an airframe and additional parts are still needed, a UND of "B" high priority is used to request serviceable replacement aircraft repair parts or components. UND of "B" high priority is used by technical supply personnel when requesting replacement PLL line items at zero balance. UND of "B," combined with an aviation unit force activity designator, will determine the highest priority to be used. Refer to DA PAM 710-2-1 for further guidance.

7-71. The commanding officer or his designated representative (in writing) of the requisitioning activity will personally review and approve all requisitions identified for expedited handling. The parts requisition classified as code "999" when used with an AOG classification is approved for processing only when it meets the following conditions:

- The requisitioning unit is assigned force activity designator I, II, or III.
- The aircraft repair parts or components required are causing aircraft mission-essential systems or subsystems to be incapable of performing any of their assigned missions (NMCS).

- Unserviceable aircraft repair parts or components have been identified during maintenance or troubleshooting, serviceable aircraft repair parts are necessary to prevent aircraft mission-essential systems or subsystems from being unable to perform assigned operational missions or tasks, or required serviceable parts are needed within five days of the date of the requisition.

7-72. Limits to the quantity of AOG requisitions per aircraft while in a theater of operations are established by the commodity command. The AOG approving authority at the DMC materiel readiness branch will validate the affected aircraft is NMCS for that particular part order with an AOG project code. Code 999 will also be used to identify items or equipment designated by the commanding officer or his designated representative as critically needed to perform the mission of the overseas unit/unit alerted for overseas deployment.

7-73. All other aircraft repair part or component requests, to include bench stock or forecasted requirements, are processed using a UND of "C." UND of "C," combined with the aviation unit force activity designator, will determine the priority to be used. Should a UND of "C" priority request change to a high priority, a modification document to reflect the higher PD must be submitted. Refer to AR 710-2 for guidance on submitting modification documents.

REQUISITION OF AIRCRAFT REPAIR PARTS

7-74. Technical supply personnel will process all aircraft repair parts or component requests. They fill aircraft parts requisitions using internal Class IX (air) assets consisting of bench stock and PLL line items. If the item is not stocked on the PLL or is at zero balance, the requisition is passed to the assigned SSA. The SSA will fill the request from internal ASL assets or pass the requisition to the DMC. Refer to section VII and the ULLS-A (E) EUM for procedural guidance on using the technical supply module.

7-75. Technical supply personnel must review all repair parts lists, to include bench stock and PLL, for availability before processing a request to a higher SOS. This review must include verification that the primary NSN being requested has no substitutes.

7-76. Technical supply personnel will refer to the interchangeability and substitutability file of FEDLOG for interchangeable or substitutable aircraft repair parts. This review can help prevent needless aircraft downtime by identifying on-hand interchangeable or substitute repair parts within the installation or command.

7-77. The technical supply section, PC, QC, and supported units coordinate their efforts when making aviation logistics management decisions. The following questions will assist in determining the total logistics requirement for a unit mission:

- How will operational pace/tempo affect maintenance operations?
- Is the Class IX (air) budget enough to sustain the unit operational pace/tempo?
- How will unscheduled maintenance requirements affect the maneuver company/troop operational pace/tempo?
- Is the unit flying aircraft based on the PC section recommended schedule in support of the aircraft flow chart?
- What TBO change components are coming due?
- What is the OR rate of the unit and what is the percentage of NMCS?
- Are serviceable repair parts available to fix an aircraft; if not, are they on-order?
- Are the document numbers assigned to these parts valid?
- Is the shipping and supply status issued against these document numbers valid?
- Has a coordinated effort been made to schedule aircraft flight hours to match scheduled maintenance and supply delivery dates?

AIRCRAFT REPAIR PARTS REQUISITION APPROVING AUTHORITY

7-78. Commanders are responsible for the accurate assignment of PDs. The commander will review or delegate this authority using a memorandum order or DA Form 1687 (Notice of Delegation of Authority-Receipt for Supplies). The PC OIC or maintenance officer/technician, operating under a delegation of authority from the commander, will certify high-priority parts requests IAW DA PAM 710-2-1.

7-79. Maintenance officers/technicians will refer to applicable TMs to verify the source, maintenance, and recoverability codes before authorizing high-priority aircraft repair part or component requests. The maintenance officer/technician will certify the request upon aircraft repair part verification. After request certification and approval, the technical supply personnel will process the repair parts request. Refer to section VII and the ULLS-A EUM for procedural guidance on using the technical supply module.

7-80. Maintenance officers/technicians enter their initials on automatically generated document registers or DA Form 2064 if using manual document registers for all high-priority UND "A" and "B" aircraft repair parts requests they have authorized. AR 725-50 and DA PAM 710-2-1 contain specific guidance.

7-81. Authorization to perform a higher level of maintenance is approved through an LOA. An LOA authorizes maintenance action and the ordering of repair parts. Technical supply personnel will not order repair parts for a higher-level maintenance action until the LOA request is approved.

ISSUE OF AIRCRAFT REPAIR PARTS

7-82. New aviation maintenance commanders will send a copy of assumption of command orders or appointing memorandum to each SSA and technical supply section at the ASC/AST providing supplies. These documents authorize the commander or accountable officer to request supplies. DA Form 1687 is used by the commander to designate additional responsible personnel to sign for and receive aircraft repair parts.

7-83. SSAs and technical supply sections at ASCs/ASTs will have assumption of command orders and DA Form 1687 on hand from supported aviation unit commanders before aircraft repair parts are released to aviation unit personnel. Logistics personnel will immediately notify requesting units when high-priority UND "A" and "B" repair parts are ready for pickup.

7-84. The AMC/AMT and ASC/AST use aircraft notebooks or logbooks to track release of aircraft repair parts to requesting units. Logbook headings should include, at a minimum, the following information:

- NSN.
- Nomenclature.
- Document number.
- Quantity.
- Date.
- Printed name and signature of the individual receiving supplies.

MANAGING UNIT DOCUMENT REGISTERS

7-85. Document registers are kept to prevent duplicating document numbers and assist in reconciliation or validation when required. Document registers are kept by each element within a unit authorized to submit supply requests to an SSA. An aviation maintenance unit will have at least two document registers, one maintained by technical supply and one by the unit supply room. The three types of document registers are nonexpendable, durable, and expendable. The nonexpendable register is kept at property book level and is used to record supply transactions for property book items (regardless of ARC) and nonexpendable components. The durable register is maintained at unit level as directed by the PBO and may be combined with the expendable document register, making an expendable/durable register. Expendable document registers are kept by each element within a unit authorized to submit supply requests to an SSA. Document registers are used to record supply transactions for expendable items. The PBO designates, by a memorandum, those elements within a unit authorized to request expendable supplies. The memorandum will specify the class of supply, DODAAC, and block of document serial numbers the element will use. Policies and procedures for maintaining the document register are outlined in DA PAM 710-2-1. Tools, repair parts, and items specifically in support of aviation maintenance operations can be ordered through the unit technical supply section; however, items other than Class IX (air) repair parts must be screened and approved by the appropriate level supervisor IAW the unit CSDP before submitting a requisition. Technical supply will process authorized and validated requests from all maintenance sections to include the unit supply room. Units order most Class II, IV, and VII items needed to support maintenance operations through their unit supply room.

SUPPLY STATUSES

7-86. When an aircraft repair part request is not filled by an SSA, a supply status is issued to the requesting unit. Supply statuses provide information to technical supply, support operations, and maintenance personnel and leaders for analysis to improve or expedite the requisition and replenishment process. The statuses of supply are shipment and exception. A shipment status displays an estimated or actual shipping date. An exception status displays a supply decision made by the supplier, such as a substitution, back-order, or request rejected. DA PAM 710-2-1 provides a complete listing of supply status codes. Supply statuses are provided by an SSA on automated forms or electronic media.

DOCUMENT NUMBER RECONCILIATIONS AND VALIDATIONS

7-87. According to AR 710-2, reconciliations are performed monthly and validations quarterly. The purpose of reconciliation is to keep due-in and due-out files synchronized, while validation ensures requests and requisitions are for legitimate requirements. Reconciliation/validation of open document registers is a process that begins when the first SOS provides its customers with a listing of due-outs requiring validation. The process continues by reconciling the supporting SSA records with the customer's validated requirements. SSA activities will provide supported units with an external SOP outlining the reconciliation and validation process. Customer validation and reconciliation procedures are evaluated during ARMS inspections and command inspection programs.

7-88. Technical and unit supply personnel will reconcile and validate open document numbers by:
- Checking TMs or applicable references to validate the authorization for aircraft repair parts or components.
- Checking if requested repair parts or components may have been obtained from another source.
- Determining if there have been any changes to PLL line items to justify an open document number listed in the assigned document register.

7-89. When items are identified as no longer required or excessive quantities are identified, requests for full or partial cancellation of the requirement are submitted to the SSA. The failure to validate a requisition for two consecutive cycles may result in the cancellation of the requisitions by the SSA, further delaying critical maintenance actions.

PROCESSING REQUISITION FOLLOW-UPS

7-90. According to AR 710-2, processing follow-ups on open document numbers is not mandatory. However, it is highly recommended to process follow-ups on all open high-priority document numbers:
- Follow-ups will not be submitted earlier than at least nine calendar days on PD 01 through 07 requests or when the estimated delivery date on the latest supply or shipment status has not been received.
- For PD 09 through 15 requests, follow-ups are conducted at the time of monthly reconciliation if supply or shipment status has not been received.
- If no status (supply or shipment) has been received, a follow-up document must be prepared.
- For high-priority PD 01 through 07 requests, contact the SSA and conduct a telephonic follow-up; for all others, submit the follow-up document to the SSA.

PROCESSING REQUISITION MODIFICATIONS

7-91. According to AR 710-2, modification documents are processed through an SSA when a—

- Document number issued against an airframe under an anticipated-NMCS has changed to an NMCS condition.
- Document number issued against an airframe under a routine priority UND "C" has changed to either an anticipated-NMCS or NMCS condition.

7-92. In addition to submitting modification documents when a shift in PDs has occurred, modification documents can also be submitted when project codes, required delivery dates, or advice codes have changed.

7-93. AOG high-priority requests are unique to aviation maintenance. Contact the assigned SSA or support operations section for guidance on modifying an aircraft parts request to an AOG request.

PROCESSING CANCELLATION OF REQUISITIONS

7-94. According to AR 710-2, a request for cancellation must be submitted when all or part of a quantity requested is no longer needed. Timely submission of cancellations will ensure the return of funds into the unit Class IX (air) budget. Technical supply personnel should know that a request for cancellation is not complete until verification is received from the SSA. Providing aviation customer units with a "BQ" status code indicates the cancellation of a specific document number has taken place. When verification is received, the following actions must be completed:

- When the entire quantity requested is cancelled, post the document register and enter "BQ" and the Julian date of the cancellation in the document register.
- When part of a quantity requested is canceled, post the document register and remove the "AC1," quantity, and Julian date of the cancellation document submitted to an SSA; enter "BQ," quantity canceled, and the Julian date of the cancellation verification in the document register.
- If no supply or shipment has been received, ensure 14 calendar days have passed before processing these requests; follow-ups on cancellation requests are not mandatory.

MANAGEMENT TOOLS

7-95. Proper use and control of the automated supply system will enhance supply customer support. Commanders at all levels, at a minimum, review the following on a regular basis:

- Average customer wait time; the average time between submissions of a customer request receipt of materiel.
- Percentage of PLL and ASL lines at zero balance.
- Percentage of PLL and ASL lines at zero balance with outstanding due out requisitions.
- Budget expenditure, remaining funds, and flying-hour program dollars relationships.
- Accuracy of readiness reports.
- Accuracy of reconciliation procedures.
- Requirement for repair parts needed against NMCS or anticipated-NMCS requirements or needed for normal replacement; document registers should also be checked to see if required items are on-order.
- Number of items above the authorized retention level (excess); excess items increase cost and reduce available storage space.

7-96. Unit document register entries should be compared to the latest customer due-out reconciliation list to ensure all requests are valid. Document register entries identified as not valid should be researched. If the part is still needed, the technical supply clerk should reorder it.

7-97. At the DMC, the following listings indicate the efficiency and effectiveness of the supply system:

- DS unit ASL lines with due outs.
- Controlled item requisition verification list.

- Cyclic input transaction statistics; delinquent count card list.
- Periodic material release order statistics list.
- Daily input-output statistics.
- Financial stockage list.
- Input transaction and error list.
- Receipt-not-due-in list.
- Stock status report.
- Supply performance report.
- Transactions register.
- ASL status review list.
- Excess report.

SECTION VI – EXCHANGE PRICING PROGRAM

7-98. Exchange pricing (EP) provides a system for returning reparable items to the supply system on a one-for-one relationship, a greater national-level visibility of reparable items, and reduces the number of financial transactions currently involved in the issue and turn-in process (by not granting credit for the return of unserviceable items). EP allows commanders to manage their budgets more effectively by eliminating the waiting period for expected credit of unserviceable items. EP publications and documents are available at http://www.ssf.army.mil/ssfweb/DesktopDefault.aspx?tabindex=5&tabid=25.

7-99. EP tracks issue and return transactions by DODAAC and primary NIIN. EP reports are accessed through logistics information warehouse (LIW) and will eventually migrate to GCSS-A.

7-100. Exchange price value, delta bill value, and serviceable exchange pricing return (SEPR) credit value (three new data elements) are added to the AMDF of the FEDLOG catalog data entries.

EXCHANGE PRICING ITEM ISSUE OR TURN-IN

7-101. An EP (in addition to standard pricing) will be established for Army managed NSNs with a maintenance repair code of F, H, D, K, and L on an existing or planned national repair program. The EP equals loaded repair cost plus cost recovery rate:

- Customer issued an EP item-
    - Army EP customer requisitions for Army managed NSNs with maintenance repair code F, H, D, K and L on an existing or planned national repair program (EP items) will be charged the EP.
    - Other Army and non-Army customer requisitions for EP items will be charged standard pricing.
    - Non-EP NSNs will have only a standard pricing and all customers will be charged standard pricing.
- Customer turn-in of an EP item-
    - If a serviceable turn-in is made against an EP item and it is matched to an issue, the customer will be issued SEPR, which equals EP minus cost recovery rate.
    - If a reparable component for an EP item is not returned within the delay days period following the requisition issue date, the customer will be assessed a Delta Bill (standard pricing minus EP).
    - There will be no unserviceable credit for Army EP customers.
    - Army customers not operating in an EP environment and non-Army customers will be given credit for serviceable and unserviceable turn-in of reparable items IAW current credit policies and/or Army Materiel Command Regulation (AMC-R) 700-99.

DELTA BILL

7-102.   A Delta Bill generates if any of these circumstances occur:

- An Army EP customer will get a Delta Bill if issued an EP item(s) and does not turn-in a reparable component within the delay period. An Army EP customer does not have to turn-in to the same SSA from which the component was issued. The customer can return the item(s) to any SSA funded by the Army working capital fund.
- An Army EP customer will get a Delta Bill if issued an EP item and subsequently matches that issue to a turn-in of an unserviceable condemned item.
- An Army EP customer will get a Delta Bill if issued an EP item and that issue matches a non-reparable/condemned transaction already in tracking.

7-103.   In all cases, the Delta Bill will be applied to the FY in which the original obligation occurred.

TRACKING

7-104.   The Army will use summary level tracking (DODAAC) and NIIN tracking for customer issues against customer returns. If a Delta Bill (obligation adjustment) is incurred, it will be made against the original issue document number. Headquarters, Department of the Army will designate by DODAAC, units as non-Army EP customers and those units will continue to pay standard price for EP items. Like all Army SARSS customers, non-Army EP customers will have their EP issues and turn-ins tracked and reported at the LIW.

7-105.   Under recoverable items tracking, the issue and turn-in of recoverable items, other than items already included in the EP process, are tracked using the same logic employed for tracking EP items. There are no financial implications to recoverable item tracking. The recoverable items reports displayed in LIW takes the place of the SARSS overage reparable item list/exception item list providing the Army with one information source to manage the recoverable item turn-in process.

SECTION VII – DISTRIBUTION MANAGEMENT CENTER

RESPONSIBILITIES

7-106.   The DMC is responsible for managing theater distribution and is the maintenance manager for deployed Army forces. It is the link between the deployed forces and the support base. The DMC may also support equipment of other services or multinational forces.

7-107.   The DMC will maintain management supervision over supply operations at the supply and maintenance activities. All operating SSAs are included, whether they are located in forward or rear areas. The Army supply system maintains its national stockage in CONUS and uses an expedient distribution and transportation system to provide resupply directly from the national sustaining base to individual SSAs worldwide, both in peacetime and during war. Distribution is accomplished by the DS system using surface transportation, sea lines of communication, and air lines of communication.

7-108.   A principal function of the DMC is to advise the command and its supported units on significant trends and deviations from established standards and to recommend necessary actions. The DMC—

- Serves as the central data collection for AV.
- Collects, maintains, analyzes, and acts on information presented in logistics and maintenance management information systems.
- Provides guidance and day-to-day planning for integrated maintenance and logistics management and policy.
- Provides SSAs with inventory management, stock control, and storage guidance.
- Provides for such services as the movement of assets/repair parts movement, cargo handling, and documentation.

- Synchronizes distribution functions through—
    - Distribution movement programs.
    - Asset management.
    - Routing information and policy.
    - Movement control distribution.

7-109. Typically, a DMC will function according to the type and level of sustainment it provides. A DMC provides sustainment to the following echelons: theater, division/corps, brigade, battalion/squadron, and company/troop.

7-110. The TSC is the highest sustainment agency for the theater Army. DCPs are a separate SRC and are a forward presence of the TSC. Their structure complements functions of the TSC. The DCP will support forces in its AO. At the theater and division/corps, distribution management is provided by the respective DMCs.

7-111. The TSC support operations DMC is broken down into several sections and branches. The supply and materiel readiness branches are essential for the aviation maintenance commander, officers/technicians, NCOICs, and assigned maintainers.

SUPPLY BRANCH

7-112. The theater-level DMC supply branch—
- Executes theater management of Classes I, II, III (packaged), V, VI, and VII.
- Performs as the expediter and problem solver on all issues involving the commodities it manages.
- Coordinates with the transportation integration branch for status on the distribution of commodities it manages.
- Provides direction for receiving, storing, and issuing theater stocks according to the combat commander support priorities.
- Passes requirements to the appropriate national inventory control point.
- Validates the requirements being considered for local procurement before forwarding them to the contracting directorate.
- Provides theater with on-hand visibility for major end items.
- Recommends priority of issue for major end items.
- Tracks and assists in the retrograde of major end items.
- Recommends cross-leveling priorities of major end items within the theater.

7-113. The ASC/AST SSA and the supporting DMC provide Class IX (air) supply to the CAB/ACS. The SSA receives, stores, issues, and turns in the parts. The materiel readiness branch of the DMC manages and accounts for the Class IX (air) inventory using demand history and command-directed actions.

7-114. SSAs are restricted to 10 days of Class IX (air) supply to prevent overstockage. The DMC determines the range of items physically stocked in the SSA/ASL. Selection is coordinated with the SSA officer/technician and ASC/AST commander. It is based on the unit PLL to be supported from the SSA and on the immediate mobility needs of forward support maintenance units.

MATERIEL READINESS BRANCH

7-115. The theater-level DMC materiel readiness branch—
- Coordinates Army maintenance functions and Class IX (air and ground) for the theater.
- Exercises staff supervision over aviation maintenance activities.
- Provides assistance on cross leveling of aviation equipment in the theater and recommends cross leveling of aviation repair parts.
- Passes requirements to the appropriate CONUS national inventory control point.

- Supervises the equipment modernization plan according to established policies.
- Operates SARSS and SAMS.
- Performs integrated materiel management for automotive equipment, tactical wheeled vehicles, general-purpose vehicles, and materiel handling equipment.
- Exercises staff supervision over maintenance operations and priorities according to the combat commander requirements.
- Coordinates the development of maintenance policy and programs.
- Conducts ongoing analysis of maintenance capabilities and requirements and makes suitable recommendations to the commander.
- Assists in determining appropriate positioning of maintenance assets to support customer units and provides technical data to the TSC.
- Recommends maintenance priorities, monitors theater maintenance operations, and provides maintenance management data and reports.

7-116.   The TSC support operations DMC materiel readiness branch consists of various sections such as ground maintenance, electronic maintenance, Class IX automation, and aviation.

7-117.   The aviation section performs materiel management for aeronautical and airdrop equipment and test equipment that is part of or used with assigned materiel. This equipment includes materiel for aircraft and airdrop, avionics, aircraft armament, and related test equipment. The aviation section, when directed, monitors and provides guidance on aviation maintenance activities.

SECTION VIII – UNIT LEVEL LOGISTICS SYSTEM–AVIATION (ENHANCED) FUNCTIONS

7-118.   The ULLS-A (E) is an inventory management tool allowing visibility of assets through all phases of supply and maintenance by Army and contractor personnel. To provide units with better AV, validation, accountability, and life-cycle management, the DOD introduced and standardized a means of direct part marking of all unique identifier items within the DOD supply system. Various unique identifier technologies will track designated assets in ULLS-A (E) throughout their lifecycle. ULLS-A (E) design accommodates—

- Unique identifier barcodes.
- RFID.
- Contact memory buttons.

7-119.   Assets within the supply system are processed into ULLS-A (E) at the point of receipt and may be marked with a bar code label with a unique identifier number, RFID tag, or contact memory button loaded with historical data. Contact memory button historical data may include—

- Asset modification status and history (as documented on DA Form 2408-5 [Equipment Modification Record]).
- Configuration (as documented on DA Form 2408-16 [Aircraft Component Historical Record]).
- Significant historical events (as documented on DA Form 2408-15 [Historical Record for Aircraft]).
- DA Form 2410 (Component Removal and Repair/Overhaul Record) component installation, removal, and repair data.
- Various aircraft component historical record data, as available (DA Form 2408-20 [Oil Analysis Log]).

7-120.   If the server is down, technical supply must be able to locate assets in its site inventory, manually submit orders, and back date orders into the ULLS-A (E), when available. By maintaining copies of specific reports and performing manual processes, the technical supply section is able to assist units in maintaining their operational pace/tempo until connectivity is restored.

TECHNICAL SUPPLY ROLE

7-121. The technical supply role is overall aviation maintenance repair parts and select tools acquisition, turn-in and oversight, including management of all PLL, bench stock, shop stock, non-shop stock, kits, and deployment packages. Technical supply also reviews specified reports associated with aviation maintenance actions for accuracy (document control register, commander exception report, and financial transaction listing).

7-122. The technical supply officer and NCOIC require command-appointed authority in writing to authorize high-priority designator (02 to 06) parts requests. Technical supply personnel will work closely with the PC section to improve overall accountability and operability.

TECHNICAL SUPPLY OPTIONS

7-123. Some technical supply options available to authorized users/personnel include the following:

- To do list.
- Asset gain (parts picked-up from higher-level supply support).
- Asset search.
- FEDLOG.
- Catalog (searches).
- Request a part.
- Technical supply menu.
- Document control register.
- Bench stock (assets).
- Non-stock (repair parts on-hand that are not demand supported).
- PLL.
- Shop stock (items).
- Reports (technical supply).

7-124. The things-to-do option allows technical supply users to view tasks requiring their attention. Actions requiring their attention may include requests awaiting processing by PC, 02 walk-through requisitions, pending issue, orders awaiting processing, orders awaiting submission, and replenishment required (PLL/bench stock).

7-125. The asset gain option provides users with the option to gain an asset for any catalog record currently residing in the database. If the catalog record is not part of the ULLS-A (E), it must be entered before processing any other action. Once the asset is gained, the user can search for the asset or view its last known physical location (for example, in-stock serviceable or unserviceable/awaiting repair).

7-126. The asset search option allows the user to locate the desired asset by part number or distinctive criteria. The distinctive criteria include serial number, NIIN, federal supply classification, and location.

7-127. The FEDLOG option allows the user to find pertinent information about a specific asset using FEDLOG data. FEDLOG data include part number, commercial and government entity code, and NSN.

7-128. The catalog option allows users to add records to the database and assign them to PLL, bench stock, or non-stock locations. The FEDLOG database can assist technical supply personnel with verifying repair parts or components information before adding records via the catalog option.

7-129. The request a part option enables users to request parts through a series of screens. Once the user fills in pertinent information, the system saves the record; once the record is saved, it goes through an approval process. This process is incorporated into the "things to do messages," to keep technical supply personnel advised of the latest information affecting the request cycle. Depending on approval and availability, requests are sent to technical supply for issuing or processing through SARSS when parts are not available. ULLS-A (E) provides users with resources that increase visibility and management of assets currently in the system. There are three means of requesting or ordering parts in ULLS-A (E):

- SARSS ordering-Current option.
- Commercial ordering-Near-future option.
- International Merchant Purchase Agreement Card (IMPAC) card-Future option.

7-130.   The technical supply menu option allows users to control basic functions associated with technical supply. The following are five options available to users:

- Order management.
- Turn-in management.
- Accept turn-in management.
- SARSS management.
- Material release order tracking links.

7-131.   The document control register option allows users to view/print all records contained in the document control register. This option enables technical supply personnel to better oversee and manage the ordering process.

7-132.   The bench stock option allows users to track and manage their assigned bench stock inventory. It also allows technical supply personnel to make changes to their minimum and maximum stockage levels based on use.

7-133.   The non-stock option allows users to track and manage their non-stock items. These items are managed by technical supply personnel and have not met the demand criteria according to DA PAM 710-2-1.

7-134.   The PLL option allows users to track and manage their PLL items. These items have met the demand criteria according to DA PAM 710-2-1.

7-135.   The shop stock option allows users to track and manage their shop stock items according to DA PAM 710-2-2.

7-136.   The reports option offers users several means for report generation. The database contains preformatted management reports, allowing users to generate custom reports. Reports generated by the ULLS-A (E) include the following:

- Bench-stock reports.
- Delinquency reports.
- Document control register reports.
- Priority 02 walk-through reports.
- Closed document control register.
- Commander exception reports.
- Commander financial transaction listing.
- Excess reports.
- Turn-in requests.
- Inventory reports.
- PLL reports.
- Request reports.
- Shop-stock reports.
- Zero-balance reports.
- Reconciliation reports.

REQUEST–APPROVAL–ORDER PROCESS

7-137.   The ULLS-A (E) technical supply request process requires the interaction of key personnel. The key personnel involved in the supply request process include the crew chief, the PC OIC, assistant PC OIC and NCOIC, and technical supply personnel (figure 7-1).

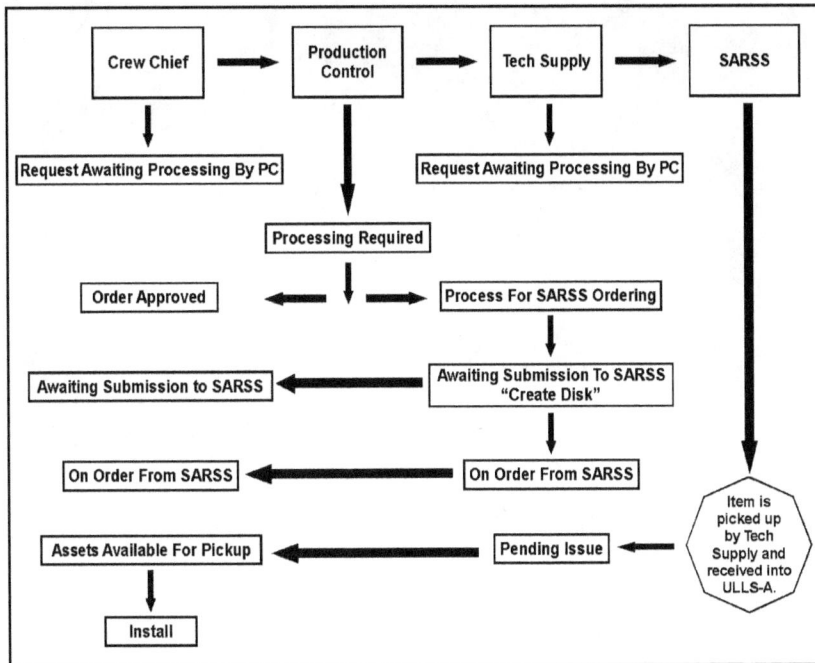

Figure 7-1. Repair parts request-approval-order process

7-138. The ULLS-A (E) request process is generally initiated by a crew chief due to a lack of parts. He or she begins a parts search for required parts; if the search is fruitless, he or she notifies PC and initiates a part request into ULLS-A (E). Once the required parts request is entered into the system, it requires an approval action from the PC office before technical supply personnel can process the request.

7-139. The ULLS-A (E) "Things-to-Do" option alerts PC that it has to review the parts request and verify that it can or should be ordered by technical supply personnel. Additionally, the PC officer or NCOIC must verify and approve the PD assigned to the repair parts request. While PC is verifying and validating the parts request for subsequent approval, the crew chief and technical supply will see "request awaiting processing by PC" when viewing their "Things-to-Do" option. After PC approves the repair parts request, the "Things-to-Do" alert of "request a waiting processing by PC" at the crew chief and technical supply stations is removed. At that time, technical supply will process the repair parts request into the SARSS. SARSS will process the request and submit an updated supply or shipping status back to the ULLS-A (E).

7-140. SARSS releases the needed part to the requesting unit, and the part is entered into the ULLS-A (E) as an asset gain. Once the part is processed into the system, it is ready for issue. At this time, the crew chief's "Things-to-Do" option will alert him or her with the following phrase: "assets available for pick up." Once the part is picked up, maintenance actions are ready to be resumed.

This page intentionally left blank.

Chapter 8

Airframe and Component Repair Platoons

This chapter provides aircraft repair platoon leaders and personnel with a "how-to" on internal management of aircraft and component repair, replacement, and maintenance functions. Maintenance and repair platoon leaders must manage their team, shop, and section operations daily to obtain optimum productivity from personnel and achieve unit MOE goals.

SECTION I – DUTIES AND RESPONSIBILITIES

PLATOON LEADER

8-1.   Aviation branch lieutenants serve as aircraft maintenance and CRP leaders in AMCs and AMTs. Due to complements of over 100 Soldiers and large equipment hand receipts, Aviation branch captains serve as platoon leaders in the ASC and AST.

8-2.   The platoon leader is responsible for internal management of all maintenance functions and activities assigned to his or her platoon. He or she ensures maintenance personnel are trained on the most current assigned maintenance equipment and prepared to operate in any operational environment.

8-3.   The platoon leader also coordinates all actions, internal and external, regarding assigned aircraft, subsystems, and component maintenance

Contents

work orders. He or she is responsible for administrative and personnel actions affecting assigned personnel. He or she manages assigned sections/shops, to include all maintenance procedures performed by aircraft and component repair personnel.

8-4.   The platoon leader coordinates priority of work in support of the MOE goals in concert with PC guidance. Work-order priority assignments are determined by the PC OIC, assistant PC OIC, or NCOIC. PC personnel coordinate any changes of these priorities with the platoon leader. The platoon leader ensures QC inspections occur for all completed maintenance.

MAINTENANCE OFFICER/TECHNICIAN

8-5.   The subordinate sections in the CRPs are led by 151A series warrant officer OICs. The maintenance officer/technician is a 151A assigned to the ASC/AST and AMC/AMT. He or she is a graduate of the aviation maintenance course and the 151A certification course. At the ASC/AST and AMC/AMT, the armament or systems repair section is led by a 151AE, a graduate from the armament technician (AH-64/OH-58D) course. Section maintenance officers are directly responsible for the internal management operations of all shops/sections assigned within the CRPs.

8-6.   The section maintenance officer/technician coordinates work-order assignments based on priority of work assigned by their platoon leader in support of PC OIC guidance. He or she manages all shop, armament, and repair section maintenance procedures involving aircraft equipment systems, subsystems, associated components, and weapons platforms. In an armament or systems repair section, he or she supervises troubleshooting, isolation, and testing procedures of weapons platforms malfunctions in assigned aircraft armament systems.

8-7.   At the ASC/AST, the maintenance officer/technician manages shop, armament, and repair section maintenance procedures listed previously. In addition, he or she manages modification and overhaul of aircraft LRUs and components when directed by ASAMs, TBs, MWOs, and higher headquarters. He or she supervises the administration of all required forms and records to ensure compliance with all pertinent regulations.

8-8.   The maintenance officer/technician distributes work and tracks all high-priority work requests to completion, including quality assurances of finished maintenance actions within the CRP. He or she coordinates for MOCs and MTFs and supports recovery/evacuation of aircraft when required. He or she notifies the platoon leader when a work stoppage has occurred on a high-priority work request due to a lack of parts. The maintenance officer/technician is responsible for engaging technical supply and PC in locating NMCS repair parts and components to include horizontal and vertical searches of critical aircraft repair parts. He or she also reviews weekly manhour reports with section chiefs.

PLATOON SERGEANT

8-9.   The aviation maintenance commander and first sergeant select the platoon sergeant based on skills, qualifications, and experience. Generally, the NCOIC will possess a 15-series MOS from an MOS-awarding TRADOC school and a skill-level 40 senior NCO.

8-10.   The platoon sergeant is responsible to the ARP/CRP platoon leader and maintenance officer/technician. He or she provides guidance and mentorship to assigned repair personnel on troubleshooting procedures for all aircraft systems, subsystems, associated weapons systems, and component repair.

8-11.   The platoon sergeant is responsible for the status of equipment on-hand and any problems that arise affecting the overall maintenance and repair operation of the sections. He or she ensures all maintenance actions and procedures are performed according to applicable aircraft TMs. He or she manages and coordinates all GSE user qualification and utilization. He or she provides guidance on procedures to complete and file required forms and records them to ensure compliance with all applicable regulations.

8-12.   The platoon sergeant ensures that platoon and shop personnel are familiar with the latest aircraft and component TMs and changes affecting maintenance and repair procedures. He or she coordinates all maintenance support and actions in the absence of the platoon leader and the maintenance officer/technician. He or she assists and advises the platoon leader and maintenance officer ensuring personnel are trained on the most current assigned maintenance equipment and prepared to operate in any operational environment.

SECTION SERGEANT

8-13.   The section sergeant supervises and assigns work within the section. He or she ensures required publications are on-hand and all applicable changes are promptly posted to support the repair functions of his assigned section. He or she coordinates all maintenance actions with the maintenance officer/technician or platoon sergeant to maintain optimum workflow of all assigned maintenance requests.

8-14.   The section sergeant is familiar with the capabilities of his or her assigned section personnel, subordinates, and equipment. He or she ensures subordinates are trained beyond AIT experience and capable of functioning within the unit. He or she manages the workload according to availability of resources and equipment.

8-15.   The section sergeant informs the platoon leader, maintenance officer/technician in the CRP, and platoon sergeant of any significant delay (maintenance, equipment, aircraft repair parts, or personnel) hindering the completion of any maintenance work requests.

8-16. The section sergeant monitors all NMCS work order requests to ensure assigned work orders have valid document numbers and supply statuses. He or she is responsible for administrative management procedures, to include filing of all aircraft required forms and records according to AR 25-400-2. He or she provides senior maintenance leaders with work-order statuses and updates.

8-17. In the CRP, the shop section sergeant reviews the shop section summary with the maintenance officer/technician weekly. He or she is responsible for maintaining and submitting a weekly manhour report to the PC office on a prearranged schedule dictated by the PC OIC.

REPAIRERS

8-18. Repairers are responsible for following all notes, warnings, and cautions listed in the TMs when performing component repairs and maintenance procedures on assigned maintenance work orders. They maintain 100 percent accountability and serviceability of all assigned tools and equipment. Personnel are familiar with all applicable aircraft maintenance manuals and corresponding changes as they are posted.

SECTION II – PROCEDURES

INSPECTIONS AND REPAIR PROCEDURES

8-19. Maintenance personnel must use only current, applicable aircraft and systems maintenance manuals to conduct inspections and troubleshooting procedures on aircraft systems or subsystems. Using current maintenance TMs ensures maintenance procedures meet current requirements. Troubleshooting of affected aircraft systems and subsystems must take place before any further maintenance action or aircraft component repair begins. Thorough and accurate troubleshooting of affected aircraft systems and subsystems narrows the scope and magnitude of maintenance and repairs, saving manhours and unnecessary component replacement.

8-20. Maintenance personnel conducting approved and authorized repairs of aircraft components must strictly adhere to established repair methodologies. These methodologies are outlined in applicable aircraft maintenance TMs.

8-21. Maintenance personnel also will use only authorized tools when conducting aircraft maintenance. Maintenance supervisors will inventory toolboxes at least monthly in the active component. ARNG and Army Reserve units will perform this inventory quarterly. Maintenance personnel assigned toolboxes will inventory their toolbox after each maintenance task to help control FOD.

8-22. A supervisor inventory is not required when toolboxes are placed in administrative storage. Corrosion control measures must be completed to ensure tools remain in a serviceable condition while in administrative storage. Annual inventories of toolboxes in administrative storage must be completed IAW AR 710-2 and DA PAM 710-2-1. Leaders will conduct replenishment operations as required following each inventory to replace missing or unserviceable tools and components.

8-23. The PC and QC OIC must seek authorization from the next higher level of maintenance support when a component repair falls out of the accepted guidelines as outlined in aircraft TMs. LOAs approving maintenance procedures or component repairs not outlined in aircraft TMs are granted to the repairer through the AMCOM LAR. AMCOM LARs can grant an LOA to the ASC/AST to perform limited, specific sustainment maintenance action according to the MAC.

8-24. While AMCOM has the authority to approve nonstandard maintenance procedures, component repairs, or authorize deviations from standard aircraft TMs the potential for errors can occur. As a result, maintenance personnel should proceed with caution when performing nonstandard, AMCOM-approved maintenance procedures or component repairs. During any portion of maintenance activity, personnel should cease the maintenance action and seek further guidance or clarification if any approved procedure does not appear to generate the desired result.

PROCESSING WORK REQUESTS

8-25. The PC office is the focal point for processing customer, intershops, or higher-level maintenance support work orders. All supported companies must initiate work orders when seeking maintenance support. The maintenance work order must be processed and accepted by the PC office before maintenance support or component repair can commence.

8-26. Maintenance work orders are authorized by the PC OIC and include a PD. Once accepted by the PC office, the PC clerk immediately distributes the work orders to the supporting platoon. Other than 01- through 03-PD maintenance, work orders are submitted to the corresponding platoon in-box or given to the shop/section maintenance technician/NCOIC according to the unit SOP after the PC meeting.

8-27. The maintenance technician or NCOIC routinely checks with the PC office for work orders. Work orders assigned to the platoon or section are processed by the automated system or logged into the platoon work order document register (DA Form 2405, when used) and distributed to the corresponding shop/section chiefs.

8-28. Once a work order is assigned to a shop, the shop/section chief ensures all necessary files, forms, and records are accurate and complete according to applicable references and publications. He or she verifies all repair parts needed to complete a maintenance procedure or component repair are on-hand or on-order. He or she must coordinate the use of special tools required to complete a job. Once all requirements to complete a job are met, he or she assigns the work to shop/section personnel.

8-29. Platoon leaders frequently receive work order status reports to ensure timely progress and identification of serious delays requiring additional resources. The platoon leader ensures the platoon meets required timelines and command MOE associated with work-order backlog reduction to sustain combat power across the brigade and ACS.

> *Note.* Work never begins on a component or item to be repaired unless it is accompanied by all required forms and records or otherwise directed by the PC OIC/NCOIC. DA Form 2410s and other historical records are maintained in the AMC/AMT QC office.

8-30. The AMC/AMT PC office initiates and generates all higher-level maintenance support work orders to include ASC/AST -level component repair. The AMC/AMT PC clerk delivers the work orders seeking maintenance support to the ASC/AST PC office.

8-31. For component repairs work orders, the PC office submits the unserviceable component with an accompanying work order to the supporting ASC/AST. In addition, the AMC/AMT PC office ensures unserviceable components meet the standards set forth in the ASC/AST external SOP before submitting the work order and unserviceable component to the ASC/AST PC office.

> *Note.* The PC clerk verifies the unserviceable component has all required documentation to include DA Form 2410 (if required) and unserviceable (reparable) tag/label (DD Form 1577-2/DD Form 1577-3 [Unserviceable (Reparable) Label Materiel]) with the corresponding TI stamp or signature. All components are cleaned before being submitted to the ASC/AST PC office. If the component is listed on the published ASC/AST RX list, then the request for issue and request for turn-in documents accompany the part to obtain a serviceable component.

AIRCRAFT TROUBLESHOOTING

8-32. The overarching principle of conducting on-site maintenance procedures and component repair as far forward as possible on the battlefield remains unchanged. Maintainers accomplish their mission by using advanced diagnostics, prognostics via embedded sensors, and troubleshooting techniques to diagnose the major component fault, at which point the component is either repaired or replaced at the breakdown site.

8-33. When the operational environment is not conducive to maintenance operations at the breakdown site, aircraft systems, subsystems, and associated component troubleshooting procedures, repairs, and replacement are conducted at a predetermined aviation maintenance support assembly area.

8-34. QC, PC, platoon leaders, maintenance officers/technicians, maintenance personnel, and when appropriate, aircraft technical representatives/contractors lend their expertise to identifying system, subsystem, or component malfunctions using accepted and by-the-book troubleshooting techniques.

8-35. When all standard published troubleshooting procedures have failed to yield an accepted and valid diagnosis for a malfunctioning system, subsystem, or component, nonstandard troubleshooting procedures must be explored. The PC OIC coordinates all troubleshooting procedures not listed in aircraft TMs and receives approval from the next higher maintenance authority (such as ASCs/ASTs, sustainment-level maintenance facilities, aircraft PMs, AMCOM, and CECOM) before proceeding. Approval for nonstandard troubleshooting and repair procedures are obtained from an AMCOM or a CECOM LAR with an LOA.

COMPONENT REPAIR PLATOON CONSIDERATIONS

8-36. The CRP performs repairs on the subcomponents and structure of the aircraft, as well as subsystems; whereas, the ARP performs component removal, replacement, and scheduled inspection operations. These platoons are complementary in their missions; however, the volume of work orders in the CRP will be significantly higher due to a higher volume of and time-expended on component repair of LRUs compared to the removal and reinstallation of the LRU on the aircraft. This higher volume requires a correspondingly larger organization than the ARP with additional leaders and technicians to delegate, manage, and lead operations. Additionally, the ULLS-A (E) shop's functions remain the same but will receive expanded engagement and utilization in the CRP directly in proportion to the higher number of work orders.

SECTION III – REPAIR POLICIES

MAINTENANCE FORMS AND RECORDS POLICIES

8-37. Entering accurate and descriptive data on all forms and records ensures that personnel receive a safe and airworthy aircraft. Personnel at all levels of maintenance, including DOD contract support, have an equal stake in maintaining accurate aircraft maintenance forms and records. QC and TIs ensure that aircraft maintenance forms and records comply with applicable publications and regulations.

Note. Refer to DA PAM 738-751 for regulatory guidance when filling out aircraft forms and records. Refer to AR 25-400-2 for filing and disposition of DA forms and records. Refer to chapter 7 for additional guidance on forms and records.

COORDINATING MAINTENANCE ACTIONS AND REPAIRS

8-38. Supported maneuver units request maintenance support for their assigned aircraft through the AMC/AMT PC office. Supported units indicate the need for scheduled and unscheduled maintenance support according to the AMC/AMT maintenance SOP. The supported unit alerts PC as soon as an aircraft system or subsystem malfunctions or the aircraft is grounded with an "X" condition.

8-39. As soon as the PC office is alerted to a malfunction, aircraft grounding condition, or an NMC aircraft, the PC clerk will generate an internal maintenance work order in ULLS-A (E) or on a DA Form 2407, record the tracking or work order number, and/or enter the work order on DA Form 2405. The maintenance work order is internally assigned to a shop or section.

Note. All required aircraft forms and records used for maintenance support are hard copies or electronically formatted, generated by the current STAMIS of record.

8-40. AMC/AMT submits maintenance work requests to the ASC/AST for maintenance support on DA Form 2407. Requests for maintenance support include but are not limited to:

- Required ASC/AST maintenance procedures and repairs as dictated in applicable TMs.
- Repairs beyond the AMC/AMT prescribed ability or capacity.
- Applications of MWOs, SOF messages, ASAMs, or TBs while aircraft or components are work ordered to the ASC/AST activity.
- Fabrication or assembly of items.
- Request for repair of aircraft components, LRUs, modules, assemblies, and subassemblies.
- Request for maintenance support from another maintenance activity or supporting unit.

8-41. All troubleshooting procedures are performed and properly documented by AMC/AMT maintenance personnel on DA Form 2408-13-1, DA Form 2408-13-2, or DA Form 2408-13-3 before work ordering an aircraft to ASC/AST for maintenance support. After completion of all applicable forms and records and verification by QC, the AMC/AMT PC OIC coordinates the maintenance request through the ASC/AST PC office.

8-42. When maintenance support is requested from an ASC/AST, all uncorrected faults on DA Forms 2408-13-1, 2408-14, and 2408-18 requiring ASC/AST-level maintenance are annotated on DA Form 2407. When the DA Form 2407 has been accepted by the ASC/AST, the aircraft equipment logbook, keys, automated system of record laptop (complete with all accessories), weight-and-balance records, and historical records accompany the aircraft. The exception to this requirement is when ASC/AST conducts on-site maintenance.

AIRCRAFT COMPONENT REMOVAL POLICIES

8-43. Removing an aircraft component can render an aircraft PMC or NMC. When an aircraft system, subsystem, or component is found unserviceable, unit maintenance personnel follow established guidelines and prescribed aircraft TMs when removing unserviceable components. Maintenance personnel will not remove a component without approval from the PC OIC or, in his absence, the PC NCOIC, except when the removal of a component is called for in the execution of a maintenance task and essential to gain access to another component with the intent being to return that item to the original position.

8-44. If, after extensive troubleshooting, an aircraft component is found to be unserviceable, the PC office coordinates all maintenance actions. Maintenance actions include coordination for QC assistance and oversight when maintenance personnel remove an unserviceable aircraft component. In addition to generating associated maintenance work requests to remove unserviceable aircraft components, the PC office coordinates sustainment actions with the technical supply officer to procure a serviceable replacement component.

8-45. The QC office and personnel have direct oversight for the accuracy of entries made on all corresponding aircraft forms and records. The entries correspond to all actions taken to remove an unserviceable aircraft component. QC personnel actions include comprehensive FOD inspections of affected aircraft system or subsystem areas where an unserviceable component was removed.

8-46. If there are no serviceable replacements in the logistics system, check the corresponding aircraft TM source, maintenance, and recoverability code to see if the component is reparable. If the component is reparable, the PC office immediately work orders the item to the ASC/AST on a high-priority maintenance work request.

8-47. Unserviceable components, once removed from an airframe, are thoroughly cleaned, preserved, inspected by a TI, tagged, and packaged. DD Form 1577-2 is filled out and attached to the unserviceable component. The unserviceable component and DD Form 1577-2 undergo a technical inspection by a qualified TI before the unserviceable component is work ordered to an ASC/AST.

TEST, MEASUREMENT, AND DIAGNOSTIC EQUIPMENT REPRESENTATIVE

8-48. Leaders ensure personnel use only prescribed, serviceable, and functional TMDE as outlined in aircraft TMs. When a maintenance procedure requires the use of calibrated items, the calibrated item must be within its calibration window.

8-49. The ARP and CRP platoon leader must appoint a platoon calibration program representative. The representative monitors the platoon TMDE and works directly with the unit TMDE coordinator in the ASES to ensure all calibrations operations are performed to standard. He or she coordinates with all platoon sections to ensure timely submission of items requiring calibration before items are overdue and rendered unusable. He or she completes and maintains the platoon master listing to include a comprehensive review for accuracy and serviceability status. He or she also requests platoon level approval to submit items requiring priority calibration.

SPECIAL TOOLS

8-50. The ARP and CRP utilize special tools to accomplish scheduled and unscheduled maintenance. Leaders will develop a list of required special tools by type, source, class, price, quantity on-hand, quantity short and funding required as defined in chapter 3 to support every aircraft, system, or component supported by the platoon. Leaders will energize the acquisition process through the commander, supply room, and technical supply to achieve a 100 percent fill of the platoon special tool kit. All special tools will be tracked in PBUSE and inventoried at least annually and during change of hand receipt holder inventories. Leaders will ensure maintenance and serviceability of all special tools in support of the unit MOE. Refer to chapter 3 for detailed information on special tools.

MAINTENANCE REFERENCE AND PUBLICATION LIBRARIES

8-51. Although the master reference and publications library is located in the QC section, every section, shop, and platoon responsible for conducting aircraft maintenance repairs and procedures is authorized a reference and publications library. Every section, shop, and platoon NCOIC is responsible for researching and verifying technical publications requirements for his assigned maintenance and component repair areas. NCOICs are responsible for ensuring their reference and publications libraries are current and updated with the latest published changes. Timely updates of assigned reference and publications libraries are essential to proper maintenance practices. NCOICs must also train their assigned maintenance personnel in posting reference/publications changes. A fielded change not promptly posted makes that corresponding TM unusable.

> *Note.* If a maintenance repair or procedure in an aircraft TM is suspected of an error, submit a DA Form 2028. The section, shops, and platoon NCOIC is responsible for coordinating all DA Form 2028 submission requirements with QC personnel.

8-52. Assigned maintenance personnel are responsible for familiarizing themselves with the appropriate TMs to include the latest changes, before conducting maintenance procedures. Section, shops, and platoon NCOICs monitor assigned maintenance personnel compliance with aircraft TM familiarization using an updated and current familiarization record. By-the-book maintenance not only includes having the corresponding aircraft TMs open but also using them to conduct maintenance procedures.

> *Note.* Refer to AR 25-30 for posting reference and publications requirements.

SECTION IV – SCHEDULED MAINTENANCE OPERATIONS

8-53. Recurring requirements for maintenance allow prediction and early planning. Since these recurring requirements are fixed by regulation, leaders can shape their organizations to efficiently perform these operations and reduce delays. Enhance scheduled maintenance operations by—

- Ensuring special tools are serviceable and on-hand in sufficient quantities.
- Isolating team personnel from duty rosters for the duration of the scheduled event.
- Coordinating with technical supply to ensure sufficient Class IX (air) is on-hand.
- Reviewing the inspection procedure prior to aircraft induction and adjusting sequencing to improve efficiency if applicable (units may submit adjustments for consideration on DA Form 2028).
- Setting measureable progress goals and ensuring on-time completion of daily tasks.
- Tracking phases by percent inspection complete/percent maintenance or tasks completed such as 65 percent inspection/25 percent maintenance.
- Coordinating with the ASES leader for support to prevent unavailability due to ASES internal scheduled or unscheduled requirements.

SECTION V – UNIT LEVEL LOGISTICS SYSTEM-AVIATION (ENHANCED) PROCEDURES

8-54. The ULLS-A (E) back shops program provides a comprehensive web-based submitting and tracking system for work orders. This system allows PC to accept and reject work orders, track work orders, check progress and statuses of work orders for maneuver units, and submit work orders to support units. Back shops accept the work orders from PC and, if necessary, submit an inter-shop work order to the appropriate shop.

Note. Refer to the ULLS-A (E) EUM for additional user information and procedural guidance.

8-55. The back shops select role screen is displayed with a drop-down menu to allow selection of—

- Production control administrator (unit production control)-back shops (PCA-BS).
- Production control user (supported unit user)-back shops (PCU-BS).
- Shop chief-back shops (SC-BS).
- Shop technician-back shops (ST-BS).
- Technical inspector-back shops (TI-BS).

PRODUCTION CONTROL ADMINISTRATOR-BACK SHOPS

8-56. Accessing the PCA-BS allows the PC administrator to—

- Create, view, and check the status of DA Form 2407 (work order).
- View the comments added by the unit submitting the work order.
- Submit the work order from the units to the back shops for repair.
- Authorize personnel generate an inter-shop work order.

8-57. Once the work order is sent to the appropriate shop, the PC administrator can view the DA Form 2407 to ensure work is done and status of the ongoing maintenance is according to the TMs. To accept the work order, the PCA-BS clicks on the "accept" button.

8-58. Once the work order is accepted internally by the back shops and a subsequent status is assigned, authorized personnel, to include PC, can view the latest status assigned to the work order by clicking on the "status history" button. If the same work order is in need of additional internal support from another shop or section, an internal work order is generated requesting support by clicking the "create" button.

Once the internal work order is generated, authorized personnel view the internal work order by clicking on the "inner shops" button.

PRODUCTION CONTROL USER-BACK SHOPS

8-59. The PC user is the supported unit PC representative. The PC user can only view work orders and corresponding statuses of work orders submitted to the support unit. The PCU-BS has a screen so he or she can highlight the work order sent to the ASC/AST unit.

SHOPS CHIEF-BACK SHOPS

8-60. The SC-BS ensures all back shops are operating correctly and safely. He or she works with PC to ensure work orders are processed and tracked to completion. The SC-BS also ensures shops are working according to all prescribed TMs and other publications.

8-61. Once a work order is accepted from the PCA-BS and goes to a specific shop, the SC-BS clicks on DA Form 2407 to view the work order and see which shop it has gone to by clicking on the "inner shops" button.

SHOPS TECHNICIAN-BACK SHOPS

8-62. The ST-BS is the shops technician doing the work. Once the ST-BS receives the work order from the PCA-BS, he or she will review it to ensure all appropriate blocks are completed.

8-63. The ST-BS will scroll to the bottom of the work order and click in Section IV, Task Requirements Data; the screen will display task requirements of DA Form 2407. The ST-BS will scroll to the top of the screen and select "add task." The "add task" fields have the following data input points:

- Quantity to be repaired.
- Work center.
- Failure code.
- Man-hours projected.
- Man-hours spent.
- Task description.
- Action code.
- Task number.
- Personal identification (PID) assignment.

TECHNICAL INSPECTOR-BACK SHOPS

8-64. The TI-BS ensures maintenance is performed correctly and according to prescribed TMs. To select the TI-BS, the user clicks on the role bar on the left side of the screen, scrolls down to the bottom, and selects TI-BS. After selection, a screen appears displaying work orders awaiting inspection.

8-65. When the TI-BS is notified, he or she inspects the maintenance performed and completes the appropriate blocks of DA Form 2407.

This page intentionally left blank.

Chapter 9

Quality Control

This chapter provides QC personnel with a "how-to" for identifying and reviewing standards of repair, overhaul, modification, SOF, and other required maintenance functions. This chapter also provides QC personnel with an overview of QC management operations procedures. Technical inspections are the command system of checks and balances. These inspections ensure high-quality maintenance and safety of Army aircraft.

SECTION I – DUTIES AND RESPONSIBILITIES

QUALITY CONTROL OFFICER-IN-CHARGE

9-1.   The QC OIC is selected, on orders, by the AMC/AMT or ASC/AST commander based on skills, qualifications, and experience. It is preferred that the QC OIC be a graduate of the aviation maintenance officer and MP course. He or she is responsible for the internal management of the QC section, to include quality assurance of all work performed by TIs. The QC OIC coordinates priority of work with the unit PC OIC and QC NCOIC. The QC OIC executes the ULLS-A (E) unit training program.

Contents

QUALITY CONTROL NONCOMMISSIONED OFFICER-IN-CHARGE

9-2.   The QC NCOIC is selected, on orders, by the AMC/AMT or ASC/AST commander based on skills, qualifications, and experience. Generally, he or she is one of the senior maintenance NCOs assigned to the unit. Preferably, the QC NCOIC is a graduate of the senior leader course. He or she is directly responsible for the operational management of the QC section. He or she coordinates and establishes priority of work with the QC OIC. In the absence of the OIC, the NCOIC performs all duties of the QC OIC. He or she distributes the work and supervises the TIs for quality assurance of work assigned. The QC NCOIC also coordinates the efforts of the QC section.

QUALITY CONTROL TECHNICAL INSPECTORS

9-3.   TIs are selected, on orders, by the unit commander based on skills, qualifications, and experience. Preferably, TIs are advanced leader course graduates. They are responsible to the QC OIC, QC NCOIC, and ultimately, the aviation maintenance commander for quality assurance. TIs are placed on orders signed by the first lieutenant colonel in the chain of command. This procedural step enables flexibility in the inspection of aircraft across the entire unit.

9-4.   TIs are under the operational control, not supervision, of the PC officer. The maintenance officer establishes priorities for TI work assignments but does not supervise the work. The QC OIC or NCOIC distributes the work and supervises the TIs to meet the PC officer operational maintenance requirements. TIs serve as primary instructors for ULLS-A (E) training program.

9-5. The QC OIC or NCOIC will serve as the TI's rater. If the QC section does not have an OIC or NCOIC, the assigned commander rates the TI. This rating scheme allows TIs to remain objective in their quality assurance duties and ensures the crew's overall safety remains their goal.

9-6. TIs are the commander-designated representatives in aircraft SOF areas and responsible for:

- Airworthiness of the aircraft.
- Component and shop inspections.
- Maintaining the master reference library.
- Reviewing publications, forms, and records for currency and accuracy.
- Ensuring all performed maintenance procedures comply with TMs and applicable references.

Note. Most aviation maintenance contracts require technical inspection completion as part of any procedure. Ensuring contractor TIs possess appropriate certification to inspect aircraft maintenance tasks is challenging when complying with ARs. The entire maintenance team, to include COR and GFR, will agree on and publish the requirements baseline for contractor TIs and determine validation and approval procedures to support their contractor mission.

SECTION II – MANAGEMENT

DELEGATION OF AUTHORITY ORDERS

9-7. Delegation of authority orders for performing specific duties must be approved by the unit commander. This authority is designated, in writing, by memorandum. The memorandum will state the functions, responsibilities, and duration of assigned duties.

9-8. Completed delegation of authority orders (memorandums) are maintained on file until revoked, rescinded, or no longer applicable. Units will maintain orders (memorandums) on:

- Commander (assumption of command orders).
- TIs (DA PAM 738-751).
- Limited TIs (DA PAM 738-751).
- MEs and MPs (AR 95-1 and TM 1-1500-328-23).
- Unit safety officer and NCO (AR 385-10).
- Personnel signing equipment and component condition tags for turning in components and equipment (aircraft maintenance only) (DA PAM 738-751).
- Personnel authorizing evacuation of aircraft with a grounding condition (X) status for a one-time evacuation mission (DA PAM 738-751).
- Personnel authorized to change an aircraft with a grounding condition (X) status to (—) status for the performance of a one-time test flight (DA PAM 738-751).
- Personnel inspecting aircraft first-aid kits (TM 1-1500-328-23).
- Weight-and-balance technician (AR 95-1).
- Technical supply officer.
- ASES OIC/NCOIC.
- TMDE support coordinator and alternate (AR 750-43).
- Publications officer or NCO (DA PAM 25-33).
- CPC program monitor (TM 1-1500-328-23).
- FOD prevention officer and NCO (AR 385-10).
- Personnel responsible for the FOD prevention plan (AR 385-10).
- AOAP monitor (TB 43-0211).
- Unit maintenance (PC) officer (AR 750-1).

- Controlled exchange officer (AR 750-1).
- Records management officer (AR 25-400-2).
- ULLS-A (E) administrator.

9-9. Army publications affecting the above designations are reviewed periodically for changes and revisions. Additions, deletions, or modifications of orders are made at that time.

LIMITED TECHNICAL INSPECTOR APPOINTMENT

9-10. The commander may appoint a Soldier on limited TI orders who has not met the recommended requirements IAW paragraph 9-3. The TI limitations are annotated on the memorandum and the Soldier is required to remain within the written limits.

COMMANDERS TECHNICAL INSPECTOR INTEGRATION

9-11. Commanders should interview or assess TI candidates to ensure proper integration into the unit QC operation. This is especially useful during high turnover or high tempo operations and provides the commander with a standard of reference when assigning duties to newly assigned or recommended TI candidates. This allows commanders to match personnel with the proper amount of TI responsibility relative to their skills and experience. Figures 9-1 and 9-2 (page 9-4) depict a sample TI integration memorandum.

DEPARTMENT OF THE ARMY
B Company, 100th Aviation Support Battalion
51st Infantry Division
Fort Spanner, SC 12345

ABCD-EF-G-COB DATE: ____________

MEMORANDUM FOR RECORD

SUBJECT; TI Request, Integration and Approval for Orders Generation

1. Platoon: ____________ Section: ____________

MOS: ____________

Major Components: ____________

2. Individual being recommended:

Name: ____________ (Last, First MI.) Rank: ____________

SSN: ____________ MOS: ____________

3. Why needed: ____________

4. Reason(s) for recommending this individual: ____________

5. Specified limitations: ____________

6. Years worked in MOS? ____________

7. How long assigned to this unit? ____________

8. How long as an NCO? ____________

9. Previous leadership positions? ____________

Figure 9-1. Sample TI integration memorandum-front page

ABCD-EF-G-COB DATE: ____________

SUBJECT: TI Request, Integration and Approval for Orders Generation

10. ALC? Yes No When Graduated? ____________

11. How many phases/PPMs completed? ________ Number led? ________

12. How many months of AMC/AMT service?________ ASC/AST service?________

13. Have you served in a flight company/troop?________ How long? ________

14. Have you served as a flight crew member?________ How many hours? ________

15. Previously a TI in a quality control shop? ________ What unit?________

How long? ________ TI start date: ________ TI end date: ________

16. Have you generated a workorder recall from a customer unit?

Yes No

If yes, explain:

____

____

____

____

Sponsor TI: Rank: ______ Last, First Middle Name: ____________________

MOS: ____________ Sponsor TI initials: ____________

17. Request/recommendation above completed: ____________ Sponsor TI Initials

18. Test Part 1 (no book) completed: ____________ Sponsor TI Initials

19. Test Part 2 (open book) completed: ____________ Sponsor TI Initials

20. Test Part 3 (filling out forms) completed: ____________ Sponsor TI Initials

21. 20 day follow along with sponsor TI: ____________ Sponsor TI Initials Date completed: ____________

22. Weight and balance/aircraft weighing practical test completed: ____________

23. SOP, DA Pam 738-751 read and understood: ____________ Sponsor TI Initials

24. Publications library operations familiarization: ____________ Sponsor TI Initials

25. Comments from sponsor TI: ____

____

____

____

____

Produce orders: Yes No

JOHN Q. PUBLIC
MAJ, AV
Commanding

Figure 9-2. Sample TI integration memorandum-back page

PROCEDURES

9-12. QC of a completed maintenance procedure with the appropriate logbook and form entries by the TI completes the maintenance cycle; these procedures are considered a management function. This process ensures maintenance is performed according to maintenance manuals for specific aircraft. QC management is coordinated with PC and matched to the maintenance workload to maintain maximum productivity, efficiency, and effectiveness.

9-13. Well-designed QC procedures assure published quality assurance standards are met and maximum effective production is balanced with quality without lowering standards.

SECTION III – RESPONSIBILITIES

AIRCRAFT AND COMPONENT INSPECTIONS

9-14. Safety of the aircraft and crew depends on—

- A rigorous aircraft inspection before, during, and after a maintenance action is conducted.
- Compliance with all applicable maintenance publications and references.

Note. TM 1-1500-328-23 contains information on the preventive maintenance inspection system, acceptance inspection, transfer inspection, and in-storage inspection.

TRACKING AIRCRAFT TIME BEFORE OVERHAUL AND RETIREMENT LIFE COMPONENTS

9-15. QC personnel use computerized printouts or a TBO and retirement life component chart to monitor the in-service time of all aircraft components requiring replacement on an hour, cycle, meter, or calendar basis. For a list of these components, refer to the applicable aircraft maintenance manual. To track TBO by MDS refer to https://tammsa.redstone.army.mil then select "MCDS" in the upper left corner of the page and follow the instructions.

9-16. TIs ensure the TBO or retirement life is not over-flown unless specifically authorized in TM 1-1500-328-23. TIs review the TBO chart or computerized printouts and update information periodically but not less than the reporting period (see AR 700-138 for reporting criteria) and when reportable components are replaced.

Note. Any method of tracking TBO or retirement components is acceptable; however, the preferred method is through ULLS-A (E). The importance of not over-flying a repair part or component cannot be overstated.

9-17. The three variations of the TBO chart are:
* Time-change component schedule chart (figure 9-3).
* Time-change bar graph component chart (figure 9-4, page 9-6).
* TBO report generated by ULLS-A (E) (table 9-1, page 9-6).

9-18. TBO reports (major component listings) produced by ULLS-A (E) track replacement of aircraft components and are generated by part number or work unit code. If computerized printouts are used, ensure they contain all required information (table 9-1, page 9-6) and maintain a separate disk copy in the QC office. QC personnel notify maintenance officers and NCOs when 100 hours remain until replacement of hourly components and/or when two months remain until replacement of calendar components. In most cases, this notification allows adequate time for advance ordering of replacement parts.

Note. Coordination and follow-up of existing aircraft TBO parts requests are made by unit maintenance personnel according to the unit maintenance SOP.

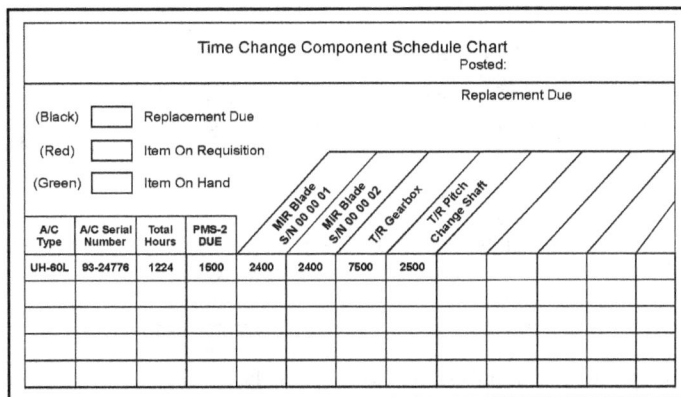

Figure 9-3. Sample format for a time-change component schedule chart

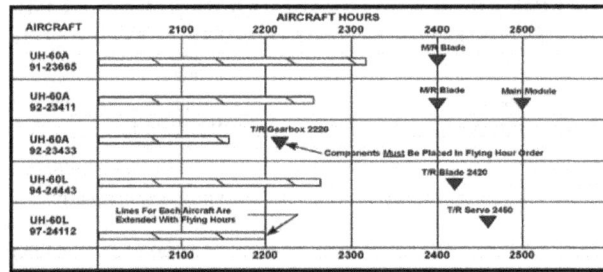

Figure 9-4. Sample format for a time-change bar graph component schedule chart

Table 9-1. Sample format for a computerized time-change computer printout

2408-16 Component Projection Report							
Product Control Number: AVAHRIGA							
Report Date: 12-MAY-05			UIC: WG31A8				
Aircraft Serial number: 6916148			Current Hours: 3576.8				
Projected Hours: 988							
WUC	Part Number	NSN	Nomenclature	Serial Number	Aircraft Hours		
					TBO Due	Until Due	
85A81H84	286-811-148-1	1615818386653	Retention strap fitting	A-4583	3695.0	118.2	
85A81H84	286-811-148-1	1615010306653	Retention strap fitting	A-1948	3695.0	118.2	
85A81H83	286-818-123-3	5315000919358	Retention strap pin	A19-38098	3695.0	118.2	
85A81H83	286-818-123-3	5315000919358	Retention strap pin	A19-38060	3695.0	118.2	
85A81H	286-811-154-101	1615010631268	Retention strap	LK-11923	3695.0	118.2	
85A81H	286-811-154-101	1615010631268	Retention strap	LK-11919	3695.0	118.2	
84A85C	6895653	2915010444551	Pump assembly, fuel	PE6398	4010.0	433.2	
84A85G	2524912-2	2915011799734	Governor assembly	86168686	4288.0	711.2	
84A85A	2524911-3	2915012510688	Fuel control	337434	4473.0	896.2	

MAINTENANCE AND SHOP SAFETY INSPECTIONS

9-19. QC inspections of maintenance and shop areas are detailed with the overall goal of establishing sound and disciplined maintenance procedures and practices. A QC inspection focuses on the maintenance facility, including maintenance and shop areas (safety).

9-20. When performing the maintenance and shop safety and equipment inspection, TIs check for cleanliness and serviceability and absence of corrosion on GSE. The inspection also includes checking for unobstructed fire lanes, serviceability of the hangar, serviceability of the fire extinguisher, and installation and use of equipment safety devices. Additional guidance for fire extinguisher inspections is found in Code of Federal Regulations (CFR) 1910.157.

Note. Active duty units will conduct these inspections monthly. National Guard and Reserve Component units will conduct these inspections quarterly.

9-21. Safety inspection forms are maintained and filed in the QC section according to AR 25-400-2. A copy of the inspection is given to the appropriate shop or maintenance section NCOIC for corrections of any deficiencies. Inspectors will forward copies of the inspection results to the ASO or unit safety manager to incorporate uncorrected deficiencies into the safety information collection and analysis program and hazard log for tracking. If deficiencies are found, shop or maintenance sections are re-inspected to ensure compliance.

9-22. For aviation safety policy, regulations, and procedures and questions or concerns related to aircraft accident prevention, go to USACRC at https://safety.army.mil or the aviation branch safety office at http://www-rucker.army.mil/abso/abso-main.htm.

> *Note.* The ARMS program provides aviation personnel with expert technical assistance and on-site evaluations, as mandated by AR 95-1, to all units assigned to FORSCOM, TRADOC, Eighth United States Army, Intelligence and Security Command, and United States Army European Command aviation units. Units seeking ARMS information or assistance can download FORSCOM ARMS commander guides and checklists at https://www.us.army.mil/suite/page/592726. For all other Army command units in need of ARMS checklists, see the Army command ARMS inspection team designated POC.

9-23. FM 10-67-1 and TM 1-1500-204-23-series manuals outline specific safety precautions. Refer to appendix B for CRM guidelines.

TEST, MEASUREMENT, AND DIAGNOSTIC EQUIPMENT UTILIZATION

9-24. QC inspectors use TMDE to obtain critical measurements and monitor maintenance procedures. Safe, economical operation of Army aircraft depends on the skilled use of TMDE in a comprehensive maintenance program.

AIRCRAFT WEIGHING REQUIREMENTS

WEIGHT-AND-BALANCE REQUIREMENTS

9-25. ASC/AST maintenance personnel perform aircraft weight-and-balancing procedures. AMC/AMT personnel appointed on aircraft weight-and-balance orders by the AMC/AMT commander can assist ASC/AST maintenance personnel when weighing their assigned aircraft.

WEIGHT-AND-BALANCE RECORDS

9-26. The assigned weight-and-balance technician maintains the aircraft weight-and-balance records. TIs coordinate with the weight-and-balance technician when maintenance on the aircraft could affect weight and balance. Refer to AR 95-1, TM 55-1500-342-23, aircraft operator manual, and aircraft TMs for additional information and guidance. The aircraft operator manual and applicable TMs contain weight-and-balance data.

> *Note.* The automated weight-and-balance system authorization and paper methods are the only authorized methods for computing weight and balance.

9-27. The manufacturer inserts all aircraft-identifying data on the various charts and completes all forms before aircraft delivery. DD Form 365 (Weight and Balance Personnel, Record of), DD Form 365-1 (Weight Checklist Record, Chart A-Basic), DD Form 365-2 (Weighing Record, Form B-Aircraft), DD Form 365-3 (Weight and Balance Record, Chart C-Basic), DD Form 365-4 (Weight and Balance Clearance Form F-Transport/Tactical), charts, and other pertinent data pertaining to aircraft weight-and-balance are maintained in a permanent binder. The binder and forms list the aircraft designation and serial number. Weight-and-balance technicians annotate any changes affecting the aircraft weight and balance on these forms.

9-28. Weight-and-balance forms for each aircraft are safeguarded and maintained according to applicable references. The aircraft serial number and information to be inserted on the charts or forms apply only to the individual aircraft. Weight-and-balance data and related forms for each aircraft are maintained according to AR 95-1 and TM 55-1500-342-23. The POC information for the aeromechanics site is www.aeromech.redstone.army.mil. This site provides aircraft weight-and-balance assistance.

PUBLICATIONS PROGRAM MANAGEMENT

PUBLICATIONS MANAGEMENT PROCEDURES

9-29. QC, shops, and maintenance personnel establish and maintain a complete, up-to-date set of technical publications for supported aircraft and equipment. These publications provide instructions on operation, maintenance, repair, modification, serviceability standards, testing, inspection, and storage of equipment. Publication personnel are appointed in the unit and responsible for ordering and maintaining unit publication accounts.

9-30. TIs perform a quarterly review of publication files (technical libraries) to ensure completeness and currency.

9-31. TIs provide guidance in preparing and submitting recommendations for changes to maintenance and administrative publications. Recommendations for changes are submitted on DA Form 2028. TIs establish and maintain a file of recommended changes IAW AR 25-400-2.

PUBLICATIONS FAMILIARIZATION RECORD

9-32. QC, shop, and maintenance personnel will maintain technical data publications to ensure maintenance personnel understand changes to publications relevant to their duties. Familiarization validations are updated quarterly or when a publication is changed. All publications used to maintain supported aircraft and related aviation equipment, and the names of maintenance personnel are listed in the familiarization record.

9-33. Shop, sections, and maintenance platoon NCOICs are responsible for tracking and announcing pertinent information updates requiring familiarization. It is the NCOIC's sole responsibility to keep assigned maintainers familiar with all changes affecting aircraft maintenance TMs and publications.

9-34. Maintenance personnel validate and record their familiarization for each publication to indicate currency. Delete shops/maintenance personnel validations as new changes are received and announced.

9-35. After a new change is announced, posted, and reviewed, shops and maintenance personnel record their currency to indicate familiarity with the new change. Each maintenance section or shop maintains separate familiarity records. TIs check the records during publication review to ensure:

- All publications used by maintenance sections or shops are listed and current to include the latest changes.
- All maintenance section or shop personnel are listed.
- All personnel have validated their familiarization with the latest change or revision to the publications.

Note. If using a printed record, IAW DA PAM 25-40, use only a black lead pencil to annotate printouts. After posting changes, write the word "posted" at the top of the change instruction sheet with initials and date.

FORMS AND RECORDS MANAGEMENT

9-36. TIs manage and monitor all forms and records for accuracy and completeness IAW DA PAM 738-751. They monitor aircraft historical records, weight-and-balance records, aircraft maintenance records, blank forms, and PQDRs. TIs, aircrew members, aviation maintainers, maintenance managers, record clerks, supervisors, and commanders (at all levels of maintenance) including DOD contract support activities, have an equal stake in maintaining forms and records.

Note. TIs ensure that a 30-day supply of blank forms is always on-hand to support maintenance operations.

AIRCRAFT HISTORICAL RECORDS

9-37. TIs maintain historical records for each aircraft assigned to their unit and ensure all essential historical records are on-file and updated according to published policies and regulations.

AIRCRAFT MAINTENANCE RECORDS

9-38. TIs check the accuracy of aircraft maintenance records each time they sign off a deficiency and as completed forms are turned into their office. Many units also establish reconciliation between the maneuver platoons and QC to assist in monitoring the accuracy of these records.

AVIATION MAINTENANCE MANAGEMENT FILE SYSTEM

9-39. The most important files maintained by QC personnel are teletype message (TWX) files such as SOF messages, ASAMs, and MIMs. These messages may ground aircraft, impose operating limitations, or provide information on aircraft maintenance techniques.

9-40. QC personnel maintain separate message files for each model of aircraft assigned or supported. They maintain one file for general messages. Messages are either informational or apply to specific models of aircraft. For more guidance on SOF messages, ASAMs, and files management, refer to AR 95-1 and AR 25-400-2.

9-41. TIs assist in preparing recommendations for changes to technical and administrative publications on DA Form 2028. The TI establishes and maintains a file of recommended changes IAW AR 25-400-2.

MANAGING QUALITY DEFICIENCY REPORTS

9-42. TIs maintain a PQDR file IAW AR 25-400-2, assigning PQDR control numbers according to DA PAM 738-751 and establishing a PQDR log (table 9-2). In addition, they check all submitted PQDRs for accuracy and completeness and assist in determining the category. TIs will submit copies of all PQDRs to the ASO or unit safety manager.

Table 9-2. Sample format for a deficiency report log

Control #	Subject & Category	Exhibit Date	Submission Date	Reply Date
W81HTW030001	(CAT I) UH-60(L), Cracks in strut housing at bearing retaining pins.	12 Jan 06	12 Jan 06	24 Jan06

9-43. If an exhibit is needed, the TI ensures all applicable forms and records accompany the exhibit (DA PAM 738-751). TIs review applicable aircraft equipment improvement and maintenance digests before submitting the PQDR.

9-44. TIs investigate all continuing deficiencies to track equipment malfunctions and trends. If a materiel defect is involved, TIs submit a PQDR IAW DA PAM 738-751 informing AMCOM of the problem. If the defect is due to an error in the maintenance procedure as found in the maintenance manual, TIs inform all maintenance personnel of the problem, the possible effects, and how it can be corrected.

9-45. TIs guide maintenance personnel in submitting a DA Form 2028 to correct shortcomings in the aviation technical maintenance manuals. If the breakdown of the repair part or component results from a manufacturer defect, TIs submit a PQDR.

MANAGING RECOMMENDED CHANGES TO PUBLICATIONS

9-46. If a maintenance malfunction occurs as the result of an improper maintenance procedure outlined in a maintenance TM, the TI notifies the PC OIC, maintenance officer, maintenance/shops NCOIC, and the maintenance personnel who performed the maintenance procedure. The TI provides a detailed description of the problem, the possible effects and, after researching the problem, guidance on how it can be corrected.

9-47. The TI provides guidance to assigned and attached unit maintenance personnel in submitting proposed recommendations to correct deficiencies outlined in the maintenance manual. The DA Form 2028 is prepared and forwarded to the agencies responsible for each manual so corrective action can be taken. The agency responsible for the TM or reference in question is listed in the suggested improvements statement in the heading of applicable manuals and publications, normally the first page.

9-48. TIs manage and track all submitted recommendations for changes to maintenance and administrative publications. Recommendations for changes are submitted on DA Form 2028. The TIs establish and maintain a file of recommended changes IAW AR 25-400-2.

Note. DA Form 2028 is found in the back of aviation technical maintenance manuals. Recommended changes can be submitted electronically at https://amcom2028.redstone.army.mil; in addition, the status of any recommended changes can be tracked at this website.

AVIATION TECHNICAL INSPECTION PROCEDURES

9-49. Technical inspection of aircraft maintenance ensures standards and practices established by applicable publications are followed. It also ensures applicable technical requirements are met, maintenance performed is documented, and quality work is performed efficiently.

9-50. Before performing an inspection, QC personnel review the latest applicable maintenance manual and regulatory policies to ensure the inspection meets current requirements. To ensure crewmember safety and equipment reliability, inspection procedures must be standardized and explicitly followed.

Status Symbols

9-51. Status symbols are used on forms and records to reflect the seriousness of faults, failures, deficiencies, and related maintenance actions and known safety hazards. The forms and records show the condition, readiness for flight, mission capabilities, operation, service, inspection, and maintenance of the aircraft system, subsystem, or associated equipment.

Note. Refer to DA PAM 738-751 for a detailed discussion of status symbols denoting aircraft airworthiness.

Grounding Condition (X) Authorization

9-52. The TI is the commander-designated representative for aircraft maintenance quality assurance and QC management. Authorization to sign off "status symbol X, grounding condition" or "circled X" conditions is designated, in writing (by memorandum or on the DA Form 1687), by the owning aviation maintenance commander. This authorization provides the name, rank, and duty position of the TI and authorizes him to inspect and sign off "status symbol X, grounding condition" or "circled X" faults on specific aircraft models and components.

9-53. The TI's initials and signature/stamp are required to release an aircraft for flight. An official memorandum listing all QC personnel with their initials, signature, and PID next to their name will help eliminate unauthorized use by other unit personnel.

Note. Aircraft status symbols may be entered in black ink.

9-54. A TI or maintenance supervisor who works on a "status symbol X, grounding condition" or "circled X" fault cannot perform quality assurance on his own work. The work must be inspected and signed off by another person designated in writing by the commander.

9-55. If no repair work or maintenance is involved and only an inspection is required, the TI performs the inspection and signs off with no recheck. The parent unit orders are sufficient authority to sign off a "status symbol X, grounding condition" or "circled X" faults on aircraft belonging to another unit (DA PAM 738-751).

Note. When authorization is given to sign off "status symbol X, grounding condition" or "circled X" faults on specific aircraft models or components, the memorandum must list these items and be signed by the commander. Keep a copy of the authorization on file in the QC office for six months after the representative departs the unit.

Inspection Stamps

9-56. An inspection stamp may be used to indicate a satisfactory condition. This stamp carries the same authority as a TI signature or PID and must be guarded against unauthorized use. If an inspection stamp is used, it is round and no larger than 1/2 inch in diameter (figure 9-5). It includes the unit designation and TI number.

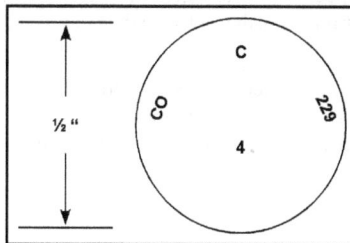

Figure 9-5. Inspection stamp sample

9-57. The following requirements must also be met:
- Keep stamps that have not been issued under lock and key.
- Destroy illegible stamps.
- Do not assign relieved stamps for six months.
- Keep a stamp inventory or register (table 9-3) in the QC section.

Table 9-3. Sample inventory register of inspection stamps

Stamp #	Assigned To	Date Assigned	Date Returned
1	Jerry H. Brown SSG	12-Jan-06	
2	John W. Doe SGT	23-Aug 04	3-Dec-04
3			
4			
5			
6	Stamp destroyed (lost)		
7	Tony L. Salazar SFC	4-Jun-05	
* All stamp numbers must be included and accounted for.			

Technical Inspections

9-58. Technical inspections are a visual, touch-and-feel inspection made by a technically qualified person (normally a QC TI). These inspections are performed on aircraft and associated equipment according to maintenance standards outlined in the aircraft TMs.

9-59. Technical inspections are also done on aviation-related equipment, maintenance and shop operations and areas, and supply facilities. The results of all technical inspections are used to—

- Assure quality maintenance is performed and in full compliance with TMs.
- Determine serviceability of aircraft systems, subsystems, repair parts, and components.
- Estimate cost of damage resulting from accidents or incidents.
- Determine how many manhours and repair parts are needed to restore equipment to a serviceable condition.
- Determine the cause of the unserviceable condition of the equipment.
- Determine the economical reparability of unserviceable equipment.

NONDESTRUCTIVE INSPECTION

9-60. NDI is a tool used by TIs to complement a QC inspection. Aircraft components may have suspected flaws that must be confirmed or denied. A defect may be visible, but the severity or extent of the defect is unknown. For example, scratches can look like cracks and hairline cracks can look like scratches. The TI must evaluate the defect to determine whether NDI methods are necessary to further evaluate the extent and severity of a defect.

9-61. NDI testing methods are used to determine the composition, integrity, dimensions, or properties of a component or structure without damaging the item. Some NDI methods include liquid penetrant, magnetic particle, electromagnetic, ultrasonic, and penetrating radiation methods. AR 750-1, TM 1-1500-204-23-7, and TM 1-1500-335-23 cover NDI details and procedures.

PROCEDURES

AIRCRAFT INSPECTIONS

9-62. Safety of the aircraft and crew depends on rigorous aircraft inspection and compliance with all applicable maintenance publications and other references. TM 1-1500-328-23 contains information on the preventive maintenance inspection system, acceptance inspection, transfer inspection, and in-storage inspection.

9-63. Aircraft are inspected to ensure published specifications are followed, maintenance requirements are complied with, and quality work is completed efficiently. If a TI is not completely familiar with the area or the item being inspected, he or she must seek supervisory guidance.

9-64. A TI must review and become familiar with the TMs on the subject area or item he or she is inspecting. A TI will never rely solely on his or her experience to conduct quality assurance on an aircraft system, subsystem, and/or equipment. TIs will always use technical references when inspecting Army aircraft and equipment.

Note. TIs, maintenance managers, maintenance personnel, and DOD contract support activities must use TMs for maintenance procedures and to ensure a safe, quality product is the end state.

PROCESSING UNIT AIRCRAFT FOR MAINTENANCE SUPPORT (AVIATION SUPPORT COMPANY/AVIATION SUPPORT TROOP ONLY)

9-65. Owning unit representatives will accompany aircraft work ordered to the ASC/AST for maintenance. They will review aircraft records with ASC/AST personnel, resolve questions, and perform a joint inventory with ASC/AST personnel. These representatives will accompany ASC/AST TIs on the initial and final inspection of the aircraft.

Note. When coordination has taken place between AMC/AMT and ASC/AST PC section personnel, AMC/AMT TIs will accompany ASC/AST TIs when conducting a final inspection of AMC/AMT owned aircraft.

9-66. Upon completion of repairs and before acceptance of the aircraft, inspectors perform a joint inventory with ASC/AST personnel, review aircraft records for accuracy and completeness, and inspect aircraft to ensure requested work was properly performed. If repairs are deferred/delayed due to unavailable parts, TIs ensure the repair parts needed to complete required maintenance procedures have valid document numbers.

9-67. TIs monitor maintenance procedures to ensure—
- Proper tools and equipment are used.
- Aircraft and components are maintained according to specific publications.
- Publications used are current.
- Forms and records are complete and accurate.
- Safety precautions are observed.
- Trained and competent maintainers are conducting aircraft maintenance.

9-68. TIs perform certain aircraft inspections at specified times. These inspections include initial, in-progress, and final (with possibly a 100 percent inspection) (ASC/AST TI initiated and performed).

Initial Inspection

9-69. ASC/AST TIs perform an initial inspection before the aircraft enters the shop for maintenance to verify aircraft or components meet specifications of published maintenance manuals. This inspection determines deficiencies, work required, economical repair of aircraft and components, and accountability of equipment to include sensitive items if installed.

Note. Minor deficiencies identified by ASC/AST TIs are not justification for refusal to accept an aircraft.

9-70. All deficiencies are entered on DA Form 2408-13-3. These forms are returned to PC after the inspection. Only those cowling and access panels necessary to inspect the faults listed on the DA Form 2407 by the ASC/AST unit are removed.

In-Progress Inspection

9-71. The in-progress inspection is a continuing inspection performed periodically while the aircraft or component is in the shop (especially important during phase/periodic inspections). TIs should be available to answer questions and resolve problems. Maintenance team chiefs set up stations, if possible, so the inspector is near the work being performed.

9-72. Equipment at each station should include all items needed to perform the inspection. All necessary forms, maintenance publications, tools, and test equipment should also be available. ASC AST TIs perform the in-progress inspection to ensure the final product is reliable; areas are inspected before they are covered with access panels or components. Maintenance procedures not performed according to applicable maintenance publications are corrected immediately upon discovery.

9-73. TIs thoroughly review logbook forms and records before performing an in-progress inspection on aircraft in phase or undergoing periodic maintenance. TIs enter deficiencies missed by the maintenance team on DA Form 2408-13-1.

Final Inspection

9-74. A final inspection is a complete inspection and functional test, if required, of all aircraft or components released after maintenance. This inspection confirms—

- Repairs meet the specifications of the maintenance manuals.
- Work requested on DA Form 2407 was completed.
- Correct tools and equipment were used.
- Entries on DA forms are complete and accurate.
- Aircraft or components conform to standards.

9-75. Major (X-grounding) deficiencies are corrected before the aircraft or component leaves the ASC/AST. Minor (diagonal) shortcomings are corrected based on the availability of parts and manhours. All deferred/delayed maintenance will have a valid requisition or work-order number before maintenance personnel enter it on a DA Form 2408-13-1. The decision to defer/delay maintenance rests with the commander or designated representative, as stated in DA PAM 738-751.

One Hundred Percent Inspection

9-76. ASC/AST TIs perform a 100 percent inspection if numerous faults are found during other inspections (such as initial inspections) not annotated in the aircraft logbook. QC personnel should coordinate with the PC OIC or maintenance officer before performing a 100 percent inspection.

9-77. The TI performs the 100 percent inspection by removing all cowling and access panels and inspecting the entire aircraft, including all systems and components. During the inspection components, repair parts, and items are checked for (to include installation on the airframe)—

- Correct assembly.
- Proper safety techniques (use of safety wire and cotter pins).
- Wear.
- Rigging.
- Leaks.
- Structural defects (such as cracks, punctures, loose rivets, and separation in honeycomb panels).
- Security of components.

FORMS AND RECORDS INSPECTION PROCEDURES

9-78. Forms and records are the first items checked in any aircraft inspection. All form entries must follow the policies in DA PAM 738-751, TM 55-1500-342-23, and TB 43-0211. All necessary forms, publications, tools, and test equipment are available at the inspection station. Refer to DA PAM 738-751 for the required locations of various forms. Some items to look for when inspecting forms are listed below.

Department of the Army Form 2408-12

9-79. Normally, the pilot or crewmember fills in the total in each block to include flight hours and landings. TIs ensure hours and landings are correctly totaled and entered on the form.

Department of the Army Form 2408-13 Series

9-80. TIs ensure—

- Hours and landings are accurate and correctly carried forward from DA Form 2408-12.
- Current aircraft hours, landings, autorotations, auxiliary power unit (APU) history, and rounds fired, if applicable, are correctly carried forward from the previous DA Form 2408-12 and DA Form 2408-13.
- The status in block 10 reflects the most serious uncorrected fault listed on DA Forms 2408-13-1, 2408-13-2, and 2408-13-3.
- All corrected X and circled-X corrective actions were inspected, according to applicable maintenance manuals, by an authorized inspector.
- All uncorrected entries signed off as carried forward from the previous DA Form 2408-13-1 are entered on the current DA Form 2408-13-1.
- Entries are carried forward word for word, and status symbols are correct.
- Inspection times are correctly carried forward from the previous DA Form 2408-13.

Department of the Army Form 2408-18

9-81. TIs ensure all required inspection items are entered. TIs update DA Form 2408-18 with correct dates or times when a TM changes or other authorization document directs the addition or deletion of a given inspection.

HISTORICAL RECORD LOGBOOK FORMS AND RECORDS INSPECTION

Department of the Army Forms 2408-5 and 2408-5-1

9-82. TIs ensure—
- DA Forms 2408-5 and 2408-5-1 (Equipment Modification Record [Component]) are reviewed for completeness and accuracy and maintained as prescribed in DA PAM 738-751.
- All applicable modifications are entered in section 4 of the form.
- The required completion date is entered, in pencil, in block 5F for modification-not-met compliance criteria (paper form only).
- Entry of applicable SOF and ASAM inspections.

Department of the Army Form 2408-15

9-83. TIs ensure—
- DA Form 2408-15 is reviewed for completeness and accuracy.
- Entry of pertinent historical data on aircraft and associated equipment throughout its service life.

Department of the Army Form 2408-15-2

9-84. TIs ensure—
- DA Form 2408-15-2 (Aircraft Vibration Record) is on-hand for the aircraft.
- Significant historical data is shown, as required by DA PAM 738-751.

Department of the Army Forms 2408-16 and 2408-16-1

9-85. TIs ensure—
- Required forms (DA Forms 2408-16 and 2408-16-1 [History Recorder, Component, Module Record]) are on-hand as listed in DA PAM 738-751.
- Serial numbers match component serial numbers on the aircraft.
- Computed replacement due times are correct and not past due.

Department of the Army Form 2408-17

9-86. TIs ensure—

- All applicable items on the master inventory guide are listed.
- Property additions and deletions made after aircraft delivery are correctly reflected.
- All equipment checks have a signature in the corresponding numbered block.
- All items added, deleted, or short are explained on the back of the form (refer to DA PAM 738-751).

Department of the Army Form 2408-19 Series

9-87. TIs ensure the appropriate series numbered forms (DA Form 2408-19 [Aircraft Engine Turbine Wheel Historical Record], DA Form 2408-19-1 [T53/T55 Turbine Engine Analysis Check Record], DA Form 2408-19-2 [T700 Series Turbine Engine Analysis Check Record], DA Form 2408-19-3 [Engine Component Operating Hours Record]) are completed according to DA PAM 738-751 and applicable publications. These DA forms are on-hand for each gas turbine and engine turbine wheel as required.

Department of the Army Form 2408-20

9-88. TIs ensure a properly completed form is on-hand for each aircraft component in the AOAP. DA Form 2408-20 is a semi-permanent historical record of oil and grease samples taken and results of laboratory test results for all aircraft components registered in the AOAP.

Department of Defense Form 365 Series

9-89. TIs ensure the appropriate series numbered forms are on-hand and up-to-date as required by AR 95-1 and TM 55-1500-342-23. Trained weight-and-balance technicians are appointed on orders signed by the aviation maintenance commander.

MANAGING TECHNICAL COMPLIANCE OF AVIATION SAFETY-RELATED MESSAGES

9-90. The TI monitors and ensures compliance with SOF messages, ASAMs, MWOs, TBs, AWRs, and ISAQs. Compliance with all aviation safety-related messages is paramount to the safety of crewmembers, aircraft, and equipment.

Safety Messages

9-91. Once safety messages are complied with, TIs make required entries on applicable DA forms according to DA PAM 738-751. All aviation maintenance units submit a safety message compliance status report according to the instructions on their assigned aircraft.

9-92. For a detailed discussion of aviation safety messages and their requirements, refer to AR 750-6 and DA PAM 738-751.

Note. For a comprehensive listing of aviation SOF messages, to include MIMs, visit the AMCOM website at https://asmprd.redstone.army.mil/SplashPage.asp. AMCOM maintains consolidated listings, by airframe, of aviation SOF messages. Users must have AKO credentials for access.

Modification Work Orders

9-93. MWOs become mandatory when—

- Providing increased safety to personnel or equipment.
- Significantly raising the operational and support features of equipment.

9-94. Refer to AR 750-10 for definitive priority criteria assigned to MWOs. There are three priorities assigned to MWOs: routine, urgent, or emergency.

9-95. Upon receipt of an MWO that applies to corresponding serial numbers of assigned aircraft, TIs enter MWO-required information on DA Form 2408-5 (refer to DA PAM 738-751). MWOs applied to assigned aircraft will normally be accomplished by sustainment-level maintenance activities such as the contract field teams, Corpus Christi Army Depot, or contract maintenance activities performing overhaul/repair. Therefore, the sustainment-level maintenance activities will complete the MWO entry when the MWO is applied. If an MWO is not applied by the specified date on the directive, TIs will enter MWO data on DA Form 2408-13-1 (refer to DA PAM 738-751).

9-96. MWOs are the only publications that authorize modification or alteration of Army equipment. MWOs are issued to—

- Provide compatibility with newer equipment.
- Prevent serious damage to equipment.
- Increase operational effectiveness.
- Reduce support requirements.

9-97. Each MWO contains specific instructions concerning—

- Time limit for compliance.
- Maintenance category to which the MWO applies.
- Parts required.
- Manhours required.
- Form entries required.
- Method for performing the modification.
- Weight-and-balance data.

TECHNICAL BULLETINS

9-98. TBs, SOFs, and ISAQs direct one-time or, in special cases, a recurring inspection of an aircraft or component. DA Forms 2408-5-1, 2408-13-1, 2408-15, 2408-16, and 2408-18 are used to ensure compliance with TBs.

9-99. TIs ensure all requirements of applicable aircraft TBs are met and required entries are made on applicable DA forms. TIs are also responsible for two actions: grounding an aircraft, if required by the TB (refer to AR 95-1), and submitting reports required by AR 95-1 to report compliance with TBs.

Department of the Army Form 2408-5-1

9-100. TIs enter TBs that apply to components on DA Form 2408-5-1 (refer to DA PAM 738-751). The procedure is the same as for MWOs.

Department of the Army Form 2408-13-1

9-101. TIs or crew chiefs use DA Form 2408-13-1 to enter the one-time inspection due on the aircraft or aircraft component. Technical inspections are performed according to the TB. Normally, if a TB is not applied within the period specified in the TB, the aircraft is grounded.

9-102. Once the inspection is completed, as outlined in the TB, and no defects are found, the inspection due is signed off on DA Form 2408-13-1. If defects are found, they are entered on DA Form 2408-13-1. Maintenance personnel are notified for corrective action. After deficiencies are corrected, the corrective action is inspected and the inspection due is signed off on DA Form 2408-13-1.

Department of the Army Form 2408-15

9-103.   TIs enter a one-time inspection of an aircraft and related systems and subsystems on this form. DA Form 2408-15 is used to record SOF messages, ASAMs, or TBs.

Department of the Army Form 2408-16

9-104.   If a TB applies to a component on which DA Form 2408-16 is maintained, TIs enter TB compliance in block 7. DA PAM 738-751 and TB 1-1500-341-01 for each MDS of aircraft list all components that require DA Form 2408-16.

Department of the Army Form 2408-18

9-105.   A TB may require a recurring inspection at specified intervals. If so, TIs enter this inspection on DA Form 2408-18 for the aircraft.

AIRWORTHINESS RELEASE

9-106.   An AWR is a technical document that provides operating instructions and limitations necessary for safe flight of an aircraft system or subsystem or associated equipment. This Army airworthiness approval is—

- Based on the results of design analysis, engineering ground test, and/or flight test.
- Required prior to operation of a new aircraft system or subsystem or associated equipment or a modification to the qualified or standard configuration.

9-107.   Aircraft specific AWRs are accessed at the following websites:

- Scout/attack AWRs at https://www.scout-attack.jatdi.mil/warrior/safety/awr/index.html.
- Blackhawk AWRs at https://www.blackhawk.jatdi.mil/safety/awr/index.html.
- Chinook AWRs at https://extranet.chinook.peoavn.army.mil.
- Apache AWRs at https://www.jtdi.mil.

Note. Refer to AR 70-62 for information on AWRs and ISAQs.

QUALITY CONTROL SUPPORT FOR MAINTENANCE EQUIPMENT AND PROGRAMS

GROUND SUPPORT EQUIPMENT

9-108.   This equipment includes all GSE needed to maintain aircraft and associated equipment. TIs will ensure the forms and records used to track maintenance and services for assigned GSE comply with DA PAM 750-8. GSE support personnel will seek the QC TI guidance when filling out GSE forms and records. Refer to chapter 3 for more information on the GSE program.

FOREIGN OBJECT DAMAGE PROGRAM

9-109.   FOD may cause materiel damage, or it may cause a system or equipment to become inoperable, unsafe, or less efficient. To eliminate potential FOD or malfunction of an aircraft system or subsystem, TIs must take an active role in enforcing the FOD program. TIs will closely monitor ongoing maintenance procedures within the scope of their responsibilities to ensure maintenance personnel are consistently practicing sound FOD procedures.

9-110.   TIs must enforce FOD directives as outlined in the unit maintenance SOP. They must work diligently with the unit assigned FOD officer/NCOIC to ensure the FOD program designed for their unit is effective, manageable, and observed by all maintainers. FOD prevention countermeasures are integrated throughout the unit SOP. Refer to chapter 3 for more information on the FOD program.

ARMY OIL ANALYSIS PROGRAM

9-111. The commander appoints an AOAP monitor who has been properly trained and certified by the supporting laboratory. The AOAP monitor manages and monitors the program in the unit. Refer to chapter 3 for more information on AOAP.

9-112. TIs will provide guidance, when called upon, to ensure maintenance personnel are adequately trained in the techniques of drawing oil samples from aircraft components. TIs will ensure all aircraft and components are entered in the program and all required records are maintained. Refer to AR 750-1, TB 43-0211, and DA PAM 738-751 for specific instructions. TIs will ensure—

- Oil samples are taken according to TB 43-0211.
- DD Form 2026 is complete and accurate.
- All samples are dispatched expeditiously to the laboratory.
- Special samples requested by the laboratory are taken immediately.
- Notification is given to the assigned servicing laboratory of replacement or removal of AOAP components.

SECTION IV – REFERENCES AND PUBLICATIONS

9-113. ARs and publications describe policies and procedures used in aircraft maintenance and logistics management. QC personnel ensure publications and reference libraries are current and updated with the latest changes. TIs set up and maintain the master reference library, consisting of many types of supporting references and publications, to assist aviation maintenance units in conducting maintenance "by the book."

Note. Electronic versions of manuals can be found at http://www.apd.army.mil.

Note. Refer to aircraft TMs for an expanded list of references and publications used by an aviation maintenance unit. Refer to DA PAM 25-30 for a detailed listing of reference and publication requirements. Refer to chapter 4 for guidance in accessing the LIDB publications module. This module contains a comprehensive listing of publications to support assigned end items. Refer to this manual for a link to the ETM's site and for more information on managing a publications account.

ARMY REGULATIONS

9-114. ARs provide policies and responsibilities that govern administrative procedures and ensure compliance at all levels. AR series numbers identify the subject matter (all ARs in the 95 series pertain to aviation.) A sub-number, preceded by a dash, indicates additional information about the basic subject (for example, a specific aviation regulation such as AR 95-1).

DEPARTMENT OF THE ARMY PAMPHLETS

9-115. DA pamphlets contain information or reference material. DA pamphlets are numbered in the same manner as ARs. All DA pamphlets in the 25 series are Army administrative publications (for example, DA PAM 25-30 is an index of publications and blank forms).

FIELD MANUALS

9-116. FMs outline military doctrine as it applies to combined arms operations and represents keystone publications for Army branches. The first digit of the manual identifies the functional area (3- represents operations). The next two digits identify the Army branch (04 represents aviation). The last set of digits preceded by a period represents a specific topic (.1 represents aviation brigades).

ARMY TACTICS, TECHNIQUES, AND PROCEDURES

9-117. Army tactics, techniques, and procedures (ATTPs) outline military tactics, techniques, and procedures for a single branch, functional area, or company/troop. ATTP numbering is the same structure as FMs.

TRAINING CIRCULARS

9-118. TCs provide individual and unit Soldier training information that does not fit standard requirements for other established types of training publications (AR 25-30). TC numbering is the same structure as FMs and ATTPs.

TECHNICAL MANUALS

9-119. TMs provide training information on a variety of subjects and on specific items of equipment. TMs for specific equipment provide instructions on operation, maintenance, and overhaul. They also provide a RPSTL and breakdown. The first one or two digits of these manuals identify the preparing technical service, (1 or 55 represents aviation manuals).

9-120. A dash and a four-digit number indicate the federal supply classification, including the equipment within the federal supply classification assigned to commodity groups and classes. Federal supply classification provides unique information regarding a specific type of equipment (-1510 represents fixed-wing aircraft and -1520 represents rotary-wing aircraft).

9-121. A dash and a three-digit number indicate the MDS of a particular aircraft (-251 represents AH-64D helicopters and -248 represents OH-58D helicopters).

9-122. A dash and a two-digit number represent the category of maintenance (such as -10 represents operators and -23 describes maintenance procedures for AMC/AMT and ASC/AST maintainers to perform).

9-123. A serial number, preceded by a dash or a slash, is added when a TM is published in more than one volume (-1, -2 or /1, /2). Each volume within a series of TMs will have its own table of contents.

9-124. The letter "P" is used as a suffix when the RPSTLs are published in a volume separate from the maintenance instructions. This volume will have the same basic number as the corresponding manuals for the same type of aircraft (TM 1-1520-248-23 is the maintenance manual for an OH-58D). Adding the suffix letter "P" to that TM, denotes a RPSTL manual (TM 1-1520-248-23&P is the RPSTL manual for the OH-58D).

TECHNICAL BULLETINS

9-125. TBs contain technical information on equipment or professional management techniques. The most common TBs encountered by QC personnel direct one-time inspection of aircraft or components.

9-126. Urgent inspection requirements are initially sent to units by a TWX. The subsequent TB then supersedes the TWX. TBs directing one-time inspection are classified by priority as urgent, limited urgent, and normal.

SAFETY-OF-FLIGHT AND AVIATION SAFETY ACTION MESSAGES

9-127. SOF messages and ASAMs provide information concerning safe operation of an entire type or specific serial numbers of Army aircraft. These messages are transmitted by TWX to all organizations concerned. The message number indicates general or specific information. General (GEN) messages apply to all aircraft while specific messages apply only to a specific series of aircraft. Examples of these messages are—

- GEN-06-02:
    - This is a general message that applies to all aircraft or maintenance facilities.
    - It was written in FY 06.
    - It was the second general message sent in FY 06.
- AH-64-06-03:
    - This is a specific message that applies to the AH-64-series aircraft.
    - It was written in FY 06.
    - It was the third AH-64 message sent in FY 06.

9-128. The three types of SOF messages are emergency, operational, and technical.

EMERGENCY

9-129. Emergency messages contain information deemed critical in nature. These messages ground affected aircraft. They usually denote hazardous aircraft conditions that, unless complied with, have the high probability of causing aircraft damage or personal injury. Emergency SOF messages are later published as TBs or MWOs.

OPERATIONAL

9-130. Operational messages apply to flight procedures, operating limits, or operational policy. These messages may ground affected aircraft for operational reasons.

TECHNICAL

9-131. Technical messages are issued by AMCOM and are later published as urgent action TBs or MWOS. When issued, these messages cause grounding of affected aircraft but allow them to fly with specific limitations.

SAFETY-OF-USE

9-132. Safety-of-use messages are high-priority notifications pertaining to any defect or hazardous condition or combination of actions, actual or potential, that can cause personal injury, death, or damage to equipment, related system, components, or repair parts. These high priority messages require an immediate action prior to the next operation.

9-133. Safety-of-use messages are developed, prepared, and electronically sent by AMCOM to all users of Army non-aircraft equipment listed in DA PAM 738-751. AR 750-10 and DA PAM 738-751 cover the procedures for issue, compliance, and management of safety-of-use messages, MWOs, and TBs.

MAINTENANCE ADVISORY MESSAGES AND MAINTENANCE INFORMATION MESSAGES

9-134. Maintenance advisory messages (MAMs) and MIMs are developed, prepared, and electrically sent by AMCOM to all users of Army aircraft. MAMs and MIMs are informational messages that apply to aviation maintenance personnel. Normally, MAMs and MIMs do not require any entries on forms and records. See DA PAM 738-751 for procedures on MAMs and MIMs.

SUPPLY BULLETINS

9-135. SBs provide important supply information to maintenance personnel and include—
- Stock number changes.
- Direct-exchange list changes.

- Reports on new materiel.

FEDERAL AVIATION ADMINISTRATION PUBLICATIONS

9-136. The Federal Aviation Administration publishes references and publications on aviation and aircraft maintenance using different standards from those applied to Army aviation assets. When conducting maintenance on Army aviation assets, aviation maintainers will use only authorized Army-approved publications and references. Do not use Federal Aviation Administrative or any other federal agency publications for Army aircraft maintenance unless authorized in writing or as part of a logistic support plan.

CHANGED, REVISED, AND RESCINDED PUBLICATIONS

9-137. Effective aircraft maintenance requires the latest technical information to be on-hand at all times. Army publications are continually updated; QC personnel must ensure units have adequate quantities of current publications. Therefore, they need to understand how the publications distribution system operates. DA PAM 25-33 provides necessary information for the TI to include—

- How initial distribution and resupply are made.
- The required DA forms for ordering publications.
- Where publications can be obtained.
- How a publications account is set up.

POSTING CHANGES

9-138. When manually posting changes to paper copy publications, personnel will—

- Ensure accuracy and neatness of the posted change.
- Use a sharp, black pencil so posting can be erased for future changes or corrections.
- Print or write the authority for changing a basic publication on the outside margin of the page by the changed portion; this authority is usually a numbered change (such as C1). If the changed portion affects more than one page, make the same notation on all pages concerned.
- Draw a line through the first and last lines of the text when three or more lines of text are affected; then, these lines are connected from top right to bottom left, forming a Z-shaped figure.
- Post change numbers in proper sequence; an urgent change may be posted out of sequence (ahead of previous numbered changes) if authority to do so is stated on its front page.
- Ensure manuals are not superseded or rescinded.

Note. DA PAM 25-40 is required reading for all TIs. It provides established guidelines and information on posting and filing publications.

INTERIM CHANGES

9-139. When there is no time to issue a printed change, a TWX is used to amend a publication. The message is identified as an interim change and prepared in the format of a published change. The message provides the exact language of the changed material. When posting the change, personnel will follow the procedures directed by the message. The message number and date are posted in the margin of the publication opposite the changed portions, such as "DA message 0614202 Mar 06."

9-140. A copy of the message is filed in front of the basic publication or the last printed change. If a copy is not available, a cross-reference sheet is inserted, showing where a copy of the message can be found. When the next printed change or revision of the publication is received, the superseded notice is checked. If the notice states the message is rescinded or superseded, the message or cross-reference sheet is removed and destroyed.

PUBLICATION REVISIONS

9-141. A publication revision is a complete new edition of an existing publication. It supersedes the preceding publication, together with all changes, supplements, and appendices.

PUBLICATION RESCISSIONS

9-142. A publication is rescinded (canceled), then destroyed, when its material becomes obsolete. DA PAM 25-30 contains a list of rescinded publications.

PUBLICATION DISPOSAL

9-143. Publications are discarded after they have been rescinded or superseded. Classified publications are discarded according to AR 380-5 and unclassified publications are discarded according to instructions from the local disposal officer. However, do not discard old publications until new ones are reviewed.

9-144. DA Form 12-series (Requirements for Distribution of Publications and Blank Forms) are used to order the quantity of publications needed. If more publications are received than needed, the DA Form 12-R (Request for Establishment of a Publications Account) and DA Form 12-99-R (Initial Distribution Requirements for Publications) are used to establish a publications account and order the quantity of publications needed. If more publications are received than needed, these forms are updated according to DA PAM 25-33.

AVIATION MAINTENANCE COMPANY/TROOP TECHNICAL LIBRARIES

9-145. Technical files and libraries are required on all assigned and attached equipment. Reference technical libraries are located in an area convenient to maintenance personnel. Immediate supervisors and QC personnel provide maintainers with the most current maintenance publications and references.

MASTER AND SHOPS TECHNICAL LIBRARIES

9-146. TIs are responsible for two types of libraries: master and shop. The master library is located in the QC office and used by all personnel. It contains publications required to maintain all series of aircraft and components owned or supported by the aviation maintenance companies. The shops library contains manuals on the specific duties of the shop. Inspectors ensure these manuals are complete and up-to-date. TIs also check the master and shop libraries quarterly to ensure—

- Libraries are located conveniently to users.
- Libraries are set up alphanumerically.
- All required manuals are on-hand or on-order.
- No unnecessary hardcopy publications are on-hand.
- Changes are posted and indexes reflect the status of publications on hand.
- No superseded or rescinded manuals are used.
- Classified manuals are controlled according to the AR 380 series.

PUBLICATIONS FILING SYSTEM

9-147. Technical publications files are maintained IAW AR 25-400-2. DA PAM 25-30 contains an index of DA publications and forms; publications are verified against the listings in the latest index to ensure currency.

INTERSERVICE PUBLICATIONS ACCOUNTS

Air Force Publications

9-148. Air Force publications can be accessed at http://www.e-publishing.af.mil.

Navy Publications

9-149. Navy publications can be accessed at https://mynatec navair.navy.mil.

https://mynatec navair.navy.mil

SECTION V – UNIT LEVEL LOGISTICS SYSTEM-AVIATION (ENHANCED) PROCEDURES

ADMINISTRATION

9-150. The ULLS-A (E) QC menu provides access to change, add, modify, and delete personnel, aircraft, and required maintenance or inspection data in the ULLS-A (E) database. Each function is addressed in the ULLS-A (E) EUM.

> *Note.* If the server is down, QC will process all logbook entries manually. Once connectivity is restored, all manual entries are uploaded in ULLS-A (E).

FUNCTIONS

9-151. Although commissioning and decommissioning of the deployed server are the responsibility of PC, QC personnel will assist in the process. The ULLS-A (E) deployed server allows the unit flexibility to push aircraft away from the primary database to support area operations. The deployed server enables TIs to have access to historical records and send information back to PC for flight hours and reporting purposes.

9-152. When the aviation maintenance unit is conducting split-based operations, the deployed server function provides a unit with the capability to deploy aircraft to support operations away from the unit primary database. The deployed server allows QC personnel access to all available QC functions, except program administrator functions.

9-153. The ULLS-A (E) automated QC program provides full data entry, editing, review, and report-generation capabilities. DA PAM 738-751 required forms and reports are provided in a paperless electronic environment.

> *Note.* Refer to the ULLS-A (E) EUM for additional user information and procedural guidance.

MAIN MENU SCREEN

9-154. Five primary areas are shown on the QC main menu screen:
- "AIRCRAFT IDENTIFICATION CARD."
- System status block.
- Menu toggle arrows.
- Main menu utilities.
- Flight/maintenance records.

AIRCRAFT IDENTIFICATION CARD

9-155. The aircraft identification card is displayed in the upper-left area of the main menu screen. Select UIC by clicking on the down arrow; from the drop-down list provided, select the assigned UIC. The same process can be used to select MDS (such as, UH-60A/L/M or AH-64A/D), as well as to select a specific aircraft serial number.

9-156. Once the UIC, MDS, and specific aircraft serial number are selected (highlighted), the data selected will appear in the field; the corresponding unit, crew chief, and supervisor names are displayed. Selecting individual aircraft allows automated QC users to browse and view all records previously saved and migrated by ULLS-A (E) automated logbook users.

SYSTEM STATUS BLOCK

9-157. The "system status" block on the lower right portion of the main menu screen provides a broad range of data for the aircraft and the current data and time. To view the data provided in the status block, click on the corresponding bullet with the mouse. The following data are provided:

- System status.
- Landings.
- Services.
- Maintenance.
- Hoist status.
- Health indicator test (HIT) summary.

Note. ULLS-A (E) uses the operating system clock as a time stamp. Do not change the computer system clock settings without the guidance of the system administrator.

9-158. The "system status" box indicates the status of aircraft hours and mission-related equipment aboard the aircraft. Once the aircraft is selected, it will show the current aircraft hours, the most critical open aircraft fault status, the most critical open weapon fault status, the most critical open electronic fault status, the most critical open hoist fault status, and the most critical related open fault status.

9-159. The "landings" status box displays the current total number of standard and autorotational landings the aircraft has executed since the last DA Form 1352 reporting period.

9-160. The "maintenance" status box is used to show either the status for preventive maintenance daily (PMD) or 10-hour/14-day inspection information, depending on the aircraft model. Information contained within this status box includes the following:

- Current preventive maintenance type.
- Date when the PMD inspection was completed.
- Aircraft hour when the PMD inspection was completed.
- PID of the individual responsible for completing the PMD inspection.
- Next phase (type) maintenance (type) due.
- Aircraft hours when the next phase maintenance is due.

9-161. The "hoist status" box displays the current status of the hoist. Information contained within this status box includes the following:

- Serial number of the hoist.
- Status of the hoist.
- Cycles of the hoist.
- Current number of hours on the hoist.
- When the last 30-day inspection of the hoist was completed.

9-162. The HIT summary status box will display engine exhaust temperature and altitude ratios measured against maintenance officer created HIT check baseline ratios for the last 26 flights. Each engine has different formulas for determining HIT check values and their acceptable deviations from baseline ratios. The HIT check summary displays the following:

- Current aircraft hours.
- Flight date.

- Flight number.
- Engine HIT check values.
- HIT baseline button.

UNIT LEVEL LOGISTICS SYSTEM-AVIATION (ENHANCED) AUTOMATED QUALITY CONTROL RECORDS

9-163.   There are three primary records menus in the automated QC program:
- Flight/maintenance records.
- Historical records and forms.
- Readiness/other records.

9-164.   Automated QC users can browse and view flight/maintenance records previously saved and migrated by ULLS-A (E) automated logbook users. ULLS-A (E) provides access to historical records, data entry, and utility features for the following records: flight/maintenance records and historical records.

9-165.   ULLS-A (E) flight/maintenance records includes the following automated forms:
- DA Form 2408-4-1 (Weapon Record Data).
- DA Form 2408-4-2 (Weapons Sighting Data [OH-58D]).
- DA Form 2408-4-3 (Weapon Sighting Data [AH-64A]).
- DA Form 2408-18.
- DA Form 2408-12.
- DA Forms 2408-13-1 and 2408-13-2.

9-166.   ULLS-A (E) historical records include the following automated forms:
- DA Forms 2408-5 and 2408-5-1.
- DA Form 2408-15.
- DA Form 2408-15-2.
- DA Forms 2408-16 and 2408-16-1 (History Recorder, Component, Module Record).
- DA Form 2408-17.
- DA Form 2408-19.
- DA Form 2408-19-1.
- DA Form 2408-19-2.
- DA Form 2408-19-3.
- DA Form 2408-20.
- DA Form 2408-33-R (Meter Tracked Component Record).

9-167.   The ULLS-A (E) QC administrative menu provides access to change, add, modify, and delete personnel, aircraft, and operational and required maintenance or inspection data in the ULLS-A (E) data base.

Appendix A

Standing Operating Procedures

This appendix proposes topics and procedures to assist leaders in drafting an SOP that provides Soldiers with continuity and standardized procedures within their unit. When producing the aviation maintenance SOP, the leadership conveys to the Soldier the guidelines and procedures to be executed in the absence of direct leadership. The commander reviews the SOP for content, context, and clarity of purpose. The commander approves the SOP by signing the document, at which time the SOP becomes a binding document.

GENERAL

A-1. Figures A-1 (page A-4) and A-2 (page A-5) contain sample SOPs for a headquarters section and PC section. Topics contained within an SOP are discussed in the following paragraphs.

- Heading.
- Applicability.
- Purpose.
- Scope.
- Objectives.
- Revisions.
- Responsibilities.
- Operations.
- Procedures.
- General information.
- References.

HEADING

A-2. The heading of the SOP varies depending on the type of internal SOP. If the SOP is part of an administrative SOP at the battalion/squadron level, then the heading will reflect the SOP as an appendix to the administrative SOP.

A-3. If the document is part of the AMC/AMT SOP, then the heading will list the name of the organization, the station, and the date. It will also include the number (if used) and type (internal or external) of SOP.

APPLICABILITY

A-4. This section identifies the unit personnel (assigned or attached).

PURPOSE

A-5. This section states the overarching concept or reason the SOP is written; such as, to provide a standardized guide for maintenance support procedures, responsibilities, operational policies, and maintenance actions in support of aircraft maintenance and related ground support system repair.

SCOPE

A-6. This section states the scope this SOP applies; garrison, field, and/or deployed to a theater of operations. If specific instructions apply while deployed, commanders and leaders convey additional instructions or policies.

> *Note.* An example of specific instructions or guidance is "The following policies are established to augment this SOP while on deployed status. The provisions of this SOP are complied with unless written deviation is authorized by the AMC/AMT commander. If this SOP is in direct conflict with a DOD or DA regulation or directive, the higher authoritative reference takes precedence."

OBJECTIVES

A-7. This section states the objectives of the AMC/AMT; such as, to provide maintenance support to assigned units, related repair parts supply, and aircraft recovery support when requested; and perform maintenance on aircraft systems or subsystems, aircraft armament, and avionics equipment.

REVISIONS

A-8. SOP relevancy is directly linked to currency. A statement such as this must be in the SOP; "This SOP must be reviewed and, if necessary, revised whenever a new or revised DA publication is fielded." In addition, explain or identify—

- Who can submit changes and how often?
- The classification of how urgent a stated change is and how soon must it be applied to the SOP.
- Who determines the criticality of the recommended change?
- Who receives and reviews recommended SOP changes?

RESPONSIBILITIES

A-9. This section identifies the responsibilities of the commander, leaders, and maintainers. Some responsibilities are to monitor—

- Supervisor application of maintenance and safety programs.
- PLL management.
- Daily flying hours and OR condition of each assigned or attached aircraft.

OPERATIONS

A-10. This section identifies the concept of operations. Additionally, this section specifically quantifies and explains, if applicable, deviations to established standard procedures. Topics include—

- What function or service is provided by each platoon, shop, or section?
- How are maintenance activities and actions conducted?
- The days and times specific operations or procedures are conducted.
- The standard procedures maintainers follow when seeking assistance.

PROCEDURES

A-11. This section provides specific steps; such as, when writing the AOAP or TMDE appendix to the SOP, the following is required:

- Samples are taken within 15 minutes after shut down (hot).
- Cold samples are explained in the circumstances block on DD Form 2026.
- Special samples are marked "SPECIAL" in red.

- DD Form 2026 is turned into QC.
- Oil sample bottles are marked with the aircraft serial number and component name.
- Oil samples are turned in the same day as taken.

GENERAL INFORMATION

A-12. This section is optional. If used, the following blanket statement can be entered: "Close coordination from the crew chiefs, MPs, platoon sergeants, and supporting sections in the AMC/AMT is essential to the success of a well-organized maintenance program." This SOP is divided into separate appendices that cover specific areas of aircraft maintenance.

A-13. All maintenance personnel are required to read and be familiar with the unit SOP. All maintenance activity is conducted according to guidance contained within this SOP.

REFERENCES

A-14. This section contains all applicable references and publications. DA PAM 25-30 contains a detailed listing of reference and publication requirements.

APPENDIX 1 (SOP Number) Headquarters, **(enter unit name)** to ANNEX C (Aircraft Maintenance) of 3rd Squadron, 7th US Cavalry, Fort Stewart GA 31314 **(enter name of parent organization and station)** 09 Jul 06 (date) Admin SOP (type of SOP)

1. Applicability:
    a. This SOP applies to all persons assigned or attached to (enter unit name).
    b. Deviation from the guidelines set forth by this SOP may be authorized by the **(parent battalion/squadron)** commander, maintenance unit commander, or the PC officer.
2. Purpose:
    To define aircraft unit maintenance SOP, responsibilities, operational policies, and maintenance procedures for personnel performing aircraft maintenance and related ground support system repair in the **(enter unit name).**
3. Scope:
    This SOP provides information and guidance to all personnel performing maintenance on **(enter unit name)** assigned/attached aircraft.
4. Objectives:
    a. Provide safe, fully mission capable aircraft to meet all training and tactical mission requirements.
    b. Ensure maximum operational readiness of equipment.
    c. Provide early detection and correction of potential equipment failure at the AMC/AMT and, if necessary, rapid evacuation to an ASC/AST for support maintenance.
    d. Enhance aircraft material readiness to achieve, as a minimum, the DA standard.
    e. Standardize applicable maintenance and administrative procedures.
    f. Coordinate recovery and evacuation of assigned/attached aircraft when airframes are NMC and must be evacuated for repairs.
5. Revisions:
    This SOP must be reviewed and, if necessary, revised whenever a new or revised DA publication affecting the contents of this SOP is fielded. If no new DA publications have been fielded, this SOP is reviewed every **(enter time)**. All personnel who are permanently assigned/attached to the **(enter unit name)** may submit proposed changes to this document to commander, **(enter unit name).**
6. Responsibilities:
    a. **(Enter unit name)** commander.
        (1) Has overall responsibility for the supervision of an effective and safe maintenance program.
        (2) Is responsible to the **(enter name of parent operational battalion/squadron)** commander for the conduct of the aviation support company/troop maintenance mission.
        (3) Is responsible for the **(enter unit name)** safety program.
        (4) Monitors a record of the daily aircraft flying hours and the operational readiness condition of each assigned/attached aircraft.
        (5) Monitors the work progress of the various maintenance sections to ensure that a balanced workload is maintained.
        (6) Monitors the preparation and submission of all required status reports to the **(enter name of parent operational battalion/squadron)** commander.
        (7) Monitors the coordination and scheduling requirements for supporting maintenance activities of all work beyond the **(enter unit name)** capability.
        (8) Monitors the management of the aircraft bench stock.
        (9) Monitors the **(enter unit name)** budget. Ensure that the Class IX (air) budget is reconciled by the unit budget officer on a regular schedule. Alerts the **(enter name of parent operational battalion/squadron)** commander whenever a budget discrepancy or short-coming is identified and no resolution is forthcoming from the resource management office.
    b. **(Enter unit name)** first sergeant:
        (1) Is responsible to **(enter unit name)** commander for coordination of all day-to-day action within the unit.
        (2) Enforces hangar safety and maintenance/shop safety procedures.
        (3) Monitors hangar space for cleanliness and safety.
        (4) Establishes and maintains required on-the-job and cross-training programs within the unit for all assigned/attached personnel.
        (5) Informs the **(enter unit name)** commander of all maintenance and personnel matters that affect the unit mission.

Figure A-1. Sample SOP for an AMC/AMT headquarters

7. Organization:
    a. **(Enter unit name)**, Headquarters.
    b. PC Section.
    c. QC Section.
8. General Information:
    Close coordination from the crew chiefs, MPs, platoon sergeants, and the supporting sections in **(enter unit name)** is essential to the success of a well-organized maintenance program. This SOP is divided into separate appendices that cover specific areas of aircraft maintenance. All maintenance personnel should become familiar with this document and conduct their daily maintenance operations according to guidance contained within this SOP.
9. References:

AR 95-1	Flight Regulations
AR 385-10	Army Safety Program
AR 700-138	Army Logistics Readiness and Sustainability
AR 710-2	Supply Policy Below the National Level
AR 750-1	Army Materiel Maintenance Policy
AR 750-43	Army Test, Measurement, and Diagnostic Equipment
DA Pam 385-10	Army Safety Program
DA Pam 385-40	Army Accident Investigation and Reporting
DA Pam 385-64	Ammunition and Explosives Safety Standards
DA Pam 385-90	Army Aviation Accident Prevention Program
DA Pam 710-2-1	Using Unit Supply System (Manual Procedures)
DA Pam 710-2-2	Supply Support Activity Supply System: Manual Procedures
DA Pam 738-751	Functional User's Manual for the Army Maintenance Management System-Aviation (TAMMS-A)
DA Pam 750-1	Commander's Maintenance Handbook
DA Pam 750-8	The Army Maintenance Management System (TAMMS) Users Manual
FM 3-04.500	Army Aviation Maintenance
TM 1-1500-328-23	Aeronautical Equipment Maintenance Management Policies and Procedures

Figure A-1. Sample SOP for an AMC/AMT headquarters (continued)

APPENDIX 2 (Production Control) to ANNEX C (Aircraft Maintenance) of 3rd Squadron, 7th US Cavalry, Fort Stewart GA 31314 **(enter name of parent organization and station)** 09 Jul 06 (date) Admin SOP (type of SOP)

1. Applicability:
   a. This SOP applies to all persons assigned or attached to (enter unit name).
   b. Deviation from the guidelines set forth by this SOP may be authorized only by the **(parent battalion/squadron)** commander, **(enter unit name)** commander, or the PC officer.
2. Purpose:
   To standardize maintenance management procedures and operations within **(enter unit name).**
3. Scope:
   This SOP provides information and guidance to all personnel performing maintenance on **(enter unit name)** aircraft.
4. Objectives:
   a. Standardize maintenance procedures.
   b. Ensure maintenance safety.
   c. Maximize aircraft and equipment operational readiness.
5. Revisions:
   All personnel who are permanently assigned to the **(enter unit name)** may submit proposed changes to this document to commander,
   (enter unit name).
6. Responsibilities of Production Control Personnel:
   a. The PC officer:.
      (1) Oversees operational readiness of all assigned aircraft and related aviation ground support equipment.
      (2) Ensures maintenance and utilization scheduling.
      (3) Ensures collection of all maintenance and readiness data.
      (4) Ensures accurate and timely submission of all required reports.
      (5) Coordinates with support maintenance activities and contract field services representatives.
      (6) Performs duties as ME, MP, and TI.
      (7) Supervises unit tech supply personnel, in the absence of an aviation logistics officer or a tech supply officer.
      (8) Performs such additional duties as may be deemed necessary by the **(enter unit name)** commander.
      (9) Chairs and conducts PC meetings.
   b. The PC NCOIC:
      (1) Oversees internal operation of the PC office and tech supply in the absence of PC officer or a tech supply officer.
      (2) Ensures accuracy of company/troop daily status reports, NMCS records, and DA Form 2408-12s and -13s.
      (3) Conducts daily PC meeting, in the absence of the PC officer.
      (4) Submits **(parent battalion/squadron name)** daily aircraft status report to the aviation brigade.
      (5) Ensure smooth and timely accomplishment of all daily battalion/squadron aircraft maintenance tasks.
      (6) Maintains accurate and up-to-the minute DA Form 1352-1s and ensures monthly DA Form 1352 report is submitted accurately and on time.
      (7) Ensures company/troop aircraft mission assignments enhance the battalion/squadron maintenance posture.
   c. PC Clerk:
      (1) Maintains an automated workorder log when STAMIS is operational. When the STAMIS is inoperable, a manual workorder log (DA Form 2405) must be used. When STAMIS resumes operation, all manual workorder entries are input into the system immediately.
      (2) Initiates and processes internal maintenance workorders. Notifies corresponding shops and sections for pickup of workorders.
      (3) initiates and processes external maintenance workorders. Submits workorders to higher-level maintenance and picks up repaired components.
      (4) Performs all duties assigned by the PC NCOIC/PC officer.
7. Production Control Operations:
   a. The PC section is the data collection, dissemination, and maintenance flow element for all field-level maintenance tasks performed on all battalion/squadron aircraft. To provide a consistent flow of information and maintenance tasks, the following standard procedures are followed by all maintenance personnel.
      (1) PC meeting: PC meeting Monday-Friday at **(enter time)** hours.
Note. Refer to FM 3-04.500, chapter 6, for information on topics of discussion, attendance requirements, and daily aircraft status reporting requirements.

Figure A-2. Sample SOP for an AMC/AMT production control

(2) Daily aircraft status reports.
(3) Work request processing: The following are procedures used by PC personnel when processing work requests for supported unit.
    (a) In-house work requests are submitted to the PC clerk/PC NCOIC on a DA Form 2407, or DA Form 2407-E if using ULLS-A (E), filled out according to DA Pam 738-751. If using ULLS-A (E), the crew chief needs to complete an aircraft migration to process the work request.
    (b) The PC officer or, in his absence, the PC NCOIC will assign the priority.
    (c) The PC clerk/PC NCOIC will log the work request, return the green copy to the originating unit or section, and forward the remaining copies to the appropriate shop for repair actions. Once the repair has been accomplished, the PC clerk/PC NCOIC will reconcile the PC workorder log.
    (d) For requests exceeding the capabilities of **(enter unit name)**, the DA Form 2407, or 2407-E if using ULLS-A (E), are turned over to the ASC/AST. Upon return of a copy of the DA Form 2407 or 2407-E indicating acceptance from ASC/AST, the unit is notified of the workorder number. The original copy of the DA Form 2407 or 2407-E will remain on file in PC until the ASC/AST completes the work.
    (e) Workorder reconciliation may be requested by any platoon sergeant, section sergeant, or crew chief from PC at any time. However, workorders for a grounding (X condition) or PMC condition are reconciled daily at the PC meeting.
(4) DA Forms 1352-1 and 1352 maintenance: The following aircraft forms are used by PC personnel to track aircraft flight hours for assigned or attached aircraft.
    (a) DA Forms 2408-12 and -13 are turned in by the unit to PC no later than **(enter time)** hours for the previous day/night flights. A unit using ULLS-A (E) would include migration of aircraft logbook data using this time as well.
    (b) PC will forward the DA Form 2408-12s and 2408-13s to the **(enter unit name)** QC section after verification of flight hours and downtime.
(5) PC board: PC personnel use the PC board to keep track of aircraft readiness as well as maintenance and logistics actions.
    (a) The PC board is used as a planning tool for daily aircraft maintenance.
    (b) The PC board is updated daily at the PC meeting.
    (c) Any activity within the battalion/squadron having updated aircraft status information will forward that information to PC immediately.
    (d) This board will serve as the battalion/squadron commander quick reference update of fleet status throughout the day.
b. Field operating procedures will mirror those operating procedures adhered to in garrison; however, flexibility is essential. PC will coordinate required deviations due to the field or tactical situation not specifically covered in this SOP.
2. References:
The following references are for both garrison and tactical SOPs. All personnel assigned or attached to the **(enter unit name)** should review references to understand the overall concern for safety and maintenance procedures. These references should be reviewed regularly so that changes or new information provided by these publications can be implemented into this SOP as necessary.

AR 700-138	Army Logistics Readiness and Sustainability
AR 710-2	Supply Policy Below the National Level
AR 750-1	Army Materiel Maintenance Policy
AR 750-43	Army Test, Management, and Diagnostic Equipment Program
DA Pam 710-2-1	Using Unit Supply System (Manual Procedures)
DA Pam 710-2-2	Supply Support Activity Supply System: Manual Procedures
DA Pam 738-751	Functional User's Manual for the Army Maintenance Management System-Aviation (TAMMS-A)
DA Pam 750-8	The Army Maintenance Management System (TAMMS) Users Manual
FM 3-04.500	Army Aviation Maintenance
TM 1-1500-328-23	Aeronautical Equipment Maintenance Management Policies and Procedures

Figure A–2. Sample SOP for an AMC/AMT production control (continued)

This page intentionally left blank.

Appendix B

Safety

This appendix explains the considerations and methods in recognizing and correcting potentially dangerous safety and operational hazards. Personnel must understand the inherent hazards of working in and around aircraft and know and apply the safety principles discussed in this appendix.

GENERAL

B-1. Aviation operations involve inherently higher risk (higher probability of accidents and more severe consequences) than most ground operations. Historically, when deployed to force application theaters, Army aviation has suffered more losses to accidents than to enemy action. Aviation accidents in force application environments are typically the same type experienced in peacetime. A sound and effective safety program for maintenance operations is a basic requirement for all Army aviation maintenance units. Aviation maintenance commanders are responsible for protecting and preserving Army personnel and equipment against accidental loss.

Note. AR 385-10 contains guidance on developing a sound and comprehensive maintenance unit safety program.

ACCIDENT CAUSES

B-2. Aviation maintenance commanders, maintenance officers/technicians and NCOICs (in combination with assigned ASOs) must evaluate maintenance operations to identify potential root causes for accidents. Particular attention must be paid to the five elements (person, task, training, material, and environment) of the system, program, or functional area during the evaluation process to ensure management induced errors receive appropriate corrections. Identifying hazards or potential causes of maintenance-related incidents will not completely eliminate accidents; however, they will mitigate ongoing maintenance operations while minimizing the potential of mission degradation, injury or loss of personnel, or damage or destruction of equipment as a consequence of aviation operations.

B-3. An aviation accident is seldom caused by a single factor. Accidents are more likely to result from a series of events and a combination of factors such as human error, materiel failure, or environment. This fact must be recognized in developing an aviation accident prevention program. The following areas are not all-inclusive but are examples of those areas requiring constant command attention to prevent aviation accidents:

- Human factors.
- Training, education, and promotion.
- Equipment design, adequacy, and supply.
- Normal and emergency procedures.
- Maintenance.
- Facilities and services.
- Environment.
- Operational pace/tempo.
- Personnel tempo.

B-4. USACRC has found that human error accounts for about 80 percent of total mishaps. Maintenance-related mishaps do account for a percentage of total mishaps in terms of both human-error related causal factors as well as materiel-related causes. As expected, more complex aircraft have higher maintenance mishap rates; however, accidents caused solely by materiel failure are considerably rarer than human-error accidents. The interface between man and machine during maintenance operations increases the potential for accidents.

B-5. At unit level, commanders and maintenance supervisors must ensure their personnel know of maintenance errors generated in their own units. They can be made aware of those in other units by examples found in the Knowledge publication, the preventative maintenance monthly magazine (PS magazine), and other publications. All maintenance activities and personnel must strictly adhere to published maintenance procedures and apply CRM at all levels of operations.

SAFETY REGULATIONS

B-6. DOD instruction 6055.1 provides the underpinnings for safety across the DOD. AR 385-10 regulates overall safety in the Army. This regulation integrates Occupational Safety and Health Act requirements into the Army safety program. DA PAM 385-90 regulates the Army aviation accident prevention program. DA PAM 385-40 covers Army accident investigation and reporting. FM 5-19 provides the doctrine and guidance for applying CRM to all Army operations.

B-7. The following personnel have major responsibilities in the unit aviation accident prevention program: the commander, the maintenance officer/technician, the unit safety officer, aviators, the flight surgeon, the unit safety NCO, and individual Soldiers/civilians. A complete knowledge of aviation personnel, materiel, and maintenance operations is necessary to establish and maintain an effective aviation accident prevention plan. The plan must be tailored to the mission and requirements of the command. Activities affecting aviation operations must be considered.

SAFETY RESPONSIBILITIES

B-8. Accidents and injuries can hamper the unit ability to complete its required mission. The unit commander must ensure all personnel know proper operation and safety-related procedures for all aircraft, vehicles, equipment, tools, and machinery. Soldiers/civilians/maintainers are responsible for protecting equipment and the lives of fellow workers; therefore, they must actively participate in safety programs and training.

B-9. The primary safety responsibility for maintenance work performed on the aircraft or on its components rests with the individual performing the work. Peers and the leadership providing oversight are equally responsible for providing an additional measure of protection. The importance of doing the right thing, policing each other, and providing direct supervision regarding safety cannot be overstated.

UNIT COMMANDER

B-10. Commanders are responsible for compliance with DOD, DA, Occupational Safety and Health Administration, National Fire Protection Association, and Environmental Protection Agency requirements. Commanders will establish other requirements, as necessary, for protection of personnel and equipment under their control.

B-11. The commander establishes a written commander safety philosophy. He develops current safety goals, objectives, and priorities, and includes them in quarterly training guidance (annually for the reserve component). The commander understands and applies the CRM process to the entire spectrum of unit operations, activities, and personnel from a holistic standpoint.

B-12. The commander ensures unit staff, subordinate leaders, individual Soldiers, and civilians are trained on the CRM process as a life skill that is applied equally to both on-duty and off-duty activities. The commander integrates identified risk controls into maintenance SOPs (a stand-alone written commander accident prevention plan is no longer required) and ensures written SOPs exist for all functional shop and maintenance areas and all operations within the command.

B-13. Aviation unit commanders are responsible for ensuring activities of their units are conducted according to established safety rules, regulations, and publications. These regulations include the aforementioned DOD instructions, ARs, and DA pamphlets as well as FMs, TBs, TMs, and other required local installation directives and policies.

B-14. Aviation unit commanders are also responsible for determining the cause of accidents and for ensuring measures are taken to prevent their recurrence. They must also be aware of and enforce safety policies and requirements established by higher headquarters.

B-15. Unit commanders are responsible for requesting permission from higher headquarters to deviate from an established safety rule or regulation. This request, including full particulars and detailed plans and specifications, is submitted to the higher headquarters commander for approval; however, unit commanders cannot rely on the safety programs of higher headquarters to ensure the safety of their people. They must also establish their own safety programs and become personally involved in implementing and enforcing them.

AVIATION MAINTENANCE OFFICER AND TECHNICIAN

B-16. The aviation maintenance officer and technician ensure an effective maintenance program is developed and maintained. The aviation maintenance officer/technician will—

- Continuously monitor QC through coordination with QC personnel, ensuring QC personnel complete SF 368 (Product Quality Deficiency Report) according to applicable references and publications.
- Ensure adequate training and cross training of maintenance personnel; ensure a formal continuing education program is available to provide maintenance personnel with current information on techniques, procedures, and modifications.
- Ensure proper and timely aircraft inspections.
- Ensure adequate program supervision to guarantee maintenance personnel are aware of, and comply with, all technical directives affecting aircraft operations.
- Ensure discrepancies (write-ups) are correctly identified as to status and they are properly cleared.
- Monitor and manage the equipment improvement recommendation program and the AOAP.
- Provide maintenance personnel with lessons-to-be-learned from accident summaries that cite maintenance as the accident cause factor.
- Ensure MPs (Army and contractor) meet the requirements of AR 95-1 and TM 1-1500-328-23 to perform MTFs, and ensure MTFs are performed according to appropriate directives.
- Ensure subordinate leaders and maintainers understand and apply the CRM process to all maintenance operations.
- Use the CRM process to mitigate or eliminate hazards associated with the personnel and activities that might affect the safe performance of maintenance operations.

UNIT NONCOMMISSIONED OFFICERS-IN-CHARGE AND SUPERVISORS

B-17. Effective supervision is the key to accident prevention. In their daily contact with Soldiers, NCOICs are in a position to personally observe working conditions and potential hazards affecting maintenance procedures. NCOICs must apply all established accident prevention measures in the performance of their duties especially when supervising daily maintenance operations.

B-18. They should conduct meetings with their subordinates at regular intervals to brief them on safety procedures, to obtain feedback/suggestions on ways of improving safety practices, and/or to announce any new safety procedures. Such meetings should be held in the work (shop or hangar) area. The agenda should include the following:

- The overall job and the results expected.
- The how, why, and when of the job and any ideas from the group on ways to improve methods and procedures.

- The part each Soldier will play; supervisors must ensure personnel understand the significance of individual roles.
- Existing and anticipated hazards and the action needed to resolve these problems.
- The need for prompt, accurate reporting of injuries, accidents, or near accidents, and the importance of first aid when required.
- The need to search constantly for, detect, and correct unsafe practices and conditions to prevent accidents and injuries.
- The need for maintainers to understand and apply the CRM process to maintenance operations.

AVIATION SAFETY OFFICER AND NONCOMMISSIONED OFFICER

B-19. The unit ASO and NCO assist, advise, and make recommendations to the unit commander regarding aviation accident-prevention matters. He observes aircraft support activities (such as POL, maintenance, operations, and enlisted crewmembers' training) to detect and report unsafe practices or procedures. The ASO and NCO participate in unit safety surveys and inspections.

B-20. The ASO and NCO provides CRM training to leaders and maintainers, ensuring unit personnel understand and apply the CRM process to operations conducted within the organization. In addition, individuals are encouraged to apply CRM to off-duty activities as a life skill.

SHOP SAFETY

B-21. Maintenance repair section and shop safety is an on-going process. Safety is to be observed not only when conducting maintenance and repair procedures but also in every phase of aviation operations. An aviation maintenance section or shop below the established standard (safety hazards, unserviceable tools and equipment, out-of-calibration TMDE, or outdated references/publications) cannot perform quality maintenance. SOF is compromised when maintainers, at any level, deviate from the established maintenance standard or fail to conduct by-the-book maintenance procedures.

B-22. Safety procedures must be adhered to by all maintenance personnel during aircraft maintenance procedures. Maintenance leaders, officers/technicians, and NCOICs are responsible for providing close supervision and correcting unsafe acts.

B-23. Fall protection is defined as maintaining "three points of contact" (one hand and two feet or two hands and one foot) on the hand holds, foot accesses/recesses, and walking/working surfaces designed into/provided on the aircraft when working on aircraft (other than home garrison maintenance pads, parking aprons, and wash racks). Fall restraint device usage is at the discretion of the maintenance supervisor or, in the absence of maintenance supervision, the PC OIC/NCOIC.

B-24. NCOICs are responsible for keeping their assigned sections/shops safe, operational, and within the established standard as outlined in the aviation maintenance commander internal SOP. In addition, it is the TI responsibility to keep assigned sections/shops within the established standard when conducting inspections of the maintenance sections, shops, and work areas, to include the hangar. These inspections are conducted monthly or more frequently when maintenance procedures are conducted.

B-25. Any shortcoming, deficiency, or safety hazard identified during a safety inspection is recorded on DA Form 2404 or unit hazard tracking log with copies given to the NCOIC and the maintenance officer/technician. The original copy of DA Form 2404 is kept by the QC section and filed IAW AR 25-400-2. Safety shortcomings, deficiencies, or hazards considered a danger to personnel or equipment are immediately brought to the attention of the NCOIC and maintenance officer/technician for corrective action. Inspectors will forward copies of all inspection results to the ASO or unit safety manager.

B-26. Routine or noncritical shortcomings, deficiencies, or hazards found during a maintenance section and shops safety inspection must receive corrective action and achieve compliance within 10 days. A completed DA Form 2404, indicating corrections resulting in compliance or recording deficiencies for future mitigation, is given to the QC section for filing with the original copy. The QC section will give recommendations and guidance to assist in correcting faults. The QC section will re-inspect to ensure shortcomings and identified deficiencies are corrected.

INDIVIDUAL SOLDIER/MAINTAINER

B-27. All personnel must be aware of the safety rules established for their individual and collective protection. Each person is responsible for reading and adhering to unit SOPs, instructions, operating procedures, checklists, and other safety-related data. They must observe and apply notes, cautions and warnings found on applicable aircraft maintenance TMs. Personnel must then apply cautions and safeguards in their everyday work areas.

B-28. Soldiers/civilians are responsible for bringing to their supervisor attention safety voids, hazards, and unsafe or incomplete maintenance procedures. Each person must follow through until the problem is corrected, then cooperate in developing and practicing safe working habits. The unit commander should make certain this spirit of cooperation prevails throughout the unit.

B-29. Soldiers/civilians are responsible for understanding and applying the CRM process to all duties and maintenance activities that could result in performance degradation, injury or illness, damage or destruction of equipment or to those off-duty activities or issues affecting their ability to report for duty and perform in a safe and effective manner.

B-30. Fall protection is defined as maintaining "three points of contact" (one hand and two feet or two hands and one foot) on the hand holds, foot accesses/recesses, and walking/working surfaces designed into/provided on the aircraft when working on aircraft (other than home garrison maintenance pads, parking aprons, and wash racks). Fall-restraint device usage is at the discretion of the maintenance supervisor or, in the absence of maintenance supervision, the PC OIC/NCOIC.

OPERATIONAL PROCEDURES

B-31. Aviation maintenance commanders/leaders, aviation maintenance officers/technicians, and NCOICs will ensure physical standards for facilities and equipment meet or exceed safety and health standards established in pertinent host government, federal, state, and local statutes and regulations and in ARs.

B-32. Ensure the CRM process is incorporated in directives, unit maintenance SOPs, special orders, training plans, and operational plans to minimize accident risk and SOPs are developed for all operations entailing risk of death, serious injury, occupational illness, property loss, or mission degradation.

B-33. Establish specific plans to assure continuity of safety and operational hazard program services during tactical operations or mobilization. These plans will address mission definition, organizational concepts, and staffing and operational procedures required to assure maximum safety function support to the force application mission. All aviation units will develop such plans.

OPERATIONAL HAZARDS

B-34. An operational hazard is any condition, action, or set of circumstances that compromises the safety of Army aircraft, associated personnel, airfields, or equipment. Operational hazards should be corrected at the lowest level possible. These hazards include inadequacies, deficiencies, or unsafe practices pertaining to aircraft operations, aircraft maintenance or inspections, or flight and maintenance training and education.

OPERATIONAL HAZARD REPORT

B-35. DA Form 2696 (Operational Hazard Report) is used to record information about hazardous acts or conditions before accidents occur. The OHR form is available on the Army electronic library disk and the APD web site. Place blank copies of the report forms in areas where they are readily available to all aviation-related personnel.

SUBMITTING OPERATIONAL HAZARD REPORTS

B-36. Any person (military or civilian) may submit an OHR. The signature and address of the individual submitting the OHR are desirable but not mandatory unless the individual wishes to have a copy of the completed report returned. An OHR is not required when an aircraft accident report is prepared according to DA PAM 385-40 or when a deficiency report is submitted according to DA PAM 738-751.

ROUTING THE OPERATIONAL HAZARD REPORT

B-37. The OHR is submitted to an ASO or Army flight operations office. A report sent to an operations office is promptly forwarded to the organization ASO.

HAZARD COMMUNICATION

B-38. Aviation unit commanders will develop and implement a unit HAZCOM program to ensure compliance with 29 CFR 1910.1200 and DOD instruction 6050.5 directives. Commanders will ensure an accurate inventory is maintained of all hazardous chemicals used by unit maintenance personnel. Additionally, units will comply with Occupational Safety and Health Administration 29 CFR 1910.1200, appendix E when identifying hazards present in the environment or facility that unit personnel may contact. All personnel must know the location of the MSDS for each hazard present, not just contained in POL or HAZMAT program storage.

B-39. The HAZCOM officer ensures MSDSs (http://www.hazard.com/msds) are readily available for and used by personnel handling or contacting hazardous chemicals. He ensures personnel handling hazardous chemicals receive training as specified by DOD and federal statute. He also ensures hazardous chemicals receive proper labels, storage, use, and disposal.

SHOP SAFETY

B-40. A shop below standard cannot put out high standard, quality work. To ensure shops/sections maintain a high safety standard, TIs will conduct an informal inspection of the various shops/sections periodically. Any deficiencies or shortcomings, identified as below-standard maintenance practices or safety hazards, are brought to the attention of the shop maintenance technician/supervisor immediately. A file of all safety inspections is kept in the QC section, and a file copy is kept in the subject area inspected. Inspectors will forward copies of all inspection results to the ASO or unit safety manager for inclusion in the unit hazard analysis and tracking program.

MAINTENANCE FACILITIES

B-41. The NCOIC supervisor responsible for facility safety will emphasize accident-prevention measures and shop equipment safety. To minimize shop-related accidents, the facility NCOIC will satisfactorily address the following questions:

- Does the facility NCOIC or supervisor emphasize accident prevention measures and check for marking and width of personnel safety aisles, safety and warning posters, and smoking and nonsmoking areas? (Refer to this publication, TM 1-1500-204-23-1, and DA PAM 385-1.)
- Is all stationary and portable shop electrical equipment properly grounded? (Refer to TM 1-1500-204-23-1 and national electrical codes.)
- Is there a program in effect to encourage reporting of problem areas such as hazards, near accidents, and unsafe practices? (Refer to AR 95-1, AR 385-10, DA PAM 385-40, and DA PAM 385-90.)
- Are equipment and vehicle operators thoroughly familiar with the equipment operation, handling, care, and preventive maintenance? (For example, do operators have permits? [Refer to AR 600-55]. Is the maintenance manual near equipment? [Refer to this publication]. Is the equipment or vehicle maintained according to organizational and operator manuals?)

- When parts or items are removed from aircraft, are they marked and stored in plain sight? (Refer to this publication.)
- Are proper safety procedures practiced to prevent FOD when maintenance is performed on turbine engines?
- Are run-up and exhaust areas policed? Are containers available for trash and loose objects? Are loose hardware and other foreign objects removed? (Refer to TM 1-1500-204-23 series.)
- Are grounding cables provided for aircraft in hangars? Are they used? Has an initial electrical resistance test been performed and recorded on grounding points? (Refer to national fire codes, TM 1-1500-204-23 series, and FM 10-67-1.)
- Are grounding safety wires visible? Are they bright yellow?
- Is adequate lighting provided for maintenance facilities and hangars?
- Are parts removed from aircraft immediately written up on appropriate forms? (Refer to DA PAM 738-751.)
- Are required numbers and types of fire extinguishers available? Are aircraft and ground fire extinguishers checked as required? Are personnel trained to use fire-fighting equipment? (Refer to this publication and TM 1-1500-204-23 series.)
- Are trained specialists available to maintain special equipment, such as ejection seat and armament, when installed in unit aircraft? (Refer to this publication and AR 95-1.)
- Are facilities clean and floors grease-free? (Refer to this publication.)
- Do personnel using power tools (for example, drills, grinders, lathes, and torches) wear safety goggles and noise-attenuating devices as required? Do repairers remove jewelry while performing maintenance? (Refer to TM 1-1500-204-23 series and ARs 40-5 and 385-10.)
- Are hoisting instructions for lifting aircraft components or aircraft followed? Are cranes, hoists, cables, slings, and forklift trucks inspected, weight-tested, and stenciled with the load rating? (Refer to TB 43-0142.)
- Are cranes, hoists, cables, slings, and forklift trucks stenciled with the date of the next required load test? (Refer to TB 43-0142 and this publication.)
- Are aircraft on jacks labeled, and is access to them restricted? Are aircraft jacks marked with the maximum lifting capacity? (Refer to this publication, TM 1-1500-204-23 series, and Occupational Safety and Health Administration standard 1910.244.)
- Do personnel in the instrument shop know the procedures for cleaning up mercury spills? (Refer to TB 385-4.)
- Are oily rags stored in closed metal containers? Are containers properly labeled? (Refer to this manual and TM 1-1500-204-23 series.)
- Are hydraulic, fuel, and oil lines protected from dirt while disconnected? (Refer to TM 1-1500-204-23 series.)
- Are all ammunition and pyrotechnics removed from aircraft before maintenance and before putting aircraft in hangars? (Refer to TM 1-1500-204-23 series.)
- Are engine, hydraulic, propeller and rotor, technical supply, and other work areas clean and well arranged? (Refer to this publication and TM 1-1500-204-23 series.)
- Are oxygen gaseous storage areas properly marked? Are oxygen gaseous cylinders stored in a separate building (area) from aircraft servicing and maintenance areas? Are empty and full cylinders stored separately? (Refer to TM 1-1500-204-23 series and national fire codes standard 410B.)
- Are sample bottles available to check fuel contamination in aircraft fuel tanks during preflight? (Refer to FM 10-67-1.)
- Are proper containers used and stored? Are containers clean and adequate? Are samples properly discarded? Is a fire point nearby? Are complete daily inspections conducted? (Use PMD/preventive maintenance services cards and orms 2408-13 and 2408-13-1.)
- Are tops of booths, shelves, and other surfaces in the paint shop clean to prevent lint accumulation? Are dope or paint deposits removed from the floor? Are there fire blankets at

strategic points and the required number (and correct type) of fire extinguishers provided throughout the paint shop? Is electrical equipment in the paint shop explosion-proof? Are smoking restrictions enforced? (Refer to TM 1-1500-204-23 series.)

- Are unsealed hydraulic fluid containers considered contaminated and destroyed? (Refer to TM 1-1500-204-23 series.)
- Are the assigned aircraft marked and painted to include warnings? (Refer to TM 55-1500-345-23.)
- Are necessary accident prevention signs posted in the shop area? (Refer to TM 1-1500-204-23 series.)
- Are aircraft parked in hangars? Are aircraft batteries disconnected? Are static ground cables attached? Are drip pans placed beneath aircraft?
- Does gasoline-powered equipment (such as tugs and APUs) parked in hangars overnight have full fuel tanks?

HAND TOOLS AND EQUIPMENT

B-42. The NCOIC supervisor, responsible for hand tools and equipment safety, will emphasize accident prevention measures and hand-tool and equipment safety. To minimize hand tools and equipment accidents, the NCOIC will satisfactorily address the following questions:

- Are racks, shelves, or toolboxes provided for tools not in use?
- Are precautions taken to prevent tools from dropping or falling from ladders, scaffolds, platforms, or other elevations?
- Are tools frequently inspected by responsible personnel? Are defective tools turned in for repair or salvage?
- Are tools with sharp cutting edges carried in protective covers?
- Are power tools equipped with guards? Are electrical contacts enclosed? Is wiring well insulated and grounded?
- Are exposed sharp edges smoothed down when work is completed?
- Are ladders used, rather than improvised ladders, such as packing cases or barrels?
- Are parts and items removed from the aircraft stowed out of the way or marked so they are visible day or night?
- Are tools stored so sharp edges do not protrude?
- Are electrical tools used inside the aircraft?
- Are nuts and bolts torqued as specified in the appropriate TM?
- Are items stored in the tool crib cleaned and lubricated to prevent rust? Are they within the calibration due date if calibration is required? (Refer to TB 43-180.)
- Are grease guns labeled with contents?

WELDING EQUIPMENT

B-43. The shop NCOIC supervisor responsible for welding equipment safety will emphasize accident-prevention measures and welding equipment safety. To minimize welding equipment accidents, the shop NCOIC will satisfactorily address the following questions:

- During welding or cutting operations, is caution observed to prevent sparks from starting fires? Is a fire extinguisher available?
- Are safety goggles provided for operators using oxyacetylene equipment?
- During electric welding operations, is the operator wearing a face shield or helmet with shaded falter glass, protective sleeves, gloves, and apron? Are welding operations screened off when other personnel are nearby?

GENERAL HOUSEKEEPING

B-44. The NCOIC supervisor responsible for general housekeeping of the work area will emphasize accident-prevention measures and housekeeping. To minimize housekeeping-related accidents, the NCOIC will satisfactorily address the following questions:

- Are covered, fire-resistant rubbish cans used in work areas?
- Are self-closing covered metal waste cans conveniently located to dispose of oil rags and waste?
- Are volatile flammable liquids used for washing or cleaning parts? Are they stored in open containers? Are working quantities of such liquids confined to approved containers?
- Is dripping or spilling of oil prevented? Are drip pans or other suitable means provided to collect excess oil?
- Are conspicuously marked fire extinguishers of the appropriate type provided in armament, maintenance, and training areas?
- Are all fire extinguishers properly charged, periodically tested, and ready for instant use?
- Are all unit personnel trained to use fire extinguishers?

This page intentionally left blank.

Appendix C

Unit Deployment and Redeployment

This appendix addresses deployment of ground vehicles, equipment, and aircraft. The capability to quickly and safely deploy aviation maintenance units and assets from CONUS to other CONUS locations, or from forward-deployment sites to another theater of operations, is critical for aviation sustainment. A maintenance unit successful deployment or redeployment is derived from thorough planning, extensive training, and a scrutinized validation of their movement plans (FM 4-01.011).

DEPLOYMENT RESPONSIBILITIES

C-1. A unit movement officer (UMO) and alternate are appointed, in writing, for each aviation maintenance unit. The alternate UMO is normally an NCO. The UMO is trained at a school or within the unit. UMOs will—

- Develop, prepare, and maintain unit movement and deployment plans and documentation including unit movement data used to generate the organizational equipment list.
- Create and process the unit deployment list.
- Supervise the preparation and execution of unit load plans, including vehicle load plans.
- Train unit load teams.
- Ensure unit personnel authorized to certify HAZMATs are available.
- Prepare and maintain documentation needed for unit movements.
- Assist in preparation of unit passenger and cargo manifests; inspect manifests for accuracy.
- Coordinate with higher headquarters and supporting units for unit movements.
- Plan convoy movements.
- Request commercial and military transportation.
- Coordinate with the arrival/departure airfield control group and contingency response element at the aerial port of embarkation and aerial port of debarkation.
- Coordinate with surface deployment and distribution command representatives at the sea port of embarkation and sea port of debarkation. Surface deployment and distribution cgommand web site at http://www.sddc.army.mil.
- Obtain 463L pallets, containers, and blocking, bracing, packing, crating, and tie-down materials.
- Ensure all cargo is properly labeled with military shipping labels and radio frequency tags when directed.
- Ensure packing lists are prepared for containers.
- Maintain a UMO movement and deployment binder.

HAZARDOUS CARGO CERTIFYING OFFICIAL

C-2. Each aviation unit requires at least one DOD-approved, school-trained hazardous cargo certifying official. The commander designates the hazardous cargo-certifying official in writing. The designation must include the scope of the hazardous cargo certifying official authority. The hazardous cargo certifying official—

- Certifies documents for commercial and military truck, rail, sea, and air shipment.

- Ensures properly prepared, packaged, and marked shipments.
- Inspects the item, then certifies and signs the HAZMAT documentation.

C-3. The hazardous cargo certifying official training must be within the past 24 months and/or completed refresher training every two years to continue to certify shipments of HAZMAT for transportation.

LOAD TEAMS

C-4. Units are required to have an appropriate number of personnel trained in vehicle, aircraft, ship/vessel, and railcar loading/unloading techniques. Training can be arranged through the installation unit movement coordinator or division transportation officer. Load teams—

- Prepare vehicle, air, container, and rail load plans.
- Prepare vehicles for shipment (purging, protecting fragile components, weighing, and marking for air and rail movement).
- Perform aircraft and railcar tie-down procedures.
- Load and unload unit vehicles.
- Load cargo into aircraft.
- Palletize cargo on 463L pallets.

C-5. Load team composition is tailored to the type and quantity of equipment and time available for loading. The following guidelines are provided for planning purposes:

- For rail movement, a well-trained team of five operators, using prefabricated tie-down devices, can complete loading and lashing of equipment on a chain-equipped flatcar; units are normally provided 72 hours for loading once the cars are spotted.
- For air movement, a six-person team can provide efficient loading and tie-down of equipment. Depending on the aircraft type, more than one team may be required.

MOVEMENT PLANNING

C-6. To meet contingency support requirements, aviation maintenance units must develop deployment movement plans and SOPs. An effective movement plan contains sufficient detail to prepare units to execute strategic deployments. The unit movement SOP is a generic document outlining functions that should occur automatically upon notification of a unit movement. In addition to movement plans and SOPs, units often maintain movement binders and battle books, which contain movement information and instructions. Movement plans can be mobilization movement plans/deployment movement plans.

UNIT MOVEMENT STANDING OPERATING PROCEDURE

C-7. SOPs address the following functions:

- Unit property disposition.
- Supply draw (unit basic load).
- Equipment maintenance.
- Vehicle and container loading.
- Security.
- Marshaling procedures.
- Purchasing authorities.
- Unit briefings.
- Other applicable deployment activities.

C-8. For deployment preparation and execution, units may use a readiness SOP or supplement their higher headquarters readiness SOP/deployment SOP. The readiness SOP normally addresses the overall deployment concept, force packages, training requirements, the alert notification system, logistics support, personnel and equipment readiness, out-load support, Soldier readiness program, and C2 at critical points (FM 71-100). This document is essential for the orderly execution of rapid force deployments in response to crises.

MOVEMENT AND DEPLOYMENT BINDER

C-9. The UMO should maintain a movement and deployment binder for reference and continuity (FM 4-01.011). The recommended contents for a deployment binder (Defense Transportation Regulation 4500.9R-Part III Mobility-Appendix A) include the following:

- Administrative section:
    - Index.
    - Unit movement SOP, including notes from previous operations.
    - Appointment orders and training certificates for UMO, load teams, and HAZMAT certifiers.
    - List of pertinent references.
    - POC, telephone numbers, and email addresses for key personnel to ensure deconfliction and smooth movement of personnel, supplies, and equipment.
    - Recall rosters and instructions.
- Operational section:
    - Index.
    - Air movement planning work sheet.
    - Weight and dimensions data on unit aircraft, vehicles, and equipment.
    - Manifest forms with copies.
    - Planning data on transport aircraft, ships, rail cars, and trucks.
    - Current automated unit equipment list.
    - Copies of load cards and container packing lists.
    - Prepared copies of transportation requests, convoy movement requests and special handling permits.
    - Blocking, bracing, packing, crating, and tie-down requirements.
    - Maps of convoy routes.
    - Plans and locations for drawing Army pre-positioned stocks.
    - Any other data required for movement of the unit.

DEPLOYMENT

C-10. Aviation unit deployment encompasses all activities from origin or home station through destination, including predeployment events, as well as intra-continental United States, inter-theater and intra-theater movement legs.

PREDEPLOYMENT ACTIVITIES

C-11. Predeployment activities prepare individuals, units, and materiel at home station or point of origin for deployment. During predeployment activities, the commander establishes movement priority that may be divided into groups, such as advance party and main body. Movement of unit personnel depends on the situation and is based on a thorough mission, enemy, terrain and weather, troops and support available, time available, and civil considerations assessment.

MOVEMENT TO PORT OF EMBARKATION

C-12. After receiving movement orders, along with any additional guidance, deploying units validate and configure for movement to the port of embarkation (POE).

C-13. The port call message identifies the date the unit must have equipment at the POE to meet the available to load dates. The deploying unit higher headquarters or the installation prepares a movement schedule or order containing unit movement times and modes for movement to the POE.

C-14. The movement mode from POE to port of debarkation determines how unit equipment is prepared for deployment. In an overseas deployment, transport of unit equipment by sea occurs two to three weeks before the unit main body personnel depart for the AO by air.

C-15. Some equipment and cargo require reconfiguration upon arrival at staging/marshaling areas enroute to the aerial port of embarkation/sea port of embarkation; such as, a unit convoying from home station to the aerial port of embarkation has organic vehicles moving on highways requiring correct configuration for safe highway movement. Equipment reaching the aerial port of embarkation staging/marshaling area then requires reconfiguration and preparation to meet airlift requirements.

C-16. Based on the unit proximity to the POE, availability of transport, and type of unit equipment; the unit moves to the POE by convoy, rail, commercial truck or bus, or a combination. Army rotary-wing aircraft typically self-deploy to the POE. Personnel move to the POE by organic vehicles or military/commercial buses. The two most used modes for moving equipment to the POE are highway and rail.

REDEPLOYMENT

C-17. Redeployment transfers forces and materiel to support joint force commander operational requirements, or returns personnel, equipment, and materiel to the home and/or demobilization stations for reintegrating and/or out-processing.

PROCEDURES

C-18. Installations have assigned redeployment responsibilities for supporting Army forces stationed in the United States. For foreign-based forces, the foreign home installation and the area support group (ASG) have redeployment responsibilities. Upon initiation of redeployment operations, installations begin preparatory actions to receive units at the port of debarkation and move them to their home/demobilization station.

C-19. Movement guidance to redeploying units addresses—
- Preparing subordinate unit movement plans.
- Updating unit movement documentation.
- Identifying and coordinating channels for any additional transportation support needed to move unit personnel and equipment to POEs.
- Preparing and submitting redeployment/deployment equipment list.

ROUTING

C-20. The redeployment plan designates redeploying unit routing to POEs. After completion of military operations, redeploying forces move to designated assembly areas. Based on the redeployment scenario, redeploying units could then move from the assembly area directly to the POE marshaling areas for loading.

C-21. The routing of units to their final destination depends on—
- Strategic lift asset availability.
- Theater transportation facilities and their throughput capacities.
- Distance/geography between unit location and POE.
- Potential for hostile action.
- Force size.
- Time available.
- Follow-on destination and mission.

C-22. Upon receiving a warning order, the unit starts the redeployment process. Units evaluate the assigned mission, current unit status, and requirements to accomplish the redeployment mission. If the unit is redeploying to another theater, it must also plan for employment in that theater. Depending on their mission and redeployment scenario, redeploying units may perform the following functions as a part of the movement to POE phase:

- Move to assembly areas. The unit normally conducts a movement to the tactical assembly area and continues to receive sustainment through normal support channels.
- Reorganize. Unit reconstitution for redeployment involves those actions required to assemble and organize the unit and to cross-level personnel, supplies, and equipment as necessary; units are consolidated under their UICs.
- Process personnel and equipment for redeployment. This process includes actions that can be completed at the assembly area, assuming availability of support assets and supplies.

C-23. Commanders/leaders should complete the following key items as early as possible in the redeployment process:

- Identify Soldiers and civilians who will deploy as individuals to supporting personnel managers.
- Conduct medical screening.
- Perform equipment checks and services according to TMs.
- Conduct an equipment inventory (Class VII, organizational clothing and individual equipment, and BIIs).
- Refine the DEL, and verify unit line number data.
- Requisition required parts.
- Schedule or defer/delay required maintenance.

C-24. The unit completes all documentation (hazardous shipping declarations, papers, labels, placards, secondary cargo load plans/cards, packing lists, and military shipping labels) before loading. The DEL is completed with actual weights, dimensions, and final destination before producing labels and applying them to equipment and containers.

REFERENCES

C-25. Table C-1 lists unit movement references.

Table C-1. Unit movement references

AR 220-1	Unit Status Reporting
AR 600-8-101	Personnel Processing (In-, Out-, Soldier Readiness, Mobilization and Deployment Processing)
AR 600-55	The Army Driver and Operator Standardization Program (Selection, Training, Testing and Licensing)
AR 710-2	Supply Policy Below Wholesale Level
Defense Transportation Regulation 4500.9-R	Part I through VII at http://www.transcom.mil/j5/pt/dtr.cfm
FM 3-0	Operations
FM 3-35.1	Army Prepositioned Operations
FM 4-01.011	Unit Movement Operations
FM 4-01.30	Movement Control
FMI 3-35	Army Deployment and Redeployment
FORSCOM/ARNG Regulation 55-1	Unit Movement Planning
FORSCOM Regulation 55-2	Unit Movement Data Reporting
JP 3-35	Deployment and Redeployment Operations
TM 38-250	Preparing Hazardous Materials for Military Air Shipments

This page intentionally left blank.

Appendix D

Environmental Management

This appendix identifies environmental issues and compliance requirements that commanders and leaders must be familiar with and adhere to in order to be successful on the battlefield. Environmental damage, in most cases, is an unavoidable consequence of force application. Commanders and their staff must identify, during the planning process, ways and means to mitigate environmental damage wherever possible. These actions ensure deployed forces conform to the environmental protection requirements of the theater commander without impairing force application effectiveness.

ENVIRONMENTAL COMPLIANCE AS A REGULATORY REQUIREMENT

D-1. The Army and its units will comply with all environmental laws and regulations applying to installations or theaters of operation. AR 200-1 and FM 3-100.4 provide an overview of the key environmental laws, regulations, and treaties that apply to unit-level operations. These come from a variety of sources to include federal, state, local host-nation, executive order, DOD policies and directives, and international agreements.

ENVIRONMENTAL RESPONSIBILITIES

D-2. Commanders, leaders, aviation maintenance officers/technicians, NCOICs, and maintainers must understand their individual duties and responsibilities for environmental protection and become environmental stewards. To practice stewardship, personnel must understand the basic environmental management responsibilities that apply to their work area or assigned duties.

COMMANDERS

D-3. The commander role in environmental stewardship centers on instilling an environmental ethic in his Soldiers and civilian contractors (if assigned) under his control. Commanders train their subordinate leaders on stewardship, counsel them on doing what is right, lead by example, and enforce compliance with laws and regulations. FM 3-100.4 identifies sources of environmental assistance available to commanders.

D-4. Commanders meet with key installation environmental personnel to obtain information on, and assistance with, environmental protection issues. Commanders look to environmental personnel for detailed guidance on regulatory compliance, environmental assessments, and to review environmental problems common to other commanders.

D-5. The primary POC is located at the installation environmental office. This office is normally part of the Directorate of Public Works at most Army installations.

MAINTENANCE OFFICER/TECHNICIAN

D-6. The maintenance officer/technician plans, coordinates, and supervises maintenance and repair activities. In many instances, these activities use significant quantities of HAZMAT and generate hazardous waste (HW). The maintenance officer/technician ensures safe use, storage, and disposal of these materials, including the operation of temporary storage areas for products such as used oils, contaminated fuels, paint residues, spill cleanup residues, and solvents. Disposal of HAZMAT and HW is accomplished IAW the unit maintenance SOP.

D-7. The maintenance officer/technician ensures all personnel comply with HAZCOM requirements. The maintenance officer/technician ensures a valid and current unit environmental plan SOP is available and unit personnel are familiar with its contents. FM 3-100.4 contains a sample unit environmental plan SOP.

MAINTENANCE PERSONNEL

D-8. Aviation maintenance personnel have the inherent professional and personal responsibility to understand and support their unit environmental program by—

- Complying with environmental requirements in unit and installation SOPs.
- Maintaining environmental awareness throughout daily activities and maintenance procedures.
- Providing recommendations to the chain of command on techniques to ensure compliance with environmental regulatory requirements.
- Identifying the environmental risks associated with individual and team tasks.
- Supporting recycling programs.
- Reporting HAZMAT and HW spills immediately.
- Making sound environmental decisions based on guidance from the chain of command and training.

ESTABLISHING A UNIT-LEVEL PROGRAM

D-9. The unit commander, with assistance from the HW coordinator, environmental compliance officer (ECO), and environmental compliance NCO, establishes an effective aviation maintenance unit environmental program by—

- Designating, in writing, a properly trained and qualified HW coordinator, ECO, and environmental compliance NCO.
- Identifying the requirements for environmental training, qualifications, and certification of unit personnel.
- Ensuring all unit personnel received or scheduled to receive environmental awareness training.
- Meeting with battalion/squadron S-3, S-4, and installation personnel who deal with environmental issues.
- Scheduling environmental compliance assessment system inspections that identify unit and common environmental problem areas and how to avoid them.
- Ensuring the unit environmental SOP adequately addresses environmental issues and procedures.
- Coordinating environmental requirements with appropriate installation and chain of command personnel.

D-10. The ECO and environmental compliance NCO is the unit POCs and responsible for environmental education, SOP updates, preparation of environmental risk assessments, and incident reporting. The ECO coordinates with environmental personnel and ensures unit compliance with environmental laws and regulations.

ARMY ENVIRONMENTAL COMPLIANCE ASSESSMENT SYSTEM

D-11. Compliance with environmental regulations is a command responsibility. All aviation maintenance units must be familiar with the regulations and publications governing environmental protection. Units also comply with environmental compliance achievement program protocol and are periodically inspected. Units obtain environmental compliance achievement program protocols from the environmental division of the installation Directorate of Public Works.

D-12. Units report alleged violations of local, state, or federal environmental laws or regulations to the commander, environmental division, or the environmental law attorney, Office of the Staff Judge Advocate. Personnel report any notice of tax, penalty, fee, fine, sanction, or other compliance order arising from local, state, or federal environmental requirements or enforcement activities to the commander, environmental division, or the environmental law attorney, Office of the Staff Judge Advocate.

HAZARDOUS MATERIALS

D-13. The Army objective is to minimize health hazards and environmental damage caused by the use and misuse of HAZMAT. A HAZMAT is one that, because of its quantity, concentration, physical, chemical, or infectious characteristics, may do the following:

- Cause or significantly contribute to an increase in mortality or an increase in serious irreversible or incapacitating reversible illness.
- Pose a substantial present or potential hazard to human health or the environment when improperly treated, stored, transported, disposed of, or otherwise managed.

HAZARDOUS WASTE

D-14. The presence of HW is a cause for concern among installation personnel and nearby residential populations. Yet, hazardous substances are an unavoidable part of Army maintenance functions and activities and ultimately result in some waste generation. The proper handling and disposal of HW minimizes danger and ensures the safety of people and the environment.

HAZARDOUS COMMUNICATION

D-15. An effective HAZCOM program will assist leaders in determining which hazardous chemicals are present in their units, how to protect their Soldiers from the hazards that those chemicals present, and how to properly store and use those chemicals. The installation safety officer is the POC for most HAZCOM matters, the MSDS program (http://www.hazard.com/msds), and the HAZCOM training program.

GOOD HOUSEKEEPING

D-16. Good housekeeping is another basic management practice and involves a number of activities in areas such as maintenance, operations, and training. For instance, preventing spills is a good housekeeping practice for both safety and environmental reasons. Keeping noise to a minimum is good OPSEC and reduces noise pollution. Recycling diminishes solid waste and helps eliminate unauthorized disposal of some types of HW.

UNIT MAINTENANCE

D-17. Unit maintenance activities may significantly affect the environment so most Army environmental programs directly affect maintenance operations. Two specific areas of concern are spill prevention and response, and HAZMAT storage and handling.

SPILL PREVENTION AND RESPONSE

D-18. Army policy, as well as federal law, requires units to prevent spills of oil and hazardous substances and to provide prompt response to contain and clean up such spills. These laws, regulations, and policies prohibit any discharge of oil or hazardous substance from installations, vehicles, aircraft, and watercraft into the environment without a discharge permit.

D-19. Installation requirements shape spill prevention and response plans for units within their jurisdiction and command. During deployments, the deployment order directs spill prevention and response procedures. During contingency operations or in a force application environment, spill prevention and response procedures are defined by the host-nation or theater guidance and unit SOP.

HAZARDOUS MATERIAL STORAGE AND HANDLING

D-20. Maintenance personnel work with a variety of HAZMAT and HW. Depending on the class of supply, the supply room or technical supply section controls requisitions and receipts for HAZMAT and prepares documentation for turn-in of HW. Maintenance personnel generate HW by lubricating, servicing, and repairing aviation and ground equipment. Maintenance personnel must—

- Requisition only the minimum amount of HAZMAT needed; when possible, substitute nonhazardous materials.
- Practice inventory control of all HAZMAT and HW (monitor HAZMAT shelf life and HW accumulation dates).
- Store HAZMAT and HW in approved containers and locations.
- Maintain an MSDS (http://www.hazard.com/msds) for each HAZMAT used.

SUPPLY

D-21. Unit supply and technical supply personnel account for all materials during HAZMAT and HW requisition, transportation, storage, and disposal. Unit commanders and leaders ensure supply personnel observe stringent HAZMAT supply economy measures. Units order only the minimum amount of HAZMAT needed. When possible, supply personnel order biodegradable, environmentally safe materials.

D-22. When storing products, supply personnel ensure first-in, first-out stock rotation to minimize the turn-in of out-of-date material. They also follow installation storage guidelines for marking materials, maintaining MSDSs, and turning in excess materials. Finally, unit leaders ensure supply personnel turn-in or dispose of HAZMAT and HW according to local regulations. Compliance includes coordinating with the local environmental office and DRMO.

PLANNING

D-23. Environmental awareness can be incorporated into the unit training program with minimal additional planning. Most topics can be reviewed by contacting the environmental division, natural resources branch, Staff Judge Advocate, and/or range control.

D-24. Table D-1 is a general point-of-contact matrix to assist personnel with environmental concerns. When overseas, refer to the U.S. agencies providing liaison with the equivalent of the points of contact. If there is no host-nation equivalent, all training and maintenance are conducted under U.S. policies and requirements. Units coordinate with these organizations to provide a briefing before deployments.

Table D-1. Environmental POC matrix

Topic	POC
Air pollution	Environmental Division
Archaeological and historic sites	Environmental Division and Natural Resources Branch
Clean and safe water	Environmental Division
Legal considerations	Environmental Law Attorney, Office of the Staff Judge Advocate
Hazardous material and waste	Directorate of Logistics, Defense Reutilization and Marketing Office, Environmental Division, and the fire department
Noise pollution	Environmental Division, Range Control (Directorate of Plans, Training, and Mobilization)
Range clearances and restrictions	Range Control (Directorate of Plans, Training, and Mobilization)
Standing operating procedures	Environmental Division
Spill reporting	Environmental Division
Threatened/endangered species	Natural Resources Branch
Water pollution	Environmental Division
Wetland protection	Natural Resources Branch, Range Control

UNIT-LEVEL ENVIRONMENTAL PROGRAMS

D-25. Unit personnel must be familiar with the various environmental programs found at the unit level. FM 3-100-4 provides information on these unit or installation programs:

- HAZMAT management.
- HW management.
- HAZCOM.
- Pollution prevention and HW minimization.
- Recycling.
- Spill prevention and response plan.

ARMY NATIONAL GUARD AND RESERVE COMPONENT CONSIDERATIONS

D-26. When collocated with active Army units or when activated, ARNG or USAR adheres to the same stringent handling, storage, and disposal criteria. When ARNG or USAR are not on active-duty status or collocated with active-duty units or their supporting HQs, their requirements may differ. ARNG units routinely operate under environmental regulations and laws of a particular state. ARNG units coordinate through their state area command for environmental guidance when deploying to installations in other states.

D-27. USAR units with subordinate units residing in different states will comply with substantially different environmental laws. The supporting HQ develops policies that account for differences in state and local laws and regulations. Units separated from their supporting installation must ensure SOPs and contingency plans adequately address local laws and regulations.

D-28. Given the distances between ARNG and USAR units and their supporting HQ, HAZMAT or HW turn-in may require alternative methods such as line haul or contractor removal. The cost of HAZMAT and HW turn-in may warrant pollution prevention initiatives to reduce, reuse, or recycle HAZMAT and HW on-site. Solvent distillation, for example, may provide significant cost savings over conventional disposal.

D-29. Disaster-relief missions present units with challenging environmental protection requirements. Units must not add their own HAZMAT and HW to the existing environmental problem. ECOs in ARNG units coordinate with their state area command HQ for HAZMAT and HW support. Unit ECOs also coordinate regularly with disaster relief HQ to determine threats from HAZMAT or HW exposure, such as polychlorinated biphenyls from transformers, POL, or decaying bodies. Unit leaders ensure Soldiers have appropriate PCE/PPE when exposed to HAZMAT or HW in the disaster area.

AWARENESS AND COMPLIANCE

D-30. AR 200-1 explains the Army environmental programs and references the additional documents that should be reviewed. TC 3-34.489 provides a comprehensive listing of all items of interest in the preparation for operating near and avoiding environmentally sensitive areas. Another good reference for environmental issues is graphic training aid 05-08-002 booklet that can be downloaded and printed. Graphic training aids can be downloaded from the United States Army Training Support Center at https://atiam.train.army.mil, look for graphic training aids under the commandant approved training section and select from the type list.

This page intentionally left blank.

Appendix E

Aviation Maintenance in Extreme and Demanding Environments

This appendix provides a discussion of the impact on aviation maintenance operations within the various environments. Each environment brings unique challenges that must be anticipated and planned for by the commander and staff. Some maintenance procedures work consistently regardless of the environment; however, the majority of maintenance activities are directly affected by the environment.

GENERAL

E-1. Operations may be conducted in desert (FM 90-3), jungle (FM 90-5), mountain (FM 3-97.6), or cold weather/northern (FM 31-70 and FM 31-71) environments. Preparing to conduct aviation maintenance; commanders, at a minimum, consider the following factors:

- Modifications to normal repair part stockage levels; such as, increased numbers of filters, bearings, and seals.
- Mobility restrictions; such, mountainous terrain, dense foliage, ice, and sandy terrain.
- Effects on personnel and equipment performance; such as, altitude and extreme heat or cold.
- Communications restrictions.
- Special shelter requirements.
- Specialized equipment and clothing requirements.
- The need for additional maintenance personnel when conducting maintenance in extreme heat or cold environments.
- Personnel work and rest cycles.
- Modifications to normal scheduled and preventive maintenance.

E-2. Preventive maintenance action frequency increases in extreme and demanding environments. Maintenance leaders and personnel monitor daily the environmental effect on aircraft and equipment to determine and apply the most effective methods of maintaining mission-ready systems. An enclosed maintenance facility provides the best conditions for efficient and productive maintenance to occur. If a permanent facility is unavailable, then a lightweight maintenance enclosure (LME) erected around that portion of the aircraft requiring maintenance is a recommended alternative. LMEs are typically part of a unit TOE and are cataloged in sufficient number to be readily available to maintenance personnel. Maintenance conducted in an exposed, unprotected environment is not recommended and has the potential to allow items receiving maintenance to become contaminated and place personnel at a higher level of risk for injuries.

E-3. Supply stockage quantities must be anticipated and reflect the increased requirements for those parts that deteriorate or experience increased wear.

DESERT ENVIRONMENT

E-4. High temperatures and low humidity are major causes of equipment failure. Wind action lifts and spreads sand and dust, affecting moving parts. Aircraft, sensors, and weapons are affected also. Rubber components, such as gaskets and seals, become brittle, and oil leaks are more frequent. For more detail on operations in desert environments, refer to FM 90-3.

ENVIRONMENTAL CONSIDERATIONS

E-5. The following characteristics are commonly found in a desert environment and will likely contribute to equipment degradation and/or failure:

- Heat.
- Sand, dirt, and dust.
- Wind.
- Extreme temperature variations.
- Static electricity.

Heat

E-6. Helicopter performance is degraded as heat and humidity increase. Aircraft canopies have been damaged or deformed under direct heat and should be covered when the aircraft is not in use. Heat soaking of sensitive electronic components ("black boxes") produces increased failures and demands on aircraft cooling systems.

Sand, Dirt, and Dust

E-7. Sand, dirt, and dust cause failures in electrical switches, digital entry keyboards, radio tuning knobs, and circuit breakers. Sand erosion causes steady wear on rotor heads, leading edges of rotor blades, Teflon® bearings, and all turbine engine blades. Blowing sand gradually degrades optical instruments and windscreens by pitting and scratching. Sand, dirt, and dust accumulation on oil cooler surfaces creates loss of cooling efficiency.

E-8. Sand mixed with oil forms an abrasive paste. Lube fittings and bearing seals require frequent monitoring and inspections. If they are damaged or missing, sand will enter the housing and cause bearing failure.

Wind

E-9. High winds can be destructive to large and relatively light/aerodynamic materiel; such as, aircraft, tentage, and antenna systems. To minimize the possibility of wind damage, provide some form or method of protection from high wind or be firmly secured to the ground; such as parking aircraft into the wind and ground staking or use natural or manmade barriers to block the wind.

Extreme Temperature Variations

E-10. In deserts with relatively high-dew points and/or high humidity, overnight condensation can occur wherever surfaces (such as metal exposed to air) are cooler than the air temperature. Condensation can affect such items as optics and fuel lines. Clean optics and weapons frequently. Weapons systems, even if not lubricated, accumulate sand and dirt caused by condensation.

Static Electricity

E-11. Static electricity occurs due to friction against the aircraft as it moves through the air. This friction strips electrons from the atmosphere and causes them to build up on the skin of the aircraft. Static electricity tends to accumulate near sharp edges; such as, the trailing edges of wings/rotor blades and tail/stabilizer surfaces.

E-12. Static electricity considerations and precautions include:

- Properly ground all equipment.
- Tape all sharp edges (tips) of antennas.

- Wear an anti-static wristband, and if available install an anti-static mat under the work bench, when working on electronic equipment away from the aircraft.

PROTECTING AIRCRAFT AND EQUIPMENT

E-13. Protective covers designed to cover the aircraft or specific items/points on the aircraft should be used at all times. Install available windscreens, blade covers, nose covers, and engine inlet covers when aircraft are not in use. Securely fasten protective covers to prevent flapping and minimize movement that may damage the item covered. Ensure all foreign material is removed from component surfaces prior to covering especially those items easily susceptible to scratching; such as windscreens and optical lens.

E-14. Hanger aircraft whenever possible or, at a minimum, cover as much of the aircraft as possible to avoid damage caused by blowing sand, dust, and dirt and heat.

E-15. During aircraft operations, optics can be provided a measure of protection by placing the device in the stow position when not in use.

E-16. Cover and protect computers, diagnostic devices, and system components removed from an aircraft when not in use.

INCREASED MAINTENANCE PROCEDURES

E-17. Rotor blade wear and turbine engine compressor blade degradation is normal in all aircraft but is greatly increased in a sandy environment causing a corresponding increase in maintenance requirements and parts replacement. Two factors that may reduce the degradation of equipment are airfield conditions and flying techniques. Component degradation can be slightly reduced by minimizing the time spent hovering over a sandy, unimproved surface or staging and operating from airfields with an improved surface.

E-18. Rotor blade wear is controlled through painting or the application of main rotor blade erosion tape. Both methods are time-consuming; require frequent inspections and reapplication, and are short-term solutions.

E-19. Aircraft rely on an inlet particle separator system to reduce engine wear but this system is less efficient at idle speed.

AIRCRAFT SURVIVABILITY EQUIPMENT

E-20. All sensors should be cleaned frequently and covered when the aircraft is not in use.

REVERSE CYCLE

E-21. Maintenance personnel consume more water and require frequent monitoring during the heat of the day. Productivity decreases as environmental extremes increase. Reverse-cycle (night-time) maintenance is a solution to adverse day-time environmental conditions.

JUNGLE ENVIRONMENT

E-22. The jungle environment is common in tropical areas of the world. Hot and humid best describes a jungle environment. Jungle climate varies with location; near the equator seasons are characterized with rain occurring throughout the year, whereas seasons become distinctly dryer farther from the equator. For more detail on operations in jungle environments refer to FM 90-5.

E-23. In a jungle environment, some considerations and precautions include:
- Lenses and dials quickly fog over with internal moisture.
- Electrical connections corrode quickly, and battery life is shorter than normal.
- Weapons tend to rust quickly and must be cleaned and oiled frequently.
- Avionics are particularly sensitive to moisture, condensation, and corrosion.

CORROSION PREVENTION

E-24. Initiate an aggressive and comprehensive corrosion-prevention program. Parts and systems are susceptible to corrosion and this susceptibility is magnified in hot and humid environments. A comprehensive corrosion preventive program should be part of the unit SOP and applied daily to maintenance activities. The unit SOP provides preventive measures and guidance to minimize the destructive effects of corrosion on unit aircraft and equipment.

FIELD SITES

E-25. Some form of engineer support is required to prepare a field site as a suitable location to conduct aircraft maintenance. In areas where heavy and/or frequent rains occur, areas suitable for aircraft maintenance may be so limited as to require the collocation with other units. Collocating units has the added benefit of sharing security requirements and the detriment of concentrating personnel and equipment.

MOUNTAINOUS ENVIRONMENT

E-26. Operations in mountainous environments present many challenges to maintenance leaders and personnel that require specialized equipment, specialized training, and acclimatization. Rugged terrain and abrupt changes in elevations limit the reliability of roads and suitable areas for maintenance operations. High altitudes and weather affect the performance of personnel and equipment. Personnel must be trained and acclimate to higher altitudes, and equipment may need adjustment to operate efficiently at higher elevations. For more detail on operations in mountainous environments, refer to FM 3-97.6.

E-27. In a mountainous environment, some considerations and precautions include:

- Aircraft may be the most efficient means to move repair parts and contact teams on-site and evacuate unserviceable items.
- ASC/AST units must be located as close as practical to the AMC/AMT units they support.
- Maintenance turn-around time increases due to high altitude effects on maintenance personnel.
- Stockpiling and caching supplies decrease resupply risks due to transportation limitations.
- Rugged terrain requires increased engineer effort to prepare area for maintenance activity and improve security measures.
- Locally obtained animals and indigenous personnel may be required to move supplies from roads and trails to unit positions (FM 3-05.213).

COLD-WEATHER/NORTHERN ENVIRONMENT

E-28. Northern operations require a considerable amount of specialized equipment; such as, tracked vehicles, sleds, heated shelters, and heated facilities. Every item of equipment is affected by extreme cold and snow in the winter and by mud and water in the summer. Extreme conditions increase wear and tear on equipment and increase the quantity and variety of parts required for maintenance. For more detail on operations in cold-weather/northern environments, refer to FMs 31-70 and 31-71.

E-29. Helicopter operation, particularly with their inherent vibrations, in temperatures below -35 degrees Fahrenheit results in a marked increase in metal fatigue. All metals become increasingly brittle as the temperature decreases. Aircraft fatigue is evidenced by an increase in the number of skin cracks and popped rivets in stress areas. Careful attention must be devoted to these areas in all stages of maintenance operations. Areas of interest to be inspected on a more frequent basis for stress cracks as a direct result of the environment include the following: engine decks, tail-boom hard points, and gearbox mounting points.

E-30. Operation of aircraft at temperatures below -50 degrees Fahrenheit should not be attempted except in emergencies; unless the aircraft has the appropriate winterization kit and auxiliary systems that have proven reliable at lower temperatures.

E-31. Unit leaders must ensure personnel and equipment can withstand the challenges of cold weather. Soldiers and their leaders must understand the effects of cold weather and adapt operations and maintenance to overcome environmental conditions. Operations in snow, ice, and extremely cold conditions require special training, personnel acclimation, and special operational techniques.

E-32. Trafficability is an issue during spring breakup and in summer when the ground thaws and ice in streams and lakes melt. Track-laying vehicles of the low-ground-pressure type may provide the only means of cross-country mobility. Mud, muskeg, swamp, marsh, and open water hamper ground movement in spring and summer.

E-33. In a cold-weather/northern environment, some considerations and precautions include:

- All tasks require more time and effort due to cold-weather effects on equipment and personnel requirements to wear cold-weather clothing and gloves. At temperatures below -20 degrees Fahrenheit, maintenance tasks may take five times as long to complete.
- Maintenance units usually require additional personnel to offset the increased time necessary to complete maintenance tasks.
- Extreme cold-weather conditions may limit the use of aircraft.
- Maintainers must allow equipment to thaw out and warm up before making repairs.
- A portable combustion type of heater, incorporating a blower and flexible hoses for application of heat to localized areas, may be used for preheating aircraft components and systems before starting.
- Heaters may be used to heat specific portions of the aircraft so maintenance personnel can work without gloves.
- When temperatures remain below freezing, aircraft batteries not in use should be removed and stored in a warm place.
- Required installation of cold-weather auxiliary equipment; such as, winter cowls, oil dilution systems, personnel heaters, and covers add time to normal maintenance operations.

MAINTENANCE ACTIVITY

E-34. Personnel efficiency is reduced by bulky clothing worn in extremely cold environments. Operators/maintainers must wear mittens or gloves at all times due to the dangers associated with handling metal objects with bare hands. Losing the sense of touch further reduces the Soldier efficiency. An even routine operation, such as handling latches or opening engine compartments, becomes a focused and time-consuming task when performed with protected hands. Complete winterization, diligent maintenance, and well-trained maintenance teams are crucial in reducing the adverse effects of cold weather and performing maintenance in a timely manner.

MAINTENANCE FACILITIES

E-35. The availability of proper maintenance facilities can be critical to the maintenance mission. Without some type of permanent or temporary shelter, even routine maintenance can become extremely difficult, if not impossible to perform.

E-36. Heated buildings or shelters are a necessity for conducting aircraft maintenance in a cold weather/northern environment. Proper and satisfactory aircraft PMCS requires personnel to work in moderate temperatures within an enclosed structure. Maintenance of many components requires careful and precise servicing and inspections, which is not possible while wearing cold-weather clothing.

E-37. When buildings are not available, LMEs are a temporary and expedient method to use for maintenance. If possible, LMEs should have wood flooring and be heated. Maintenance leaders and supervisors closely monitor personnel working in these conditions, responding immediately to the first indication(s) of any cold-related symptoms or injuries.

E-38. During certain times of the year, hours of daylight in a northern environment are short. Lighting equipment must be available and in sufficient quantity to furnish adequate illumination for maintenance services. Lights with ample cable extensions, attachment plugs, connectors, and spare bulbs are a necessity.

NIGHT OPERATIONS

E-39. Aircraft maintenance performed at night on aircraft flown that day has the potential to ensure those aircraft are available the next day. Maintenance leaders must establish an efficient maintenance schedule that cycles aircraft through inspection, repair, and placement back on the flightline while avoiding a stacking or lining-up of aircraft awaiting maintenance. An SOP that is understood and practiced by all personnel and a sound fighter management program provides for the consistent and continued success of the unit maintenance program.

E-40. During night-time maintenance, some considerations and precautions include:

- Night-time work performance is not equal with daytime because of mental fatigue associated with disruptions in the body internal clock, known as shift lag. Shift lag is a disruption of the circadian cycle affecting personnel that have a changed work/sleep schedule.
- Work performance is restricted when working in subdued (red or green) lighting, compared to white light.
- MOCs and MTFs may have to wait until daytime.
- The potential for "missing something" increases as light levels diminish and the fatigue level of night workers increases.

TRANSITION BETWEEN SHIFTS

E-41. The chances of an incomplete or inadequate maintenance task occurring increases during shift changes. Supervisors must avoid the tendency to complete a specific task quickly in order to reach a point that permits a smoother shift change transition. A detailed coordination between shift supervisors will avoid the potential for incomplete or inadequate maintenance.

PHYSIOLOGICAL FACTORS

E-42. Vision is obviously reduced at night; however, other human factors affect night maintenance. Supervisors and maintenance personnel should receive instruction on physiological factors affecting night operations. The commander can institute a program that provides training in conjunction with personnel shifting to a night-time work cycle as part of an adjustment period.

E-43. Physiological factors that must be considered in night aircraft maintenance include:

- Eyes require about 40 minutes to fully adapt to darkness.
- Adjustment to a new work schedule requires about one day for each hour of shift change.
- Forward shift rotations (days to evenings to nights) allow faster adjustment than backward rotations (nights to evenings to days).
- The body clock is set by exposure to the daylight, most night workers never fully adjust.
- Fatigue affects personnel night vision, muscular actions, and mental abilities.
- Personnel experience a loss of depth perception and color distinction at night.
- Smoking three cigarettes in rapid succession or 20 to 30 cigarettes a day reduces night vision by approximately 20 percent.
- FOD incidents increase at night.
- Diet affects night vision; individuals should eat only nutritious foods, avoiding "junk foods."

CHEMICAL, BIOLOGICAL, RADIOLOGICAL, AND NUCLEAR OPERATIONS

E-44. Aircraft maintenance personnel have the potential to be exposed to or work on aircraft exposed to CBRN agents. The use of chemical or biological agents against U.S. maintenance facilities and units by threat forces has the tactical advantages of isolating important battlefield systems and demoralizing personnel. Maintenance leaders and personnel must consider ways to resume operations at the earliest opportunity. CBRN defense, avoidance, protection, and decontamination of unit personnel, equipment, supplies, and operating areas is a time-consuming task requiring careful, realistic planning (FMs 3-11, 3-11.3, 3-11.4, and 3-11.5).

E-45. Units should establish SOPs for contaminated aircraft and equipment maintenance procedures as follows:

- Inspection and contaminated maintenance collection point procedures.
- Procedures for performing immediate decontamination or requesting deliberate equipment decontamination from a CBRN defense company.
- Procedures for repair without electronic test equipment (if equipment is destroyed by blast or electromagnetic pulse).
- Responsibilities and procedures for establishing and operating a contaminated-equipment holding area.

E-46. Maintenance on contaminated equipment considerations and precautions include:

- Petroleum products tend to trap chemical contaminants.
- An aircraft that is safe for an operator to use without MOPP-4 protection may be unsafe for maintenance personnel to repair.
- Chemical contaminants may collect in bolt threads, hydraulic fluids, and closed assemblies. Maintenance personnel could open a component and be exposed to lethal concentrations of hazardous vapors. Injuries or casualties could occur unless all repairs and preventive maintenance on previously contaminated aircraft and components are done in MOPP-4.
- Oil, grease, and dirt seriously degrade the protective qualities of the chemical protective suit; maintenance personnel must keep themselves as clean as possible. Extra protective suits should be on-hand to replace dirty ones.
- Wet-weather gear helps keep protective suits clean but increases heat buildup and will eventually be penetrated. The combination of protective gear and wet-weather gear provides good protection from a combination of toxic chemicals, grease, and oil contamination; fuel handler aprons and field-expedient rubber sleeves can provide some added protection with less heat buildup.

CONTAMINATION CONTROL

E-47. Contamination must not be spread. Contaminated equipment is not taken into a clean area. Maintenance personnel repair contaminated equipment only in an area specified for contaminated aircraft and/or equipment. Repaired, contaminated equipment is marked and returned to contaminated units only.

E-48. Equipment immediately decontaminated can still be hazardous to handle. A previously contaminated unit conducting periodic contamination checks is able to use the equipment safely because of the precautions being taken.

E-49. After tools and equipment are used on contaminated aircraft or equipment, they are marked and treated as contaminated from that point. Segregate contaminated tools and equipment from uncontaminated tools and equipment. Protection from contaminated equipment is mandatory. Contaminated tools and equipment must be stored at a separate location downwind of clean areas. Every effort must be made to minimize and control the spread of contamination.

E-50. Contaminated aircraft and equipment should not be evacuated for repairs. If AMC/AMT or ASC/AST maintenance is required, a maintenance team in MOPP-4 is sent forward to effect repairs in the contaminated aircraft area and must test the equipment for contamination. If contamination exists, the maintenance team must decide whether repairs can be made in MOPP-4. If they cannot, the equipment must be decontaminated. Safeguards must be taken to protect personnel inside and outside contaminated areas. Chemical-agent detection equipment should be operated while contaminated equipment is being repaired. The testing must be a continuous process.

E-51. Mark contaminated aircraft and equipment. Aircraft and equipment that are contaminated or that have been decontaminated to low-risk levels for operators and crews could still present a serious hazard to mechanics.

E-52. Contaminated aircraft must be identified with standard triangular contamination signs on all four sides and at the flight controls. Write the type and date of contamination on the signs, which should be easily visible from the outside of the aircraft. For nonpersistent agents, signs may not be removed until decontamination has been verified by a detailed inspection. Contamination signs on aircraft and equipment contaminated with persistent agents will not be removed even after decontamination.

E-53. Any surfaces the maintenance team must touch to repair or recover the aircraft must be given an operator spray down with an approved decontamination apparatus. This spray down will not reduce the level of MOPP needed but offers some additional protection and limits spread. Maintenance teams must carry extra onboard decontaminants for this purpose. The objective is to limit transferring liquid contamination from the equipment being repaired to the maintenance or recovery team or its equipment.

E-54. Support from a contaminated area is limited to the amount of time Soldiers can operate in MOPP-4. This time restriction severely limits the maintenance support within a contaminated area. It may be possible to extend the time the unit can continue to support from the contaminated location by scheduling periodic withdrawal of personnel to a clean area for complete personnel decontamination and a rest period at a reduced MOPP-level. For continued effectiveness, however, the unit must leave the area, go through a detailed equipment and decontamination process, and set up shop in a clean area.

E-55. Maintenance personnel repairing equipment contaminated with radiation should wear dosimeters and be closely monitored for exposure. They must never exceed exposure levels. When the highest acceptable levels are reached, personnel should be replaced, mission permitting. The amount of radiological contamination that personnel can be exposed to varies. It depends on operational exposure guidance and the tactical situation.

Appendix F

Unmanned Aircraft Systems

This appendix identifies UAS specific maintenance requirements and operations. As in manned systems, UAS operations consist of many interrelated functions that depend on a responsive supply system and thorough maintenance program.

LOGISTICAL REQUIREMENTS

F-1. Unlike other organizations on the battlefield, a UAS deployed and dispersed geographically across the theater, corps, and division (brigade, battalion/squadron, company/troop) requires focused sustainment from forward units regardless of the C2 relationships that exist (FMI 3-04.155).

F-2. UAS units have the same responsibilities as other units to request and obtain supplies and logistics support. The initial entry force will carry 24 hours of Class I (food and water) and Class III (POL); it will have 72 hours of Class IX (air). Table F-1 provides UAS logistic responsibilities for each class of supply.

Table F-1. UAS logistic requirements

Class	MQ-1C Company	MQ-5B Hunter Company	RQ-7B Shadow Platoon
Class I	Organic unit	Organic unit	Supported unit
Class II	Organic unit	Organic unit	Organic unit
Class III	Organic unit JP-8	Organic unit JP-8 or Diesel #2	Supported unit 100 Low Lead (AVGAS)
Class IV	Organic unit	Organic unit	Supported unit
Class V	Organic unit	Organic unit	N/A
Class VI	Organic unit	Organic unit	Supported unit
Class VII	Organic unit	Organic unit	Organic unit
Class VIII	Organic unit	Organic unit	Supported unit
Class IX/IX(A)	Organic unit	Organic unit	Supported/organic/CLS where appropriate.

F-3. All system-peculiar and specific repair parts, including Class IX (air), are coordinated for delivery or delivered by contractor logistics support (CLS) contact teams. When deployed away from the battalion/squadron, the supported unit or forward support battalion provides common items.

TWO-LEVEL MAINTENANCE

F-4. UAS are maintained under the two-level maintenance concept. Field maintenance is performed by UAS unit military and/or contractor personnel. UAS maintenance personnel perform authorized maintenance procedures within their capability. Depot or forward repair activities generally perform sustainment maintenance beyond unit-level repair. CLS may or may not be provided by OEM representatives. If the supportability strategy calls for CLS, these elements generally co-locate in the brigade support area along with the ASB.

FIELD-LEVEL MAINTENANCE

F-5. The OH-58D armament/electrical/avionics systems repairer (MOS 15J with UAS additional skill identifier) performs the following maintenance functions on the UAS:

- Fault detection and isolation.
- Removal and replacement of inoperative chassis-mounted components and LRUs down to card level.
- Functional tests and built-in tests.
- Periodic inspection or replacement to comply with scheduled maintenance requirements, corrosion prevention, detection, and removal.
- Electronic maintenance covering payloads and electronic-based components repair by removal and replacement of LRUs.

F-6. UAS operator (MOS 15W) maintenance tasks are intended to keep the system operational and prevent deterioration. Operators will perform—

- PMCS.
- Preoperational tests to verify the system is ready to operate using built-in tests.
- Visual inspection and built-in test analyzer.

F-7. The RQ-11B Raven and the one system remote video terminal do not have an operator/maintainer MOS structure. Soldiers trained/certified to operate these systems also perform field-level maintenance. Operators perform—

- PMCS.
- Preoperational tests to verify the system is ready to operate via checklist.
- Minor fault detection and isolation at the LRU level.
- Removal and replacement of LRUs and minor component adjustments.

SUSTAINMENT-LEVEL MAINTENANCE

F-8. Sustainment maintenance personnel perform UAS component repair, part replacement, fault detection, and fault isolation of specific parts. At this level of maintenance, maintainers focus on repair of component items and their return to the distribution system. Component repair includes items such as major assemblies, LRUs, and repairable line items. Corps and theater maintenance activities, special repair activities, or contractors on the battlefield can perform sustainment maintenance.

F-9. Sustainment maintenance actions typically involve repair of reparable Class IX components, off-system, for return to the supply system. Soldiers, DA civilians, or contractors perform sustainment maintenance. The decision to have sustainment maintenance includes detailed off-system, inside-the-box repair of LRUs through shop replaceable unit repair/replacement; and rebuild of engines or transmissions.

CONTRACT LOGISTICS SUPPORT

F-10. Contractors play a key role in the Army ability to support their mission, and provide a responsive alternative to increasing the number of support personnel necessary to perform the mission. During each phase of an operation, contracting support is used to augment the support structure. Contracting personnel establish their operations with, or near, the local vendor base to support deployed forces. Contracting support bridges gaps that occur as military logistics support resources mobilize, and may be necessary for the duration of the contingency.

F-11. Commanders must understand their role in directing contractors on the battlefield, and train their staff to recognize, plan, and implement contractor requirements. FM 3-100.21 provides basic understanding of contracting and contractor management.

AVIATION RESOURCE MANAGEMENT SURVEY

F-12. UAS organizations have the same annual internal ARMS requirements as aviation maintenance units. Brigade aviation elements assigned to brigade combat teams perform annual internal ARMS for Shadow and Raven units/teams.

PRODUCTION CONTROL

F-13. Commanders select PC OICs and NCOICs based on their skills, qualifications, and experience. The PC OIC/NCOIC oversees and supervises the unit UAS equipment and maintenance operations. The PC OIC/NCOIC tracks maintenance and sustainment statuses directly affecting assigned UAS. He manages all maintenance actions and scheduled maintenance flow.

QUALITY CONTROL

F-14. Commanders select QC personnel based on their skills, qualifications, and experience to perform quality assurance on all UAS maintenance. Commanders assign qualified and experienced UAS ground crewmembers (mechanics and technicians) to perform QC inspector duties. This inspector ensures completion of maintenance on the unit systems according to The Army Maintenance Management System procedures.

FORMS AND RECORDS

F-15. This section covers the preparation, management and historical record keeping of forms and records needed to manage maintenance, control the use, and report warranty actions and deficiencies on the (Army) UAS.

F-16. DA PAM 738-751 and DA PAM 750-8 provide the model for evaluating the material condition in support of UAS readiness and safety. The forms cited in DA PAM 738-751 require deviations to the instructions for completing the data fields and blocks to accommodate the UAS; such as, no onboard cockpit; the ground control station performs ground-to-air control and air-to-air control via data link.

F-17. UAS units use forms and records to—
- Control and manage maintenance.
- Track UAS components, modules, and flight safety-related parts, by serial number, to support reconstruction of UAS component historical records for component configuration, and maintenance and failure analysis.
- Track configuration, application of ECPs, MWOs, reportable components, and TUAS field notices (flight safety notices, safety action messages, safety of use messages, and TBs).
- Collect maintenance performance and related logistic data to perform maintenance analysis for possible redesign and improvement of fielded UAS equipment according to AR 750-1.
- Submit deficiency reports such as equipment improvement recommendations and PQDRs.

LOGBOOK AND HISTORICAL RECORDS

LOGBOOK FORMS AND RECORDS

F-18. Forms and records filed in the UAS logbook ensure easy access by operators, maintenance, and QC personnel. Operational and maintenance forms and records provide a record of—
- Aircrew flight information and servicing data.
- Engine operational data.
- Payloads and other subsystems status.

- When the next scheduled maintenance inspection is due.
- When the next special inspection or item replacement is due.
- Faults and correcting information.
- Equipment condition status.
- Related maintenance actions.
- Uncorrected faults or maintenance.

Note: All DA operational, maintenance, and historical forms used in ULLS-A or LAS Programs have been revised to include an "E" following the number, for example, DA Form 2408-15-E. The "E" forms are electronically generated and filled with data at the same time. The "E" forms are filled out the same as the DA hard copy forms, except a few of the electronic forms have been designed to add, delete, or combine information automatically. Only the DA hard copy forms, without the "E," will be preprinted, stocked, stored, and issued. The hard copy forms will be used as a back-up system when the ULLS-A or LAS computer hardware or software becomes inoperative.

HISTORICAL RECORDS

F-19. Historical records contain permanent component data. The QC shop maintains a record of—
- Configuration changes, application of ECPs, MWOs, reportable components, and TUAS field notices (flight safety notices, safety action messages, safety of use messages, and TBs).
- Components, modules, and flight safety related parts, by serial number, to support reconstruction of historical records for configuration and maintenance or failure analysis.
- Maintenance performance, related logistic data and all significant events.
- Results of engine analysis checks and maximum power checks.
- Receipt, transfer, and disposal of mission equipment.
- Software versions installed on UAS subsystems.

UNMANNED AIRCRAFT SYSTEM MODIFIED UNIT LEVEL LOGISTICS SYSTEM–AVIATION (ENHANCED)

F-20. UAS modified ULLS-A (E) assists maintenance personnel with various tools that enhance aircraft reporting, status, and flying hours according to AR 700-138. Furthermore, UAS modified ULLS-A (E) processes aircraft transfers, maintains operational and historical records, processes Class IX (air) repair parts, and enhances overall maintenance operations. It automates bench stock listings by shop codes (stocked and maintained manually with an automated reordering process), reportable component management, and maintenance management processes performed by PC.

F-21. Enhanced logbook automated system is fielded to Army UAS units. ULLS-A (E) as modified for UAS, once fielded, will be the system of record tracking sustainment and maintenance actions for all aviation maintenance units. The manual system (hard copies of forms and records) will be used as a backup if ULLS-A (E) as modified for UAS becomes nonfunctional. The PC office is responsible for coordinating the input and update of all maintenance and sustainment actions into ULLS-A (E) as modified for UAS once the system is fully operational.

F-22. RQ-11B and the one system remote video terminal are supported through the SAMS-E and ULLS-G. SAMS-E was primarily designed to support Army motor pools, not aviation maintenance which requires a partially mission-capable category. Systems will only be reported as FMC or NMC; however, units will have an automated parts-ordering and reporting capability.

Appendix G

Bench Stock Management

This appendix addresses bench stock specific procedures. Bench stock items are authorized for all aviation maintenance activities. Aviation maintenance officers /technicians establish a level of bench stock availability based on unit requirements and usage; ensuring maintenance procedures are not interrupted due to a lack of bench stock items.

GENERAL

G-1. According to AR 710-2, bench stocks are authorized at AMC/AMT - and ASC/AST -level units. These items are stored near the work area providing maintenance personnel with direct access to supplies. Management of bench stock items is a maintenance team effort, beginning with aviation unit maintainers /crew chiefs, ending with the maintenance officer/technician.

> *Note.* AR 710-2, DA PAM 710-2-2, and DA PAM 738-751 contain additional regulatory management policy on bench stock items.

G-2. Bench stocks are composed of low-cost, high-use; consumable Classes II, III (packaged), IV, and IX (air) (less components) items used by maintenance personnel at an unpredictable rate. Examples of these items are common hardware, resistors, transistors, wire, tubing, hose, thread, welding rods, sandpaper, sheet metal, rivets, seals, oils, grease, and repair kits.

G-3. Two records are required for bench stock management: a bench stock list and bench stock replenishment tags.

PREPARING A BENCH STOCK LIST

MANUALLY

G-4. Manually prepare the bench stock list on a memorandum or plain bond paper and include the date prepared, unit/activity, and UIC. The essential data elements are provided in table G-1 (page G-2) IAW AR 710-2. The person preparing the list signs it and sends it to the unit commander or unit/installation maintenance officer for approval and signature.

Table G-1. Sample of a bench stock list

Bench Stock List					
Prepared Date:	20060614	**UIC:**	WCMFD0	**Highlight Price:**	$150.00
Organization:	D CO 159TH AVN REGT			**DODAAC:**	W36N0T
'*' = Exceeds Highlight Price					

Shop Code	NIIN	Noun	Location	Quantity	Price	Unit of Issue
*A	000344641	Circuit	A0001	4	$262.00	EA
E	000364197	Light, in	E0001	50	$.85	EA
E	000364421	Connector	E0002	50	$1.20	EA
M	000366967	Screw, as	M0001	20	$2.39	HD
G	000366995	Seal, non	G0001	100	$.59	FT
C	001255256	Battery	C0001	2	$12.48	EA
K	001433115	Lamp, inc	K0003	50	$.12	EA
G	001436234	Rivet, bl	G0003	100	$.09	EA
*A	002542199	Connection	A0005	2	$278.23	EA
D	010102536	Chain as	D0007	5	$109.29	EA

Prepared by:	Approved by:
Stephen Jones, CW4, AV Shops Officer	James Smith, CW5, AV Maintenance Officer (or CDR)

ELECTRONICALLY

G-5. Change minimum and maximum stockage levels using ULLS-A (E) by accessing the supply module within ULLS-A (E), clicking on the bench stock icon, and selecting change min/max stock levels. When quantities have been adjusted, print a bench stock report. At the end of the printed report, the technical supply manager can indicate who prepared the list and who authorized the list.

BENCH STOCK REPLENISHMENT TAGS

G-6. Technical supply personnel provide instructions to maintenance personnel on how to use DA Form 1300-4 (Reorder Point Record) as a bench stock replenishment tag. Place the tag in or near the location of each bench stock item or in a consolidated file collocated with the items. Essential data elements of the bench stock replenishment tag are stock number, unit of issue, item noun, basic stockage level (BSL), minimum stockage level (MSL), location, Julian date ordered, and quantity ordered.

G-7. When a replenishment request for a bench stock item is submitted, enter the date and quantity from the request on the tag. Use of an alternate form is authorized when conditions such as bin size preclude the use of DA Form 1300-4 (Reorder Point Record); however, all data elements must be used to ensure continuity if an alternative or locally prepared form is used.

G-8. The bench stock replenishment tag captures usage of bench stock at the user level. This information is necessary to establish a 30-day stock and an MSL (reorder point). Units should establish a method to determine actual usage for two review periods, and divide this quantity by 12 (12 months, two review periods) to determine an average 30-day stock.

G-9. For example, during the first review period, 50 nuts were used and during the second review period, 40 of the same nuts were used. During the two review periods (12 months), 90 nuts were used. Dividing this by 12, the requirement for 30 days would be 7.5, rounded to 8 each. If the nut comes in an issue of each, then 8 would be the maximum stock level and the minimum would be the established MSL. For items with an issue of one hundred, then one hundred (or 1) would be the maximum stockage level and the minimum would be the established MSL.

G-10. To establish an MSL, technical supply personnel determine the order-to-ship time and how many bench stock items are used during the order-to-ship time; that number would be the reorder point. To effectively manage the unit bench stock, eliminate excess, and establish a go-to-war bench stock, the user must first identify actual usage of this class of supply.

G-11. The authorized stock level or BSL is the maximum level authorized by the maintenance officer. When the MSL level is reached, it is time to reorder the amount sufficient to return the stock level to the maximum or BSL.

REPLENISHMENT OF BENCH STOCK ITEMS

G-12. ULLS-A (E) users will use the MSL method of replenishing bench stock as the STAMIS is defaulted to this method. Manual users can use replenish as used, replenish on a schedule, a combination of as used or schedule, or the MSL system.

G-13. The MSL system is preferable because it is easier to manage and track usage of bench stock items. Tracking usage via the MSL facilitates technical supply personnel conducting semiannual reviews. The MSL replenishment system parallels the reorder point philosophy.

G-14. The recommended procedure for processing the replenishment is for technical supply to have the mechanics or crew chiefs pull the DA Form 1300-4 from the item location bin when the stockage level reaches the MSL. Technical supply personnel would then run the replenishment process in ULLS-A (E). Once the replenishment screen appears in NIIN sequence, technical supply personnel would tag the item and the system would run the replenishment request. ULLS-A (E) will use the difference between the maximum level and minimum level to order the shortages.

G-15. The minimum and maximum stockage levels should match the numbers reported on the corresponding DA Form 1300-4.

BENCH STOCK REVIEW PROCESS

G-16. The commander or maintenance officer/technician is required to conduct a semiannual review of the bench stock according to AR 710-2 (table G-2, page G-4). This process is accomplished by reviewing the bench stock list and the usage/replenishment data on the DA Form 1300-4. The using unit should ensure all replenishment requests are recorded on the replenishment tag.

Table G-2. ULLS-A (E) example of a bench stock replenishment review list

Prepared: 20060614										
UIC: WCMFD0					Organization Name: D CO 159TH AVN REGT DODAAC: W36N0T					
Shop code instructions: If part is to be replenished, indicate by placing a 'Y' in the REPL DSG field.										
Shop Code	LOC	NIIN	Noun	Min Stock Level	Date Last Replenish	Date Last Reviewed	Repl Dsg	Repl Rev	Qty Rev
A	A0005	002542199	Connecti	2	20051124	20006023		1	3
A	A0001	000344641	Circuit	4	20050922	20006023		0	0
A	A0002	000368617	Connecto	20	20051124	20006023		1	20
D	D0001	000573740	Packing	10	20051124	20006023		1	10
D	D0005	008460504	Packing	50	20051124	20006023		1	50
D	D0006	009093020	Yoke, BU	10	20050922	20006023		0	0
E	E0001	000364197	Light, IN	50	20051124	20006023		1	50
E	E0003	000383914	Cable AS	5	20050922	20006023		0	0
G	G0001	000366995	Seal, NON	100	20051124	20006023		1	100
G	G0004	001539838	Handle, E	2	20050922	20006023		0	0
K	K0005	009115652	Harness	5	20050922	20006023		0	0
K	K0004	001433133	Lamp, INC	25	20050922	20006023		0	0
M	M0002	000531078	ScrewXMA	50	20050922	20006023		0	0
M	M0003	009230439	Filter E	5	20051124	20006023		1	5
P	P0003	008571729	Hose, NON	25	20050922	20006023		0	0

Glossary

SECTION I – ACRONYMS AND ABBREVIATIONS

1LT	first lieutenant
AAR	after-action review
ABCS	Army Battle Command System
ACOR	administrative contracting officer representative
ACS	air calvary squadron
ADMRU	aviation depot maintenance roundout unit
AFMA	aviation field maintenance activity
AFMD	Aviation Field Maintenance Directorate
AGPU	aviation ground power unit
AHB	assault helicopter battalion
AIT	advanced individual training
AKO	Army Knowledge Online
ALSE	aviation life support equipment
ALSS	Aviation Life Support System
AMC	aviation maintenance company
AMCOM	Aviation and Missile Command
AMDF	Army master data file
AMO	aviation materiel officer
AMT	aviation maintenance troop
AO	area of operations
AOAP	Army oil analysis program
AOG	aircraft on ground
APU	auxiliary power unit
AR	Army regulation
ARA	aircraft repair authorization
ARB	attack reconnaissance battalion
ARC	accounting requirements code
ARMS	aviation resource management survey
ARNG	Army National Guard
ARP	airframe repair platoon
ARS	attack reconnaissance squadron
ASAM	aviation safety action message
ASB	aviation support battalion
ASC	aviation support company

ASES	aviation support equipment section
ASL	authorized stockage list
ASO	aviation safety officer
AST	aviation support troop
ATST	area test, measurement, and diagnostic equipment support team
AV	asset visibility
AVCRAD	aviation classification repair activity depot
AWR	airworthiness release
BAMO	brigade aviation materiel officer
BCS3	Battle Command Sustainment and Support System
BDAR	battle damage assessment and repair
BII	basic issue item
BSL	basic stockage level
C2	command and control
CAB	combat aviation brigade
CBM+	condition-based maintenance plus
CBRN	chemical, biological, radiological, and nuclear
CBU	calibrate before use
CECOM	communications-electronics command
CFR	Code of Federal Regulations
CFSR	contractor field service representative
CLS	contractor logistics support
CONUS	continental United States
COR	contracting officer representative
CPC	corrosion prevention and control
CRM	composite risk management
CRP	component repair platoon
CSDP	command supply discipline program
CTA	common table of allowance
CTASC	Corps/Theater Automated Data Processing Service Center
CW3	chief warrant officer three
CW4	chief warrant officer four
CW5	chief warrant officer five
DA	Department of the Army
DA PAM	Department of the Army pamphlet
DART	downed aircraft recovery team
DESX	defense supply expert
DLA	Defense Logistics Agency

DMC	distribution management center
DOD	Department of Defense
DODAAC	Department of Defense activity address code
DS	direct support
DSCC	Defense Supply Center, Columbus
DSCP	Defense Supply Center, Philadelphia
DSCR	Defense Supply Center, Richmond
ECO	environmental compliance officer
ECP	emergency change proposal
EETF	electronic equipment test facility
EP	exchange pricing
ETM	electronic technical manual
EUM	end users manual
FARP	forward arming and refueling point
FBCB2	Force XXI Battle Command Brigade and Below
FEDLOG	federal logistics
FM	field manual
FMC	fully mission capable
FMT	field maintenance team
FOD	foreign object damage
FORSCOM	Forces Command
F/T	field/tactical
FY	fiscal year
GCSS-A	Global Combat Support System-Army
GS	general support
GSA	General Services Administration
GSAB	general support aviation battalion
GSC	group support company
GSE	ground support equipment
HAZCOM	hazardous communication
HAZMAT	hazardous material
HIT	health indicator test
HQ	headquarters
HW	hazardous waste
IAW	in accordance with
ILAP	integrated logistics analysis program
IMPAC	International Merchant Purchasing Agreement Card
IMRF	instrument master record file

ISAQ	interim statement of airworthiness qualification
ITV	in-transit visibility
LAO	logistics assistance office
LAP	logistics assistance program
LAR	logistics assistance representative
LIDB	logistics integrated data base
LIW	logistics information warehouse
LME	lightweight maintenance enclosure
LOA	letter of authorization
LOG911	logistics-911
LOGSA	logistics support activity
LRU	line replaceable unit
MAC	maintenance allocation chart
MAM	maintenance advisory message
MDS	mission-design-series
ME	maintenance test pilot evaluator
METL	mission essential task list
MHE	material handling equipment
MIM	maintenance information message
MOC	maintenance operational check
MOE	measures of effectiveness
MOPP-4	mission-oriented protective posture-level 4
MOS	military occupational specialty
MP	maintenance test pilot
MSC	major support command
MSDS	material safety data sheet
MSL	minimum stockage level
MTF	maintenance test flight
MTOE	modified table of organization and equipment
MWO	modification work order
NCO	noncommissioned officers
NCOIC	noncommissioned officer-in-charge
NDI	nondestructive inspection
NIIN	national item identification number
NMC	not mission capable
NMCS	not mission capable supply
NM	national maintenance
NMP	national maintenance program

NSN	national stock number
OCONUS	outside continental United States
OEM	original equipment manufacturer
OHR	operational hazard report
OIC	officer-in-charge
OJT	on-the-job training
OR	operational readiness
ORF	operational readiness float
OTR	one time repair
P4T3	problem, plan, people, parts, time, tools, and training
PBO	property book officer
PBUSE	property book unit supply enhanced
PC	production control
PCA-BS	production control administrator-back shops
PCE	protective clothing and equipment
PCU-BS	production control user-back shops
PD	priority designator
PGSE	peculiar ground support equipment
PID	personal identification
PLL	prescribed load list
PLM+	product lifecycle management plus
PMC	partial mission capable
PMCS	preventive maintenance checks and services
PMD	preventive maintenance daily
POC	point of contact
POE	port of embarkation
POL	petroleum, oils, and lubricants
PPE	personal protective equipment
PPM	progressive phase maintenance
PQDR	product quality deficiency report
QC	quality control
QDR	quality deficiency report
QSS	quick supply store
RASM	regional aviation sustainment manager
RFID	radio frequency identification
RPSTL	repair parts and special tools list
RSOI	reception, staging, onward movement, and intergation
RTF	ready-to-fight

RTL	ready-to-launch
RX	reparable exchange
S-2	intelligence staff officer
S-3	operations staff officer
S-4	logistics staff officer
S-6	signal staff officer
SALE	single Army logistics enterprise
SAMO	squadron aviation materiel officer
SAMS	Standard Army Maintenance System
SAMS-1	Standard Army Maintenance System-Level 1
SAMS-2	Standard Army Maintenance System-Level 2
SAMS-E	Standard Army Maintenance System-Enhanced
SAR	system access request
SARSS	Standard Army Retail Supply System
SARSS-1	Standard Army Retail Supply System–Level 1
SARSS-2A/C	Standard Army Retail Supply System–Level 2A/C
SARSS-2B	Standard Army Retail Supply System–Level 2B
SARSS-Gateway	Standard Army Retail Supply System–Gateway
SB	supply bulletin
SC-BS	shop chief-back shops
SFC	sergeant first class
SKOT	sets, kits, outfits, and tools
SOF	safety-of-flight
SOP	standing operating procedure
SOR	source of repair
SOS	source of supply
SRA	specialized repair authorization
SSA	supply support activity
SSF	single stock fund
SSG	staff sergeant
STAMIS	Standard Army Management Information System
ST-BS	shop technician-back shops
STP	Soldier training publication
TAMMS-A	The Army Maintenance Management System-Aviation
TAMP	theater aviation maintenance program
TASM	theater aviation sustainment manager
TASMG	Theater Aviation Sustainment Maintenance Group
TB	technical bulletin

TBO	time between overhaul
TDA	table of distribution and allowances
tech	technical
TI	techical inspector
TI-BS	technical inspector-back shops
TM	technical manual
TMDE	test, measurement, and diagnostic equipment
TOE	table of organization and equipment
TRADOC	Training and Doctrine Command
TSC	theater sustainment command
TWX	teletype message
UAS	unmanned aircraft system
UCMJ	Uniform Code of Military Justice
UIC	unit identification code
ULLS-A (E)	Unit Level Logistics System-Aviation (Enhanced)
ULLS-G	Unit Level Logistics System-Ground
UMO	unit movement officer
UND	urgency of need
USACRC	United States Army Combat Readiness Center
USAMC	United States Army Materiel Command
USAR	United States Army Reserve
USATA	United States Army test measurement and diagnostic equipment activity
UTL	unit task list
WARCO	warranty control officer
WebLOG	web logistics

SECTION II – TERMS

Accountable officer

Person officially appointed in writing to maintain a formal set of accounting records of property or funds. This person may or may not have physical possession of the property or funds. There are three types of supply accountable officers as defined below:

- Transportation officer-accountable for property entrusted to him or her for shipment.
- Stock record officer- accountable for supplies being held for issue from time of receipt until issued, shipped, or dropped from accountability.
- Property book officer-accountable for property upon receipt and until subsequently turned in, used (consumed) for authorized purposes, or dropped from accountability. (Hand receipt holders are not considered accountable officers.)

Aerial port of embarkation

A station which serves as an authorized port to process and clear aircraft (scheduled, tactical, and ferried) and traffic for departure from the country in which located.

Army exchange price customer

Customers designated by Headquarters, Department of the Army, to pay the exchange price for EP items.

Arrival/departure airfield control group

A provisional organization provided by the designated installation to perform aerial port functions during unit deployment, employment, and redeployment.

Authorized stockage list

A list of items that a direct support unit is authorized to stock based on established criteria. Criteria are usually crafted based on demands for the item to be supplied. ASL stockage for Class IX is restricted to essentiality code C, D, E, and J items. Items with an essentiality code of "G" may be stocked if a QSS is established.

Authorized stockage list depth

Quantity of a single line stocked on an ASL.

Authorized stockage list range

Size of an ASL in terms of the number of different lines stocked.

Average customer wait time

Average time in days, developed at a supply support activity, required to satisfy customer demands, regardless of whether the demand was for a stocked or unstocked item, or whether or not the demand was satisfied from stock on hand at the supply support activity.

Backorder

That portion of requested stock not immediately available for issue and not passed to another source of supply for action. Record of obligation to file the backorder is known as a backorder or due-out.

Basic load

Supplies kept by using units for use in combat (for other than ammunition). The quantity of each item of supply in a basic load is related to the number of days in combat the unit may be sustained without resupply.

Bench stock

Consumable Class II, III (packaged), IV, and IX supplies used by maintenance personnel at an unpredictable rate. Bench stocks are authorized for support level maintenance activities, including aviation unit maintenance activities.

Cost recovery rate

The first nine cost recovery elements identified in paragraph 55.I.2.b, V 11-B, DOD 7000.14-R. Note: cost recovery elements 10 (retail losses) discontinued. If the ninth cost recovery element (carcass attrition [washouts and losses]) is not included in cost recovery elements, add this attribute to the EP formula.

Command responsibility

The obligation of a commander to ensure all government property within his or her command is properly used and cared for and provide for proper custody and safekeeping of government property. Command responsibility is inherent in command and cannot be delegated. It is evidenced by assignment to command at any level and includes:
- Ensuring the security of all property of the command, whether in use or in storage.
- Observing subordinates to ensure that their activities contribute to the proper custody, care, use, and safekeeping of all property within the command.
- Enforcing all security, safety, and accounting requirements.
- Taking administrative or disciplinary measures when necessary.

Common tables of allowances

An equipment authorization document which prescribes basic allowances of organizational and individual equipment; and does not pertain to major military equipment.

Components of assemblages

Items identified in a supply catalog component listing as a part of an SKO, or other assemblage.

Components of end items

Items identified in technical publications (such as TMs) as part of an end item. (Items troop installed or separately authorized, and special tools and test and support equipment are not components.)

Credit denial

The process where credit is not allowed for a turn-in that is not matched with a corresponding issue within the delay days period during phases II and III.

Delay days period

Parameter specified period of time allotted that an issue is available to be matched to a turn-in (initial parameter set at 60 days).

Delta bill

An additional obligation to an EP customer as a result of an issue of an EP item in Tracking exceeding the delay days period without a matching turn-in or matching an issue against a condemned turn in; based on standard price minus EP.

Department of Defense activity address codes

A unique six-position alphanumeric code assigned to identify specific units, activities, or organizations as found in DOD activity address directory.

Exchange price

Loaded repair cost plus cost recovery rate.

Exchange price item

An Army managed NSN with a maintenance repair code of F, H, D, K, and L that is on an existing or planned national repair program that will have an exchange price as well as a standard price.

Hazardous material

A substance or material that has been determined by the Secretary of Transportation to be capable of posing an unreasonable risk to health, safety, and property when transported in commerce and that has been so designated.

History

Repository for all transactions once they are closed in tracking. Transactions in history can no longer be matched.

Loaded repair cost

(Average repair cost multiplied by final recovery rate percentage) plus (latest acquisition cost multiplied by [one minus final recovery rate percentage]).

Local purchase

Authorized purchase of supplies requested by an SSA for its own use or for issue to a supported activity in lieu of requisitioning through the supply distribution system.

Measures of effectiveness

A criterion that measures the attainment of an operation end state, achievement of objective(s), or creation of an effect that is used to assess changes in the operational environment (are we doing the right things right?).

Movement control element

Any organization responsible for the planning, routing, scheduling, and control of personnel and cargo movements over lines of communications.

Movement control team

Movement control teams are Army units that regulate the movement of personnel and materiel as well as the coordination of bulk fuel and water transportation at the pipeline and production take-off points.

Modification work order (current)

A MWO that has been published, released, and for which the required resources are available for application within a specified time (fiscal year). Required resources, as a minimum, include the availability of funds, kits, and manpower.

Non Army exchange price customer

Customers designated by Headquarters, Department of the Army, to pay the standard price for EP items.

Organizational equipment list

A computerized listing (in printed and data file formats) of on-hand equipment, personnel, and supplies in a unit. The organizational equipment list supports cargo manifesting for movements and provides input to transportation managers to identify movement requirements.

Personal responsibility

The obligation of a person to exercise reasonable and prudent actions to properly use, care for, and safeguard all government property in his or her possession. Applies to all government property issued for, acquired for, or converted to a person's exclusive use, with or without receipt.

Prescribed load list

A PLL is kept to support a unit's daily organizational maintenance operations. Technically, it is a list of unit maintenance repair parts that are demand supported, nondemand supported, and specified initial stockage repair parts for newly introduced end items. Normally, this is for a prescribed number of days of supply. In practice, the term PLL is often used to refer to the actual body of materiel that the list delineates.

Primary hand receipt holder

A person who is hand-receipted property directly from the accountable officer.

Port of debarkation

Geographic point (seaport or airport) in the routing scheme where a movement transitions from air or sea back to land.

Port of embarkation

Geographic point (seaport or airport) in the routing scheme where a movement transitions from ground to air or sea.

Serviceable credit value

The dollar value shown in FEDLOG for serviceable credit.

Serviceable exchange price return

Exchange price minus cost recovery rate.

Shop stock

Repair parts and consumable supplies stocked within a support-level maintenance activity for internal use during accomplishment of maintenance requests. It is similar in purpose to repair parts kept by a unit in support of organizational maintenance, in that it is for internal use only and has been issued from an ASL at an SSA.

Standard price

Latest acquisition cost plus cost recovery rate.

Subhand receipt

A hand receipt between a primary hand receipt holder and a person subsequently given the property for use. It does not transfer direct responsibility for property to the subhand receipt holder.

Supply support activity

Units assigned a DODAAC and a supply support mission; such as, aviation maintenance support units or direct support supply units.

Table of organization and equipment

Prescribes the doctrinal organization, personnel, and equipment required for a particular type of a unit. Fielded units operate in terms of a MTOE. MTOEs form the "go-to-war" units of the Army, whether those units are combat (infantry, armor, artillery), support (engineer, signal, military police) or sustainment (quartermaster, maintenance, medical) units.

Tracking

EP relevant transactions resident in EP tracking that have not exceeded delay days period. Transactions in tracking have the potential to be matched.

Transportation control number

A 17-position alphanumeric character set assigned to control a shipment throughout the transportation cycle of the defense transportation system.

Unserviceable credit value

The dollar value shown in FEDLOG for unserviceable credit.

This page intentionally left blank.

References

These publications are sources for additional information on the topics in this FM. Find most JPs at http://www.dtic.mil/doctrine/doctrine.htm. Most Army publications are found online at http://www.apd.army.mil.

SOURCES USED

These are the sources quoted or paraphrased in this publication.

ARMY PUBLICATIONS

AR 25-30. *The Army Publishing Program*. 27 March 2006.

AR 25-400-2. *The Army Records Information Management System (ARIMS)*. 2 October 2007.

AR 70-62. *Airworthiness Qualification of Aircraft Systems*. 21 May 2007.

AR 95-1. *Flight Regulations*. 12 November 2008.

AR 190-51. *Security of Unclassified Army Property (Sensitive and Nonsensitive)*. 30 September 1993.

AR 200-1. *Environmental Protection and Enhancement*. 13 December 2007.

AR 220-1. *Unit Status Reporting*. 19 December 2006.

AR 380-5. *Department of the Army Information Security Program*. 29 September 2000.

AR 385-10. *The Army Safety Program*. 27 August 2007.

AR 600-8-101. *Personnel Processing (In-, Out-, Soldier Readiness, Mobilization and Deployment Processing)*. 18 July 2003.

AR 600-55. *The Army Driver and Operator Standardization Program (Selection, Training, Testing, and Licensing)*. 18 June 2007.

AR 700-4. *Logistics Assistance*. 14 December 2007.

AR 700-127. *Integrated Logistics Support*. 17 July 2008.

AR 700-138. *Army Logistics Readiness and Sustainability*. 26 February 2004.

AR 700-139. *Army Warranty Program*. 7 October 2005.

AR 710-2. *Supply Policy Below the National Level*. 28 March 2008.

AR 725-50. *Requisition, Receipt, and Issue System*. 15 November 1995.

AR 735-5. *Policies and Procedures for Property Accountability*. 28 February 2005.

AR 740-1. *Storage and Supply Activity Operations*. 26 August 2008.

AR 740-3. *Stock Readiness*. 6 January 2003.

AR 750-1. *Army Materiel Maintenance Policy*. 20 September 2007.

AR 750-10. *Army Modification Program*. 24 February 2006.

AR 750-43. *Army Test, Measurement, and Diagnostic Equipment*. 3 November 2006.

AR 750-59. *Army Corrosion Prevention and Control Program*. 9 December 2005.

ARMY TACTICS, TECHNIQUES, AND PROCEDURES PUBLICATIONS

ATTP 3-04.155. *Army Unmanned Aircraft System Operations*. 31 August 2009.

DEPARTMENT OF THE ARMY PAMPHLETS

DA PAM 25-30. *Consolidated Index of Army Publications and Blank Forms.*14 July 2009.

DA PAM 25-33. *User's Guide for Army Publications and Forms.* 15 September 1996.

DA PAM 25-40. *Army Publishing: Action Officers Guide.* 7 November 2006.

DA PAM 385-10. *Army Safety Program.* 23 May 2008.

DA PAM 385-40. *Army Accident Investigations and Reporting.* 6 March 2009.

DA PAM 385-64. *Ammunition and Explosives Safety Standards.* 15 December 1999.

DA PAM 385-90. *Army Aviation Accident Prevention Program.* 28 August 2007.

DA PAM 611-21. *Military Occupational Classification and Structure.* 22 January 2007.

DA PAM 710-2-1. *Using Unit Supply System (Manual Procedures).* 31 December 1997.

DA PAM 710-2-2. *Supply Support Activity Supply System: Manual Procedures.* 30 September 1998.

DA PAM 738-751. *Functional Users Manual for the Army Maintenance Management System-Aviation (TAMMS-A).* 15 March 1999.

DA PAM 750-1. *Commanders' Maintenance Handbook.* 2 February 2007.

DA PAM 750-8. *The Army Maintenance Management System (TAMMS) Users Manual.* 22 August 2005.

FIELD MANUALS

FM 1. *The Army.* 14 June 2005.

FM 3-0. *Operations.* 27 February 2008.

FM 3-04.513. *Aircraft Recovery Operations.* 21 July 2008.

FM 3-05.213. *Special Forces Use of Pack Animals.* 16 June 2004.

FM 3-07. *Stability Operations.* 6 October 2008.

FM 3-11. *Multiservice Tactics, Techniques, and Procedures for Nuclear, Biological, and Chemical Defense Operations.* 10 March 2003.

FM 3-11.3. *Multiservice Tactics, Techniques, and Procedures for Chemical, Biological, Radiological, and Nuclear Contamination Avoidance.* 2 February 2006.

FM 3-11.4. *Multiservice Tactics, Techniques, and Procedures for Nuclear, Biological, and Chemical (NBC) Protection.* 2 June 2003.

FM 3-11.5. *Multiservice Tactics, Techniques, and Procedures for Chemical, Biological, Radiological, and Nuclear Decontamination.* 4 April 2006.

FM 3-35.1. *Army Pre-Positioned Operations.* 1 July 2008.

FM 3-97.6. *Mountain Operations.* 28 November 2000.

FM 3-100.4. *Environmental Considerations in Military Operations.* 15 June 2000.

FM 3-100.21. *Contractors on the Battlefield.* 3 January 2003.

FM 4-0. *Sustainment.* 30 April 2009.

FM 4-01.011. *Unit Movement Operations.* 31 October 2002.

FM 4-01.30. *Movement Control.* 1 September 2003.

FM 5-19. *Composite Risk Management.* 21 August 2006.

FM 10-67-1. *Concepts and Equipment of Petroleum Operations.* 2 April 1998.

FM 31-70. *Basic Cold Weather Manual.* 12 April 1968.

FM 31-71. *Northern Operations.* 21 June 1971.

FM 71-100. *Division Operations.* 28 August 1996.

FM 90-3. *Desert Operations.* 24 August 1993.

FM 90-5. *Jungle Operations.* 16 August 1982.

FMI 3-35. *Army Deployment and Redeployment.* 15 June 2007.

JOINT PUBLICATIONS

JP 3-35. *Deployment and Redeployment Operations.* 7 May 2007.

TECHNICAL BULLETINS

TB 43-180. *Calibration and Repair Requirements for the Maintenance of Army Materiel.* 1 January 2010.

TB 43-0211. *Army Oil Analysis Program (AOAP) Guide for Leaders and Users.* 1 December 2004.

TB 750-25. *Maintenance of Supplies and Equipment Army Test, Measurement and Diagnostic Equipment (TMDE) Calibration and Repair Support (C&RS) Program.* 7 October 2008.

TB 1-1500-341-01. *Aircraft Components Requiring Maintenance Management and Historical Data Reports.* 31 December 2007.

TECHNICAL MANUALS

TM 1-1500-204-23-1. *Aviation Unit Maintenance (AVUM) and Aviation Intermediate Maintenance (AVIM) Manual for General Aircraft Maintenance (General Maintenance and Practices) Volume 1.* 31 July 1992.

TM 1-1500-204-23-7. *Aviation Unit Maintenance (AVUM) and Aviation Intermediate Maintenance (AVIM) Manual for General Aircraft Maintenance (Nondestructive Testing and Flaw Detection Procedures and Practices) Volume 7.* 31 July 1992.

TM 1-1500-204-23-9. *Aviation Unit Maintenance (AVUM) and Aviation Intermediate Maintenance (AVIM) Manual for General Aircraft Maintenance (Tools and Ground Support Equipment) Volume 9.* 31 July 1992.

TM 1-1500-328-23. *Aeronautical Equipment Maintenance Management Policies and Procedures.* 30 July 1999.

TM 1-1500-335-23. *Nondestructive Inspection Methods, Basic Theory.* 15 June 2007.

TM 1-1500-344-23-1. *Cleaning and Corrosion Control Volume I Corrosion Program and Corrosion Theory.* 1 March 2005.

TM 1-1500-344-23-2. *Cleaning and Corrosion Control Volume II Aircraft.* 1 March 2005.

TM 1-1500-344-23-3. *Cleaning and Corrosion Control Volume III Avionic and Electronics.* 1 March 2005.

TM 1-1500-344-23-4. *Cleaning and Corrosion Control Volume IV Consumable Materials and Equipment for Aircraft and Avionics.* 1 March 2005.

TM 38-250. *Preparing Hazardous Materials for Military Air Shipments.* 15 April 2007.

TM 55-1500-342-23. *Army Aviation Maintenance Engineering Manual Weight and Balance.* 29 August 1986.

TM 55-1500-345-23. *Painting and Marking of Army Aircraft.* 12 June 1986.

TRAINING CIRCULARS

TC 3-04.72. *Aviation Life Support System Management Program.* 15 October 2009.

TC 3-34.489. *The Soldier and the Environment.* 8 May 2001.

OTHER PUBLICATIONS

CTA 50-909. *Field and Garrison Furnishings and Equipment.* 1 August 1993.

CTA 50-970. *Expendable/Durable Items (Except Medical, Class V, Repair Parts, and Heraldic Items).* 28 January 2005.

DOD 4145.19-R-1. *Storage and Materials Handling.* 15 September 1979.

DODI 6050.5. *DOD Hazard Communication (HAZCOM) Program.* 15 August 2006.

DODI 6055.1. *DOD Safety and Occupational Health (SOH) Program.* 19 August 1998.

Defense Transportation Regulation (DTR) 4500.9-R. *Defense Transportation Regulation* series.

FORSCOM/ARNG Regulation 55-1. *Unit Movement Planning.* 1 June 2006.

FORSCOM Regulation 55-2. *Unit Movement Data Reporting.* 31 October 1997.

GTA 05-08-002. *Enviromental-Related Risk Assessment.* 1 March 2008.

DOCUMENTS NEEDED

These documents must be available to the intended users of this publication. DA Forms are available on the APD website (www.apd.army.mil). DD forms are available on the OSD website (www.dtic.mil/whs/directives/infomgt/forms/formsprogram.htm).

DEPARTMENT OF THE ARMY FORMS

DA Form 12-R. *Request for Establishment of a Publications Account.*

DA Form 12-99-R. *Initial Distribution Requirements for Publications.*

DA Form 581. *Request for Issue and Turn-in of Ammunition.*

DA Form 1300-4. *Reorder Point Record.*

DA Form 1352. *Army Aircraft Inventory, Status and Flying Time.*

DA Form 1352-1. *Daily Aircraft Status Record.*

DA Form 1687. *Notice of Delegation of Authority-Receipt for Supplies.*

DA Form 2028. *Recommended Changes to Publications and Blank Forms.*

DA Form 2062. *Hand Receipt/Annex Number.*

DA Form 2064. *Document Register for Supply Actions.*

DA Form 2404. *Equipment Inspection and Maintenance Worksheet.*

DA Form 2405. *Maintenance Request Register.*

DA Form 2407. *Maintenance Request.*

DA Form 2407-1. *Maintenance Request-Continuation Sheet.*

DA Form 2408-4-1. *Weapon Record Data.*

DA Form 2408-4-2. *Weapon Sighting Data (OH-58D).*

DA Form 2408-4-3. *Weapon Sighting Data (AH-64A).*

DA Form 2408-5. *Equipment Modification Record.*

DA Form 2408-5-1. *Equipment Modification Record (Component).*

DA Form 2408-12. *Army Aviator's Flight Record.*

DA Form 2408-13-1. *Aircraft Inspection and Maintenance Record.*

DA Form 2408-13-2. *Related Maintenance Actions Record.*

DA Form 2408-13-3. *Aircraft Technical Inspection Worksheet.*

DA Form 2408-14-1. *Uncorrected Fault Record (Aircraft).*

DA Form 2408-15. *Historical Record for Aircraft.*

DA Form 2408-15-2. *Aircraft Vibration Record.*

DA Form 2408-16. *Aircraft Component Historical Record.*

DA Form 2408-16-1. *History Recorder, Component, Module Record.*

DA Form 2408-17. *Aircraft Inventory Record.*

DA Form 2408-18. *Equipment Inspection List.*

DA Form 2408-19. *Aircraft Engine Turbine Wheel Historical Record.*

DA Form 2408-19-1. *T53/T55 Turbine Engine Analysis Check Record.*

DA Form 2408-19-2. *T700 Series Turbine Engine Analysis Check Record.*

DA Form 2408-19-3. *Engine Component Operating Hours Record.*

DA Form 2408-20. *Oil Analysis Log.*

DA Form 2408-33-R. *Meter Tracked Component Record.*

DA Form 2410. *Component Removal and Repair/Overhaul Record.*

DA Form 2696. *Operational Hazard Report.*

DA Form 2765-1. *Request for Issue or Turn-in.*

DA Form 5988. *Equipment Inspection and Maintenance Worksheet.*

DA Label 80. *U.S. Army Calibrated Instrument.*

DA Label 163. *U.S. Army Limited or Special Calibration.*

DEPARTMENT OF DEFENSE FORMS

DD Form 314. *Preventive Maintenance Schedule and Record.*

DD Form 365. *Weight and Balance Personnel, Record of.*

DD Form 365-1. *Weight Checklist Record, Chart A-Basic.*

DD Form 365-2. *Weighing Record, Form B-Aircraft.*

DD Form 365-3. *Weight and Balance Record, Chart C-Basic.*

DD Form 365-4. *Weight and Balance Clearance Form F-Transport/Tactical.*

DD Form 1577. *Unserviceable (Condemned) Tag-Materiel.*

DD Form 1577-2. *Unserviceable (Reparable) Tag-Materiel.*

DD Form 1577-3. *Unserviceable (Reparable) Label-Materiel.*

DD Form 2026. *Oil Analysis Request.*

STANDARD FORMS

SF 368. *Product Quality Deficiency Report.*

This page intentionally left blank.

Index

This page intentionally left blank.

By order of the Secretary of the Army:

GEORGE W. CASEY, JR.
General, United States Army
Chief of Staff

Official:

Joyce E. Morrow

JOYCE E. MORROW
Administrative Assistant to the
Secretary of the Army
1001202

DISTRIBUTION:

Active Army, Army National Guard, and U.S. Army Reserve: To be distributed in accordance with the initial distribution number (IDN) 113827, requirements for TC 3-04.7.

www.ingramcontent.com/pod-product-compliance
Lightning Source LLC
Chambersburg PA
CBHW081358270326
41930CB00015B/3338